D1246884

HISTORY OF CIVILISATION

The World of the Phoenicians

The World of the Phoenicians

SABATINO MOSCATI

Professor of Semitic Philology in the University of Rome

Translated from the Italian by

ALASTAIR HAMILTON

WEIDENFELD AND NICOLSON

5 WINSLEY STREET LONDON WI

SBN 297 17049 X

Printed in Great Britain
by W & J Mackay & Co Ltd, Chatham

CONTENTS

CONTENTS

LIST OF ILLUSTRATIONS

vii

LIST OF FIGURES

LIST OF MAPS

TRANSLATOR'S NOTE

In quotations from classical authors and inscriptions I have used existing translations whenever possible. I have quoted from the following translations in Heinemann's Loeb's Classics Series: Columella, translated by E.S.Forster and Edward H.Heffner (1955); Diodorus Siculus, translated by Russel M.Geer (1954); Herodotus, translated by A.D.Godley (1928); Josephus, translated by H.St J.Thackery and Ralph Marcus (1934); Pausanias, translated by W.H.S.Jones (1935); Polybius, translated by W.R.Paton (1922); Thucydides, translated by Charles Forster Smith (1921). I have also quoted from Herbert A.Strong's translation of Lucian (London, 1913), John Selby Watson's translation of Justin (London, 1875), and Horace White's translation of Appian (London, 1899). I have used Donald Harden's translation of the 'Tariff of Marseilles' and the 'Voyage of Hanno' which appeared in *The Phoenicians*, Thames & Hudson (London, 1962). Finally, I have quoted from the Authorized King James version of the Bible.

PREFACE

Long before I wrote this book the title, *The World of the Phoenicians*, was devised as part of a series to be published by Weidenfeld and Nicolson; and, were it not for the title, the book, or at least my book, would never have been written. It was when I looked back on the publisher's suggestion that I decided to write it, as I realized that those very words could provide new and stimulating lines of research. I saw two main aspects to the subject: the characteristics peculiar to the Phoenician civilization, which seems so varied and incoherent, and the persistence and development of those characteristics in the Phoenician colonies and settlements abroad.

I have tried to follow these two lines of research through material which has proved extremely uneven. It is scanty and uncertain on the Phoenicians in the East and almost too vast on the subject of Carthage, but here, with the exception of Carthaginian art, the sources are principally indirect and historical-political. And finally, the material has been scattered and mainly archeological on the Phoenician colonies. I have, of course, had to rearrange the material for the purpose of this book, and have therefore dealt in detail with the actual Phoenician world, in the East, where the characteristic elements of this civilization were formed. I have reduced to a bare minimum the well-known facts about Carthage, giving special emphasis to the lesser known ones (particularly in the artistic field), and I have concentrated on the persistence and development of originally Phoenician elements. I have dealt at length with the Mediterranean colonies, especially in cases where no conclusions have yet been drawn, but always with the intention of individuating and revealing the historical-political, religious and artistic characteristics which have made the colonies an important part of the world of the Phoenicians.

Needless to say, this book is not an historical or monumental catalogue. The material, however, is ample enough to avoid distorted or incorrect perspectives, and to exemplify the main characteristics of the Phoenician civilization. My basic purpose is to document and illustrate these characteristics, and I think this was what the publisher intended with the title.

It is up to the reader to decide on the results of the finished work, but I would like to add a further point. In my opinion, the historian's duty, in a field of study like this, is to produce a general synthesis, provided, of course, that it contains original ideas. This is essential, because such a synthesis stimulates the scholars of the future, no matter whether they approve of or criticize it. A synthetical work inevitably contains debatable opinions and imperfections, and while I admit the existence of these defects I sincerely hope I shall be forgiven for them.

Rome, December 1965

ACKNOWLEDGEMENTS

In a book covering such extensive material as this there are many people who have collaborated with me. I would like, in particular, to express my gratitude to Prof. G. Levi Della Vida for his valuable general suggestions; to Prof. Mario Liverani, who helped me to assemble the documentary sources; to Prof. Paolo Matthiae, who collaborated with me in the section on art; to Prof. Giovanni Garbini for much information on the colonies; to Dr Ferruccio Barreca for his advice on Sardinia; to Dr Antonia Ciasca, who assembled material on the complex problem of pottery. I would also mention all my collaborators in the archeological missions which I have directed in recent years in the Mediterranean area, without whom I would have been unable to gain experience which has proved most important.

I am indebted to all the Institutions which have provided the photographs and which are specified in the list of illustrations, as well as the directors of the Institutions and the photographers. Of the directors I am particularly indebted to Emir Maurice Chéhab of the Museum of Beirut; to Prof. Gennaro Pesce of the Department of Antiquities in Cagliari; to Prof. Vincenzo Tusa of the Department of Antiquities in western Sicily. The drawings are by Piero Bartoloni, to whom I am most grateful.

INTRODUCTION

The people and civilization of the Phoenicians have always aroused great interest in the West. From the time when Homer revealed their nautical and commercial qualities, and when it was realized that our own alphabet was derived from them, they became the centre of as much attention as has ever been accorded to an ancient people of the East, and greater attention than has been accorded to nations of far vaster cultural and political productivity.

This interest in the Phoenicians, however, does not seem ever to have corresponded to sufficient attention to the distinctive characteristics of their culture, to those historical, political, religious, literary and artistic facts which both condition and define a civilization. So the unity, autonomy and consistency of the Phoenicians as a people have been taken for granted rather than analysed and established, with the result that the geographical area and the extent of Phoenician civilization have been indiscriminately varied. The excavations in Ugarit, for example, have induced scholars to ascribe the Phoenician civilization to a far earlier date and to alter its basic consistency without wondering whether they were justified in classifying the Ugaritic material as Phoenician. Another example of this is the increase in Phoenician and Punic excavations in the Mediterranean. The main problem – to what extent these discoveries actually reflect the Phoenician civilization or whether they result from the expansion of Carthage – has hardly been touched upon. It is pointless to stress that the solution of both these problems is far from simple, but if we see the prehistoric culture of Ugarit and that of the final Punic phase juxtaposed in a panorama of Phoenician civilization we can assess the extent of the misunderstandings to which the Phoenician problem leads on account of its size alone.

Apart from the most obvious aspects of the question, however, there remains the problem of the unity and coherence which characterizes any civilization if it is to become more than a name. This problem appears primarily in East Phoenicia, where the autonomy of individual city-states prevails and it is difficult to distinguish the links between these cities from the environment; and continues in the West, where importation frequently renders it impossible to determine the distinctive elements of the culture, while the large-scale penetration of foreign elements (mainly Greek) destroys all coherence.

These problems are the basis of this book, but before going any farther we must establish the limits in time and space which I have attributed to the civilization in question.

I have decided to start by dealing with the period c. 1200 BC, the date of the invasion of the 'peoples of the sea' and the beginning of the Iron Age. This event undoubtedly produced a deep rift in the ancient Near East which marks the start of actual Phoenician history and civilization. Restricted to the strip of land between the Mediterranean and the mountain chain of the Lebanon, hemmed in by the arrival of powerful states (the Hebrews and Aramaeans), the peoples on the coast found themselves both united and compelled towards the Mediterranean, and this nautical venture was to be one of their characteristics.

Geographically, I have located the Phoenician area between Shukshu (Tell Suqas) and Akka, taking into account temporary expansion beyond this region. As for colonization, it is unquestionably an intrinsic phenomenon of Phoenician civilization which must be examined both in its temporal and secondary developments. It is difficult to establish a time when actual Phoenician civilization ends and Punic civilization begins, and in many cases the problem is irrelevant, since the one is a continuation and development of the other. I have, however, tried to distinguish inherited characteristics from innovations in historical and cultural phenomena.

The end of Phoenician civilization can be placed approximately at the advent of Hellenism, which gradually but entirely abolished the cultural independence of Phoenician cities. In the West the colonies survived little longer – the crisis, initiated by Hellenism, was brought to a head by the conquests of Rome.

I

THE PHOENICIANS IN THE EAST

CHAPTER 1

NAME, PEOPLE, AND REGION

1 The name

A people is primarily defined by its name, the origins of which are invariably significant enough for an investigation of the meaning to be necessary. The name φοίνικες for the people and φοινίκη for the region is of Greek origin, going back as far as Homer, if not farther. Lacking any correspondence amongst the people to whom it refers, it remains a name used by foreigners, while it is undoubtedly connected etymologically with φοῖνιξ, meaning 'purple', and therefore with the industry of dyeing fabrics with purple typical of Phoenician cities.

Although the Greek name goes back to Homer the Mycenaean texts that have recently been deciphered contain a feminine adjective, *po-ni-ki-ja*, which means 'red' and refers to a cart. This adjective may already have contained an ethnic value, particularly since a noun, *po-ni-ki-jo*, is used to denote a herb which could be the *herba Phoenicea* mentioned by Pliny.[1] So if the ethnic value existed in Mycenaean times the Greek documentation would be a few centuries earlier.

In local sources we find the name *Canaanite* for the people and *Canaan* for the land in the fifteenth century BC (Akkadian inscription on the statue of Idrimi, Egyptian stele of Amenophis II from Memphis). It continues to be documented, however sporadically, through the ages (especially in the Bible, even if its meaning frequently embraces the whole pre-Israelite area and people), and it is found in the Hellenistic period in Phoenicia (inscriptions on coins: 'Laodicea in the Canaan'). It appears frequently in the classical sources (Philo of Byblos) and is encountered in the African territory as the name retained by the settlers of Phoenician descent (St Augustine: 'Unde interrogati rustici nostri quid sint, punice respondentes *Chanani* . . .').[2]

E.A.Speiser observed that in the Akkadian texts of Nuzi *kinaḫḫu* means 'purple', and this bears a significant similarity to φοῖνιξ. There are no linguistic reasons for supposing that *kinaḫḫu* derives from *knʿn*, and not vice-versa, so we can suggest the following origin of the name: Canaan is the indigenous term for the Phoenician territory, and from it the word for 'purple' is derived, on account of the local dye-making industry; in Greek the local name is borrowed both for the region and the colour.

If *Canaanite* was a name used by the Phoenicians to describe themselves it was certainly not the only one and maybe not the main one. The name *Sidonian*, for instance, connected with the city of the same name, is used frequently and haphazardly instead of Phoenician in Homer and in the Bible, where it is supported by the genealogy in Genesis (Canaan has two sons, Sidon and Heth).[3]

On the whole the names which designate the Phoenicians as a unity are rarely used, at least as far as the Phoenicians themselves are concerned, and this stresses the division of the area and the prevalence of city consciousness over national consciousness. What there was of a unitary consciousness appears in the second half of the second millennium and continues from then on, and the relative lateness of names like Canaanite and Sidonian merely confirms the time limits attributed to the Phoenician civilization.

2 The people

The American scholar, William Foxwell Albright, wrote that the time is past when we need discuss the Erythraean theory of the origin of the Phoenicians or the more recent hypotheses which brought them from the south of Palestine, or the question of the home of the Semites. Albright is right, but even the most recent and prominent writers are concerned with the 'home' of the Phoenicians. Otto Eissfeldt, who discusses it at length, maintains that it must be situated in the Sinai Peninsula or in the adjacent Arab steppe whence the Phoenicians would have emigrated *c.* 3000 BC to occupy their future historical sites. Georges Contenau devotes many pages to the *berceau des Phéniciens* and although he does not commit himself, he does not hesitate to ascribe the existence and individuality of a Phoenician people to early historic, if not prehistoric times; he even claims that the ethnic data become increasingly clear the earlier the period; so it is quite likely that at the dawn of history there was a Semitic race speaking Semitic. Donald Harden has also recently referred to the various waves of migrating Semites, coming, it is thought, from Arabia or the Persian Gulf (as his source he quotes Herodotus and neglects the recent studies on Semitic origins). Finally, the numerous studies following the publication of the Ugaritic texts provide renewed support for the theories on southern origins.

In fact, most hypotheses are based on the classical authors. Philo of Byblos claims that the Phoenicians were autochthonous, and that not only the men but also the gods and the whole of human culture hail from

4

their area.[4] Herodotus locates them primarily on the Eritrean sea.[5] Strabo maintains that on the Persian Gulf there were temples and cities similar to Phoenician ones[6] and Pliny confirms it.[7] Justin tells how, driven from their homeland by an earthquake, the Phoenicians settled first on the Syrian Lake (the Dead Sea?) and then on the Mediterranean coast.[8]

This combination of traditions and studies attempting to identify the origins of the Phoenician nation is based on the indemonstrable assumption that the nation existed as such before its historical appearance on the Mediterranean coast; but since no historical and cultural coherence of the Phoenician cities must be ascribed to pre- or even early historic times, the problem of the origins deeply changes. The formation of the Phoenician nation, within fairly loose limits, seems to result from an historical evolution in the Syro-Palestinian area and not a migration of people from outside. It could even be said that it was a migration of other peoples (Philistines, Hebrews, Aramaeans), which compressed the Phoenician towns into a certain coherence.

It is obviously difficult, therefore, to claim a large-scale immigration of new peoples as the genesis of the Phoenician nation, and to search for distinctive racial characteristics. In the anthropological complex of the Syro-Palestinian area, which witnesses the encounter between Arab and Armenian types, the Phoenicians have no special characteristics. The language, like that of their neighbours, is Semitic. Finally, the independence of the Phoenicians as a people is determined as a result of particular geographical and historical-political conditions, but can be based on neither home nor race.

3 The region

The history of the Phoenicians begins in the Syro-Palestinian coastal area. The northern boundary of this region can be marked level with Tell Suqas, because north of this town there are no stable Phoenician settlements. There is, of course, the great city of Ugarit, but this cannot be attributed to Phoenician civilization, as it is defined in this book. Besides, the history of Ugarit ends before 1200 BC. The southern boundary, on the other hand, can be placed level with Akka. Admittedly Eshmunazar's inscription mentions the annexation to Sidon of Dor and Jaffa[9] in the Persian period, but these towns cannot be considered stable Phoenician settlements.

The eastern and western boundaries of Phoenicia are evident – the Mediterranean sea to the west, the mountain chain of the Lebanon to the east. Following the strip of the Nosairis mountains, the Lebanon chain stretches for about sixty miles parallel to the sea, attaining in places a height of nine thousand feet or more. The distance from the mountains to the sea varies from thirty to seven miles, interspersed with rocky promontories stretching into the water. Small valleys open up between these promontories and the watercourses descending from the mountains, which are usually little springs swelling in the rainy season and drying up in the summer.

The historical implications of this geographical situation are obvious. In the first place the entire region is hemmed in between the mountains and the sea, and this resulted in an historical separation from the interior often emphasized by the arrival of powerful peoples and their states c. 1200 BC. In the second place, the internal fragmentation of the area hinders the formation of political unity and even more unitary consciousness, and allows city-states and communities to prevail. In the third place, the natural expansion route for the people of this land is the Mediterranean. This proved true with the fall of other peoples who had formerly controlled navigation, and remained so until new and better-organized nations came on to the scene.

The necessity for navigating the Mediterranean stems from the problem of communications. With the mountains dropping straight into the sea, passage by land becomes difficult. A narrow path was sometimes cut on the inner flank of the promontories, but navigation remained the easiest and surest means of transport both from town to town and country to country.

Phoenician cities often had a characteristic topography: they were usually built on rocky promontories so as to contain harbours, one to the north and one to the south, used according to the winds and seasons. The Phoenicians also preferred islets lying just off the coast, where fortification, isolation, and lengthy defence in case of siege were easier. Such are the two large Phoenician cities, Aradus and Tyre, the latter being subsequently joined to the mainland by a mole constructed by Alexander the Great.

Phoenician navigation, resulting from geographical and historical-political conditions, determined their expansion across the Mediterranean and the foundation of a series of landing-stages or trading-posts. Throughout this expansion, which extended beyond the Pillars of Hercules, the Phoenicians sought the sites to which they were accustomed – promontories such as Carthage, Nora, and Bythia; and islets, such as S. Antioco, Motya, Cadiz, and Mogador. Finally, in order to have suitable landing-stages for their long voyages, they tried to found their settlements at regular distances apart.

The climate of ancient Phoenicia was more or less the same as it is today. In the winter there is a high rainfall which penetrates deep into the loamy soil and fertilizes it. The spring begins in March, and by May the corn is ripe. The rains diminish in March and cease almost completely between May and September. Summer lasts for four or five months and parches the vegetation, although it is irrigated at many points by the watercourses. In October the weather becomes cooler, the rains resume and the annual cycle is repeated. On the whole, therefore, Phoenicia shares the general climatic conditions of the Near East, with certain mitigations and improvements owing to the particular geographical situation.

As a result Phoenicia appears to be one of the most fertile countries of the Levant. In spite of the limited extent of arable land, agriculture is well developed: wheat, olives and vines, fruit trees (especially fig trees and sycamores) grow there. The palm tree, which is now rare, abounded in ancient times, while the orange tree, which is now common, was then unknown.

But according to historical texts the greatest riches of Phoenicia were the forests of the Lebanon. They abounded in pines, cypresses, and, above all, cedars, famous throughout the Near East. Expeditions from Mesopotamia or Egypt continued through the ages in order to procure this precious material which scented its surroundings. Nowadays hardly anything is left of those splendid forests, which have been gradually exhausted by exploitation, and a concentrated effort to reforest the area has been thwarted by the herds of goats which destroy the shoots.

The fauna of ancient Phoenicia corresponded to the surroundings and the climate. The mountains were infested with panthers, bears, hyenas, wolves, jackals, and hares, while the commonest domestic animals were donkeys, oxen, sheep, and goats. There were plenty of fish from the sea, and notably the purple murex fish which gave its name to the region.

The subsoil was mainly composed of soft, crumbly limestone. In the mountains, however, there were strata of marble, lignite, and iron, and the fine sand provided useful material for the glass industry.

On the whole the country provided the ancient inhabitants of Phoenicia with excellent resources. But these resources were only serviceable on the basis of active exchange, which was first practised with the neighbouring nations and, soon after, with the whole of the Mediterranean, turning the Phoenicians into the most celebrated and able merchants of the ancient world.

CHAPTER 2

HISTORY

1 Introduction

On the whole, early Phoenician history can be reconstructed from indirect sources. The historical facts to be deduced from the brief inscriptions in the Phoenician language are minimal – names of sovereigns of single cities, dynastic successions, dedications of monuments, references to protective deities. Besides, these earliest inscriptions come from Byblos, where a group of tenth-century texts was found, while the other cities provide equally scanty information considerably later.

One source, which must originally have been direct, but which has been transmitted to us in an indirect and fragmentary form, are the annals of Tyre, quoted by Josephus in certain passages from Menander of Ephesus. These passages refer to two periods, the tenth to eighth centuries and the sixth century, and provide numerous facts about the history of the cities – names of kings, and some detailed information about local events. The intermediate transmission of these facts obviously adds to the risk of misunderstandings, but comparison with further data, and particularly with the biblical information about the earliest epoch, suggests that the annals are accurate. In all events, these annals show a local historiographical tradition which may become in the future an excellent source of information.

The Phoenician cities are also mentioned in both the Egyptian and Mesopotamian sources. These are mainly Assyrian annals which contain facts about the subjugation of the Syro-Palestinian towns, and although they seem to be accurate it must be kept in mind that the conquests were normally mere recognitions of authority and are therefore frequently repeated. Few important facts can be deduced from the other Egyptian and Mesopotamian sources, apart from the Egyptian tale of Wenamun which casts a light on Phoenicia's relationship with Egypt around the middle of the eleventh century.

A very important indirect source for Phoenician history in the East is the Old Testament. The historical books give much information about the relations with Phoenician cities and, in particular, with Tyre; and

8

however sporadic the data, the Old Testament provides more continuous narratives than any other source. It contains by far the most extensive information about certain periods, such as the age of Solomon and his relations with Tyre, and we must remember that Hebrew historiography of that time is notoriously accurate and reliable.

Apart from Josephus's references to the annals of Tyre, the late classical sources contain useful information about the final phase of Phoenician history, while mentions of early phases are scanty and not always reliable.

In reconstructing the main events of Phoenician history from these sources the immediate problem is to assess the extent to which unitary elements overcome the city divisions and justify the treatment of the area as a whole. Division prevails, because we are faced with the history of individual cities, but there are certain indications of links and unitary consciousness which must be emphasized if we are to establish an historical coherence of Phoenician cities.

2 The age of independence

The invasion of the 'peoples of the sea' *c.* 1200 BC had a direct effect on certain coastal cities: Aradus was destroyed and so was Sidon, according to a statement by Justin[1] which seems to be confirmed by archeological discoveries. The political and military situation after the invasion, however, marked the beginning of an era of independence. The great powers were temporarily inactive in the Syro-Palestinian area: Assyria was confined within her frontiers and Egypt was defeated: the Hebrew and Aramaic states prospered and the Phoenician cities were compressed on to the coast.

The leading cities of this new phase are Aradus, Byblos, Sidon, Tyre, and Akka (Berytus is not mentioned until the Persian epoch). Various indications suggest that Sidon initially dominated the other cities. To start with, there is the name, *Sidonians*, which both the Old Testament and Homer use for the Phoenicians. In view of the unlikelihood of the name first being used to designate the whole people and then restricted to one of the towns founded by them, it probably either implies supremacy, or, and this is particularly relevant, a relative cohesion of the cities, even if this cohesion were the result of external rather than internal forces.

The other indication of the supremacy of Sidon is in the account which Josephus hands down from Timaeus – two hundred and forty years before the temple of Jerusalem was built, therefore soon after 1200 BC, the inhabitants of Sidon, defeated by the king of the 'Ascalonians' (probably the 'peoples of the sea'), fled in their ships and founded Tyre.[2]

The account is inaccurate, because we know that Tyre existed far earlier, but it might have an historical basis if groups of Sidonians moved to the area of Tyre, under pressure from the 'peoples of the sea', and restored the town, which may have been sacked by the conquerors themselves. In all events, according to various sources, the Tyrian era began *c.* 1200 BC, while the supremacy of Sidon over the other cities probably lasted until *c.* 1000 BC, after which the importance of Tyre gradually increased and prevailed.

The decline of Egyptian rule, which had dominated the area for centuries, is shown *c.* 1100 by various facts. It was in this period that the Assyrian king, Tiglatpileser I (1112–1074), led an expedition to Upper Syria, where he also received tributes from Aradus, Byblos, and Sidon.

To Mount Lebanon I went. Logs of cedar for the temple of Anu and Adad, the great gods, my lords, I cut and brought away. Against Amurru I returned. Amurru in its entirety I conquered. The tribute of Byblos, Sidon and Aradus I received. I crossed over in ships of Aradus, from Aradus which is on the sea-shore, to Simyra of the land of Amurru . . . I killed a *nahiru*, which they call a 'sea-horse', in the midst of the sea.[3]

It is obvious from this account that the aim of Tiglatpileser I's mission was to collect cedar wood. There is no mention of battle, and 'conquest' and 'tribute' are terms which can be used to denote a commercial connexion. The killing of the dolphin suggests a fishing expedition organized by the Phoenician cities for their illustrious guest. Besides, the political situation of the time would not have enabled Tiglatpileser I to maintain lasting dominion over Syria, while the wars with the states of the Upper Tigris and the Aramaic tribes from the western borders prove that he did not then control the approaches to Syrian territory.

Another important indication of the independence of the Phoenician states (particularly from Egypt) is provided by the tale of Wenamun. It tells of the disrespectful welcome that the prince of Byblos, Zekarbaal, accorded to the protagonist, who had been sent to procure cedar wood for the sacred vessel of the god Amon. Referring to the sovereign of Egypt, the prince says, 'Nor am I the servant of him that sent thee'.[4]

Again in Byblos, in the tenth century, brief inscriptions give us the names of a succession of sovereigns: Ahiram, Ittobaal, Abibaal, Yehimilk, Elibaal, Shipitbaal.[5] In the case of Ahiram it is a funerary inscription on his coffin, and in other cases dedications of buildings or statues added to invocations of divine protection. The characters, the language, the relationship between the sovereigns suggested by the inscriptions, make them an unquestionably homogeneous group, which can be dated by the fact that two of the inscriptions, of Abibaal and Elibaal, are cut on Egyptian statues, of Sheshonq 1 (950–929) and Osorkon 1 (929–893) respectively. The actual coffin of Ahiram, which bears the earliest inscription, must be a couple of centuries earlier, and the inscription is probably the result of further use. The succession of sovereigns and their dates can be reconstructed as follows:

c. 1000	Ahiram
980	Ittobaal
940	Abibaal
920	Yehimilk
900	Elibaal
880	Shipitbaal

It is worth noting that of these sovereigns Yehimilk does not mention the name of his father and might therefore be the founder of a new dynasty. The title of the sovereigns, 'King of Byblos', suggests their autonomy; and it has been proved (by W. Herrmann) that the inscriptions are formulated in such a way as to suggest substantial independence from Egypt. The fact that Abibaal and Elibaal should use statues of pharaohs for their inscriptions, dedicating them to the goddess of Byblos, may simply point to good relations with their powerful neighbours. What Herrmann does not manage to prove, on the other hand, is his theory of the expansion of the sovereigns of Byblos in the surrounding territory and their supremacy in the Phoenician area which would have passed on later to Tyre.

The immediate opponents of the Phoenician cities in the area of their expansion were naturally the Philistines and the Israelites. Concerning their relations with the former, however, we only have the account of the destruction of Sidon by the Ascalonians. The Old Testament, on the other hand, provides extensive information about the Israelites which is appropriately confirmed by the annals of Tyre. It is possible that David (*c.* 1000–961) included a large part of the Phoenician coast when he expanded his state: at least, the biblical account of the census ordered by the king says that his envoys 'came to Gilead, and to the land of Tahtimhodshi; and they came to Danjaan, and about to Sidon, and came to the strong hold of Tyre, and to all the cities of the Hivites, and of the Canaanites: and they went out to the south of Judah, even to Beersheba'.[6] The passage can obviously be interpreted in different ways and the text is uncertain; but nevertheless it does give some idea of the extent of the state of David. Tyre, the largest Phoenician city, on the other hand, certainly remained independent, as is suggested by the account of the king, Hiram, who sent David craftsmen and cedar wood to build his palace.[7]

At the time of Solomon (*c.* 961–922) information increases. In Tyre,

Hiram, or Ahiram, son of Abibaal, was probably still reigning between 969 and 936 BC. The annals tell us that he enlarged his city, erected a gold column in the temple of Zeus Olympus (the god Baal Shamem), joined the islet on which stood the temple of Melqart to the larger island of Tyre, and built new temples to Heracles (Melqart) and Astarte.[8] The only war mentioned in the annals is an expedition against the inhabitants of Kition, the Phoenician colony in Cyprus, because they had refused to pay tribute.[9] (The name of the inhabitants is uncertain, but this interpretation seems far more likely than the theory that they were the inhabitants of distant Utica.) Relations with Solomon were good, and he persuaded Hiram to provide him with material and craftsmen to build his temple and palace. His generous rewards seem to prove the reciprocal independence of the two sovereigns.

Now, for the first time, there are numerous historical accounts which deserve detailed examination. According to the annals:

These works Solomon completed in twenty years, and, since Hiram, the king of Tyre, had contributed much gold and more silver to their building, as well as wood of cedar and pine trees, he too presented Hiram in return with great gifts, sending him every year grain and wine and oil, of which, because, as we have already said before, he inhabited an island, he was always particularly in need.[10]

And here is the biblical account, which is still more extensive and establishes the relations between the two sovereigns:

And Hiram king of Tyre sent his servants unto Solomon; for he had heard that they had anointed him king in the room of his father; for Hiram was ever a lover of David. And Solomon sent to Hiram, saying, Thou knowest how that David my father could not build an house unto the name of the Lord his God for the wars which were about him on every side, until the Lord put them under the soles of his feet. But now the Lord my God hath given me rest on every side, so that there is neither adversary nor evil occurrent. And, behold, I purpose to build an house unto the name of the Lord my God, as the Lord spake unto David my father, saying, Thy son, whom I will set upon thy throne in thy room, he shall build an house unto my name. Now therefore command thou that they hew me cedar trees out of Lebanon; and my servants shall be with thy servants: and unto thee will I give hire for thy servants according to all that thou shalt appoint: for thou knowest that there is not among us any that can skill to hew timber like unto the Sidonians. And it came to pass, when Hiram heard the words of Solomon, that he rejoiced greatly, and said, Blessed be the Lord this day, which hath given unto David a wise son over this great people. And Hiram sent to Solomon, saying, I have considered the things which thou sentest to me for: and I will do all thy desire concerning timber of cedar, and concerning timber of fir. My servant shall bring them down from Lebanon unto the sea: and I will convey them by sea in floats unto the place that thou shalt appoint me, and will cause them to be discharged there, and thou shalt receive them: and thou shalt accomplish my desire, in giving food for my household. So Hiram gave Solomon cedar trees and fir trees according to all his desire. And Solomon gave Hiram twenty thousand measures of wheat for food to his household, and twenty measures of pure oil: thus gave Solomon to Hiram year by year.[11]

The autonomy of the two kingdoms and the interdependence of their economy which emerges from this biblical passage, is confirmed by a parallel passage in the Book of Chronicles. It is also confirmed by other facts, such as the curious episode when Hiram refuses several cities presented to him by Solomon. The annals say:

Besides these he (Solomon) made him a present of some cities in Galilee, twenty in number, which lay not far from Tyre; but when Hiram went to them and looked them over, he was ill pleased with the gift and sent word to Solomon that he had no use for the cities.[12]

The same account exists in the Bible:

And it came to pass at the end of twenty years, when Solomon had built the two houses, the house of the Lord and the king's house, (Now Hiram the king of Tyre had furnished Solomon with cedar trees and fir trees, and with gold, according to all his desire,) that then king Solomon gave Hiram twenty cities in the land of Galilee. And Hiram came out from Tyre to see the cities which Solomon had given him; and they pleased him not. And he said, What cities are these which thou hast given me, my brother? And he called them the land of Cabul unto this day. And Hiram sent to the king six-score talents of gold.[13]

An interesting incident, in the Oriental tradition of story-telling, recorded in the annals of Tyre, is worth noting: the contests of wisdom between Hiram and Solomon. Although the Bible does not mention this episode, it does, of course, stress the wisdom of the Israelite king. The annals say that Hiram sent Solomon problems and riddles, asking him to solve them. Since Solomon was very wise, he succeeded.[14] The account given by the historian Dio, quoted in *Contra Apionem*, is slightly different: Solomon sent riddles to Hiram and asked for others in return: whoever failed to guess them would pay a sum of money. Hiram accepted and, at first unable to solve the riddles, spent most of his treasures paying the fine. But he subsequently managed to answer the questions and proposed others himself. Solomon could not answer them and had to return everything and pay a large additional sum to Hiram.[15]

Then there is the naval expedition to the land of Ophir, which, according to the Bible, was planned and performed by the two kings:

And king Solomon made a navy of ships in Eziongeber, which is beside Eloth, on the shore of the Red sea, in the land of Edom. And Hiram sent in the navy his servants, shipmen that had knowledge of the sea, with the servants of

Solomon. And they came to Ophir, and fetched from thence gold, four hundred and twenty talents, and brought it to king Solomon.[16]

Other passages add further details:

And the navy also of Hiram, that brought gold from Ophir, brought in from Ophir great plenty of almug trees, and precious stones.[17]

For the king had at sea a navy of Tarshish with the navy of Hiram: once in three years came the navy of Tarshish, bringing gold, and silver, ivory, and apes, and peacocks.[18]

These passages give an idea of the naval prestige of the Phoenicians: in the tenth century they were already undertaking long nautical voyages and this is of considerable importance with regard to their subsequent maritime dispersion. Ophir is usually situated in the Yemen, if not in Somaliland, and the expression 'gold of Ophir' appears on a Hebrew ostrakon from Tell Qasile. The problem of Tarshish is more complex. It can probably be identified with the Tartessus of the classical sources and situated in the south of Spain, which would give a significant dimension to Phoenician expansion, even if the term 'navy of Tarshish' may have a generic meaning ('ocean-going navy').

The annals of Tyre tell us of the successors of Hiram: Baleazar, who lived forty-three years and reigned seventeen (935–919); Abdastratos, who lived twenty-nine years, reigned nine (918–910), and was killed by the sons of his nurse. The first of these to reign was Methustratos, who lived fifty-four years and reigned twelve (909–898); then Astharymos, who lived fifty-eight years and reigned nine (897–889); then, after murdering his brother, Phelles, who lived fifty years and reigned eight months (888). Phelles was overthrown and murdered by a priest of Astarte, Ittobaal, who lived sixty-eight years and reigned thirty-two (887–856), starting a new dynasty which was to last for at least a century.[19] The period of tumults and civil wars which ended with the accession of Ittobaal was significantly accompanied by an equally dark period in Israel, where the monarchy was split and palace disputes raged. The accession of Ittobaal in Tyre also corresponded to the accession of Omri in Israel, the foundation of a dynasty which lasted a few decades, and the resumption of friendly relations between the two states.

Here the Old Testament accounts begin again. Ittobaal married his daughter Jezebel to Ahab, son of Omri. This marriage may have extended the political influence of the state of Israel to the Phoenician coast, and certainly extended Phoenician religious influence in Israel, as we see from the condemnation in the Bible:

And Ahab the son of Omri did evil in the sight of the Lord above all that were before him. And it came to pass, as if it had been a light thing for him to walk in the sins of Jeroboam the son of Nebat, that he took to wife Jezebel the daughter of Ethbaal king of the Sidonians, and went and served Baal, and worshipped him. And he reared up an altar for Baal in the house of Baal, which he had built in Samaria.[20]

If we add that Atalia, daughter of Jezebel, married Joram, king of Judah, we get some idea of the diffusion of Phoenician beliefs and cults.

The power of Tyre under Ittobaal is confirmed by numerous indications. In the Bible he is referred to as 'King of the Sidonians'[21] while Hiram was called 'King of Tyre'. This is no mere coincidence, because Josephus designates Ittobaal as 'the king of Tyre and Sidon',[22] thereby confirming the extent of his rule to the Phoenician area. Josephus also gives us an account of this king's foundation of Botrys, north of Byblos, and of the colony of Auza in Libya.[23] Since Botrys is already known as Batruna in the letters of El Amarna, it must be a refoundation or fortification, similar to the older fortification of Tyre by Sidon, and it gives us some idea of the power attained by Ittobaal. Auza, on the other hand, had not yet been located, but this does not make Tyre any the less powerful.

3 Assyrian expansion

Assyria's return to power and her progressive expansion in the ancient Near East mark the reduction of the independence of the Phoenician cities. If the homages and tributes repeatedly mentioned probably applied to occasional raids, and the repetition of the Assyrian expeditions shows that they only temporarily satisfied their aims, these expeditions must, however, have radically altered the balance of power in which the independence of the Phoenician cities could prosper. To this must be added the progressive decline of the small Hebrew and Aramaic states, which constituted an internal boundary for the cities themselves, and a protective strip between Phoenicia and the larger neighbouring powers.

Tiglatpileser I's expedition, mentioned as early as 1100, was a herald of Assyrian expansion which only began to develop continuously after Assurnasirpal II (883–859). His annals say:

At that time I marched along the side of Mount Lebanon, and to the Great Sea of the land of Amurru I went up. In the Great Sea I washed my weapons, and I made offerings unto the gods. The tribute of the kings of the seacoast, of the people of Tyre, Sidon, Byblos, Makhalata, Maisa, Kaisa, Amurru, and Aradus, which lies in the midst of the sea, – silver, gold, lead, copper, vessels of bronze, garments made of brightly coloured wool, linen garments, a great monkey, and a small monkey, maple-wood, boxwood, and ivory, and a *nahiru*, a creature of the sea, I received as tribute from them, and they embraced my feet.[24]

The expedition into Phoenicia to which this passage refers can be dated *c.* 875. The Phoenician cities do not seem to offer any armed resistance and there is no mention of battle. This would be in character with the traditional policy of the small states, which preferred to satisfy their powerful neighbours with homages and tributes. The expedition, however, differs from that of Tiglatpileser I in that it was obviously performed to enforce submission to the local kings. As for the towns mentioned, some are known (Tyre, Sidon, Byblos, Aradus), while the others (Makhalata, Maisa, Kaisa) are unknown and any identification can only be theoretical (Makhalata – Tripoli). Amurru must have been a region and seems out of place in a list of cities, so that the alteration to Simyra, which has been suggested, seems possible.

It is interesting to examine the tributes paid by the Phoenician cities to the Assyrian sovereigns. The garments of coloured wool suggest the celebrated local industry of purple dye, and local, too, must have been the wood and the working and production of bronze and ivory. The linen garments, gold, and monkeys were from Egypt. Some of the other metals, such as copper, were from Cyprus. Finally, the list of tributes is a significant indication of the commercial development of the Phoenician cities and of the products from the neighbouring regions which converged there.

The fact that the Assyrians used Phoenician wood for building purposes is confirmed by an inscription of Balawat, which also suggests a commercial rather than military expedition:

I marched unto Mount Lebanon and cut down beams of cedar, cypresses and juniper, with the beams of cedar I roofed this temple, door-leaves of cedar I fashioned, and with a sheathing (bands) of copper I bound them, and I hung them in its gates.[25]

Finally, still under Assurnasirpal II, a stele from the palace of Nimrud shows that Phoenician craftsmen from Tyre and Sidon were amongst those employed in building the palace itself.[26] So, as Solomon had done for his temple, the Assyrians seem to have used skilled Phoenician workmen in the field of peaceful agreements.

Information becomes more abundant under Salmanassar III (858–824). The Assyrian king marched on various occasions against the states of the west (Hama and Damascus in particular), and subsequently proceeded farther and imposed tributes on the Phoenician cities. The first campaign in which contact with the Phoenicians is confirmed is that of the sixth year (852): the inscription on the monolith of Kurkh specifies the composition of the Syrian army, mentioning '10 chariots, 10,000 soldiers of the Irkateans, 200 soldiers of Matinu-ba'il, the Arvadite, 200 soldiers of the Usnateans, 30 chariots, (?),000 soldiers of Adunu-Ba'il, the Shianean'.[27] It is interesting to note the numeric contrast between the large Irkatean and Shianean forces, and the tiny Arvadite and Usnatean contingents: the various states were by no means in agreement, since some of them intended to fight the Assyrian king, while others were reluctant to do so. The two names of the Phoenician sovereigns mentioned in the inscription are also of interest: the first is something like Matten-Baal, the second Adoni-Baal. The encounter took place at Qarqar, but although the Assyrians spoke of it as a victory for Salmanassar, who allegedly killed 14,000 of the enemy, the advance stopped at Qarqar, so the battle must have been indecisive.

In the campaigns of the tenth, eleventh, and fourteenth years the mentions of the expeditions against Damascus and Hama are accompanied by a reference to twelve kings of the coast amongst the adversaries of the Assyrian king. But the next prominent battle only took place in the eighteenth year (840). We read in the annals:

I advanced as far as Mount Hauran. Countless cities I destroyed, I devastated, I burned with fire. Their spoil, without number, I carried off. To Mount Ba'li-ra'si, a headland of the sea, I marched. My royal image I set up there. At that time I received the tribute of the men of Tyre, Sidon and of Jehu, son of Omri.[28]

In another edition of the same annals the name of the king of Tyre is given, Ba'li-manzer, and mention is made of a further regal image erected by the Assyrian sovereign in the Lebanon.[29]

Yet another campaign in Phoenicia is mentioned in the twenty-first year (837): the king received tribute from Tyre, Sidon, and Byblos.[30] A king, Ba'li, is also referred to – his name is apparently Phoenician, but the name of his state is lost and that of the capital, La-ru(?)-ba, cannot be identified.

At this point we must return to the annals of Tyre, which mention the successors of Ittobaal and indicate the length of their reign: Balezoros, who lived forty-five years and reigned six (855–850); Mettenos, who lived thirty-two years and reigned twenty-nine (849–821); Pygmalion, who lived fifty-six years and reigned forty-seven (820–774). In the seventh year of Pygmalion's reign (814–813), add the annals, his sister fled and founded the city of Carthage in Libya.[31] Now comes the problem of the connexions with the Assyrian inscriptions, according to which Ba'li-manzer reigned in Tyre in the year 840: the most similar name is Balezoros, but there are chronological complications for which various explanations have been suggested. In each case the chronology of the annals of Tyre needs to be altered.

The death of Salmanassar III (824) was followed by several decades during which Syria and Phoenicia enjoyed relative tranquillity. In this period, which lasted until the succession of Tiglatpileser III in 745, the only expedition worth noting was undertaken by Adadnirari III (809–782), in the fifth year of his reign (805). Adadnivari explicitly declares that the tribute was denied to his father, Shamshi-Adad V, and claims to have advanced as far as the region of the Philistines and Edomites, and imposed taxes on Tyre and Sidon.[32]

So far, therefore, Assyrian expansion had not taken the form of lasting conquest in Phoenicia so much as control from a distance and imposition of tributes. No unitary consciousness appears in the Phoenician world as described in the Assyrian annals. A series of conquered cities (city-states) are mentioned at random, but none of these cities are classified in groups and no differentiation is made between the cities of the interior and those on the coast, those on the non-Phoenician coast and those on the Phoenician coast. There is no unitary denomination for the Phoenicians and no organic limitation or concept.

4 The Assyrian conquest

Assyrian pressure increased in the reign of Tiglatpileser III (754–727) and a policy of territorial annexation commenced. Certain references in the annals to the western cities are most significant: 'I brought them within the border of Assyria'; 'my officials I set over them as governors'; '. . . people I carried off from their cities and placed them in the province of . . .'[33]

In Phoenicia a great victory was won over the Urarteans and the Syrians in the third year of the reign (743). On this occasion the Assyrians made a province of territory which included the Phoenician cities of Usnu, Siannu, Simira, and Kashpuna, the latter unidentifiable, but always 'on the seacoast'.[34] Another passage of the annals probably refers to the same event: it names the cities of Byblos, Simira, Arqa, Usnu, and Siannu, in addition to other unknown towns like Zimarra, Ri'-saba, and Ri'-sisu.[35] Some of these cities were probably residences of Assyrian governors: indeed, a governor of Simyra is explicitly mentioned in another fragment.[36]

Byblos was in a special position. It is sometimes mentioned among the annexed cities and sometimes referred to as an independent tributary with its own king, Sibitti-bi'li.[37] In fact, it probably retained that form of partial autonomy which had for years been characteristic of local city-states, as did Aradus, whose king, Mattan-bi'li,[38] is mentioned, but which is not on the list of annexed cities.

Finally we can say that Assyrian annexation under Tiglatpileser extended to the north of Phoenicia, as far as Byblos, leaving Byblos and Aradus in a state of relative autonomy. No mention is made, on the other hand, of annexations south of Byblos. Tyre paid tribute under king Hiram II,[39] whose name reappears in a Phoenician inscription from Cyprus,[40] in which a local governor calls himself 'servant of Hiram, king of the Sidonians'. This fact is noteworthy: it seems to imply that Tyre had retained substantial independence and ruled over the neighbouring region. No mention is made of Sidon in Tiglatpileser's inscriptions. Hiram was succeeded by Mitinna, who also paid tribute.[41]

Salmanassar v (726–722) conquered Samaria in the last year of his reign, and Sargon II (721–705) took possession of Cyprus. He mentions the tributes paid to him by the Cypriots on several occasions, and had a basalt stele bearing his name erected in Kition.[42] The remarkable development of Sargon's Mediterranean ventures, related in the annals, altered the attitude of the Cypriot cities and suggests an essential change in the economic policy of the eastern Mediterranean. The Phoenicians were no longer able to retain sole control of the trade routes and fell under the aegis of greater powers.

In spite of this, the strength of the Phoenician cities was still remarkable: the province of Simyra attempted to rebel at the beginning of the reign, taking part in a revolt headed by Hama, which included the provinces of Arpad, Damascus, and Samaria.[43] This uprising of northern and central Syria was led by the provinces instituted by Tiglatpileser III, as well as by Samaria, which had only just been conquered, but remained unsettled. The most likely cause of the revolt was the rapid retreat of Salmanassar v's army. Sargon II intervened in the second year of his reign and rapidly quelled the rebellion.

No further events on the Phoenician coast under this king are known. In the seventh year the annals refer to the payment of tribute by a few kings, including 'the kings of the seacoast';[44] the isolated inscription on a foundation cylinder of the palace of Khorsabad, which defines Sargon as he 'who subdued Cilicia (Kue) and Tyre',[45] refers at most to one of the usual acts of formal homage. On the whole we do not have the impression that Sargon was particularly hostile to Phoenicia; on the contrary, he may even have used her in the vast Mediterranean venture which he undertook.

Under Sennacherib (705–681) a coalition of Syrian cities was formed against Assyria, and these included the Phoenician cities:

In my third campaign I went against the Hittite land (Syria). Luli, king of Sidon, – the terrors of the splendours of my sovereignty overcame him and far off in the midst of the sea he fled. There he died. Great Sidon, Little Sidon, Bit-Zitti, Sarepta, Mahalliba, Ushu, Akzib, Akka, his strong, walled cities where there were fodder and drinking-places for his garrisons, – the terrors of the weapons of Assur, my lord, overpowered them and they bowed in submission at my feet. Tuba'lu I seated on the royal throne over them, and tribute, gifts for my majesty, I imposed upon him for all time, without ceasing. From Menahem, the Shamsimurunite, Tuba'lu, the Sidonite, Abdi-bi'ti, the Arvadite, Uru-milki, the Gublite, Mitinti, the Ashdodite, Budu-ilu, the Beth-Ammonite, Kammusunadbi, the Moabite, Malik-rammu, the Edomite, – kings of Amurru, all of them, lavish gifts, as their heavy tribute, they brought before me for the fourth time, and kissed my feet.[46]

Elsewhere it is specified that 'Luli from Tyre fled to Cyprus', where he died.[47] The campaign in question took place in 701 or 700. Luli is the Elulaeus mentioned in the annals of Tyre and said to have reigned for thirty-six years.[48] The term 'king of Sidon' in the Assyrian annals can only refer to the extent of his dominion. There is no doubt that he was king of Tyre, as Josephus says, and even the Assyrian annals state that he fled from Tyre to Cyprus. Josephus also gives an interesting account[49] of the other Phoenician cities which broke away from Tyre, placing sixty ships at the disposal of the Assyrian king in order to besiege the island. We may well ask the reason for this confederation of the other Phoenician towns against the greatest city, and, if it was not actually formed under pressure from Assyria, this pressure might have been added to feelings of hostility and local rivalry. According to Josephus, Tyre resisted the siege for five years and defeated the fleet sent to conquer her. But even so, the flight of Elulaeus and the installation in Sidon of a new king chosen by the Assyrians (Tuba'lu, or Ittobaal II) was a blow for the power of the mightiest Phoenician city.[50]

There are no further references to expeditions made by Sennacherib in the Phoenician area. The mention of 'Tyrian, Sidonian, and Cyprian sailors, captives of my hand'[51] used in subsequent ventures must refer to prisoners in the campaign of the year 701 or 700.

Under Asarhaddon (681–668), Abdi-Milkutti, the successor of Ittobaal, was king of Sidon. He allied himself with Sanduarri, a king of Cilicia, against the Assyrian sovereign:

Abdi-Milkutti, king of Sidon, who did not fear my majesty, did not heed the word of my lips, who trusted in the fearful sea and cast off my yoke, – Sidon, his garrison city, which lies in the midst of the sea, I razed to the ground, its walls and houses I destroyed and cast into the sea, the site I annihilated. By the aid of Assur my lord, I caught up Abdi-Milkutti, who had fled from my arms, out of the sea like a fish and cut off his head. His wife, his sons, the people of his palace, property and goods, precious stones, garments of coloured wool and line, elephant skins and elephant tusks, maple and box-wood, all kinds of treasures from his palace, in great abundance I carried off. His widespreading people, – there was no numbering them, cattle and sheep and asses, in great number, I transported to Assyria. And I gathered together the kings of Khatti (Syria) and the seacoast, all of them, and in another place I had a city built. Its name I called Kar-Esarhaddon. The inhabitants of

. . . , cities in Sidon's environment, where there was fodder and water, his garrison towns, which, by the aid of Assur, my lord, my hand had captured, – the people, spoil of my bow, of mountain and sea of the setting sun, therein I settled, and I returned to Assyria. That province I reorganised and set my official as governor over them, laying upon them a tribute greater than that of former days. Those cities of his – Ma'rubbu and Sarepta, I turned over to Ba'li, king of Tyre.[52]

This passage from the annals contains certain facts of considerable interest. To begin with, Sidon, formerly loyal to Assyria, has become hostile, while Tyre, formerly hostile, helped the Assyrians under the new king, Baal. Furthermore, the territory of Sidon included Sarepta, which was then transferred to Tyre, which obviously again controlled an area in the south. This time the conquest of the rebel cities was followed by destruction, the departure of the population and foundation in another locality. And although no further mention is made of this new foundation, while the ancient city is referred to at a later date, there is no doubt that this measure was far more drastic than the usual subjugation and enforced tribute. Another interesting fact is the appointment of an Assyrian governor.

According to the chronicle of Asarhaddon and the Babylon chronicle, the capture of Sidon took place in 677 and the execution of Abdi-Milkutti in 676.[53] From 676 to 671, when Tyre rebelled, relative tranquillity ensued, and we have a list of vassal kings of this period who provided the Assyrian king with material for constructing his new palace at Nineveh. These included Ba'lu of Tyre, Milkiashapa of Byblos, and Mattan-Baal of Aradus.[54] A treaty between Asarhaddon and Baal of Tyre, in fragmentary condition, but which gives a good idea of Assyrian and Phoenician policy, is also of this period.[55] In the first part the obligations of Baal to Asarhaddon are established and criteria are suggested by which to settle the questions raised by the two states. In the second part the gods are invoked as guarantors of the agreement and a curse laid on whoever breaks it. The position of the Assyrian governor in Tyre, in charge of all Assyrian affairs, is clearly defined. There is also a council of ancients ('the ancients of thy land') which assists the king in all his functions. Special attention is paid to the problems of navigation, in which Tyre is obviously particularly interested: the ports are named in the Syrian region where Tyrian ships can call after obtaining permission to trade in the territory under Assyrian control.

The treaty must have been very onerous for Tyre: in the tenth year of the reign of Asarhaddon (671) she allied herself to Taharqa, king of Egypt, and revolted against Assyria.[56] In an inscription from Assur, Asarhaddon declares: 'I captured Tyre which is in the midst of the sea. Ba'lu, its king, who had trusted in Taharqa, king of Ethiopia, – all of his cities, his property, I took away from him. I conquered Egypt, Upper Egypt, and Ethiopia.'⁵⁷

Several fragments from the annals, however, give the impression that on this occasion, too, the subjugation consisted of the imposition of a tribute after provisions had been cut off from the island of Tyre,⁵⁸ besides, under Asarhaddon's successor, Assurbanipal, Tyre still appears to be autonomous and ruled by Baal.

In all events, Asarhaddon's reign marked a further decline of Phoenician independence. The territory was now divided into Assyrian provinces: Simyra in the north, the zone of Sidon (Kar-Esarhaddon) in the centre, the zone of Tyre (Ushu) in the south. Only few, isolated, independent city-states remained: Aradus, Byblos, and the island of Tyre.

Under Assurbanipal (668–626), Baal of Tyre rebelled again:

In my third campaign I marched against Baal, king of Tyre, who dwells in the midst of the sea, when he did not observe my royal command and did not obey the word of my lips. I threw up earthworks against him, by sea and land I seized his approaches. I pressed them sorely and made their lives miserable. I made them submit to my yoke. A daughter, the offspring of his loins and the daughters of his brothers he brought into my presence, to serve as my concubines. Yahi-Milki, his son, who had never before crossed the sea, he had them bring to me, for the first time, to render me service. His daughter and his brothers' daughters I received from him, with large dowries. I had mercy upon him and gave him back his son, the offspring of his loins.⁵⁹

According to all the evidence, the rebellion of Tyre was connected with the Egyptian attempt to overthrow Assyrian supremacy. Both rebellions were quelled, although Tyre was not occupied and merely had to send homages and tributes. Immediately after the subjugation of Tyre the Assyrian inscriptions mention the submission of Aradus: 'Yakinlu, king of Aradus, who dwells in the midst of the sea, who had not submitted to the kings, my fathers, I brought under my yoke. His daughter, with a large dowry, he brought to Nineveh, to serve as my concubine, and kissed my feet.'⁶⁰ And another inscription specifies: 'Gold, dark red wool, black wool, fish and birds, I imposed upon him as yearly tribute.'⁶¹

As a precedent of the revolt of Aradus it is worth quoting an important letter from a governor, Itti-Shamash-balatu, to the Assyrian king:

Ikki-lu (probably Yakinlu) does not permit the ships to leave the port of the king my master. All ships he wards off to his own ports. Whoever comes to him he consents to his voyage, but whever goes to a port in the land of Assyria, he comes and destroys his ships.⁶²

In another passage Ikki-lu seriously impedes the Assyrian naval trade. Subsequently, after the death of the sovereign of Aradus, his sons went with rich gifts to pay homage to Assurbanipal, who chose Azi-Baal as the successor and gave the other sons gifts.[63] It seems that the Assyrian king was either bound by treaty to designate the successor or else that Yakinlu had not chosen an heir and that his sons preferred to rely on Assurbanipal's advice.

Later, on his return from his ninth campaign against the Arab tribes, Assurbanipal was faced with another rebellion in Phoenicia:

On my return march I captured the city of Ushu, which is located on the shore of the sea. The people of Ushu, who had not cowered before their governors, and had not paid their tribute, their yearly gifts, I slew. Among those insubmissive people I applied the rod. Their gods, their people I carried off to Assyria. The insubmissive people of Akka I slaughtered. Their corpses I hung on stakes, surrounding the city with them. Those who were left I carried away to Assyria, joined them to my military organisation, adding them to the many troops which Assur had given me.[64]

There is no further mention of Phoenicia under the successors of Assurbanipal. So, at the fall of the Assyrian empire (612), the area seems to have been in the same situation as at the time of Asarhaddon: the three provinces of Simyra, Sidon, and Ushu, in addition to three cities which were autonomous, but paid tribute to Syria – Aradus, Byblos, and Tyre.

5 The Babylonian and Persian age

There are no historical references to the Phoenician cities between 640 and 590. It seems likely, however, that the decline of the Assyrian empire and its destruction by the Medes in 612 granted them temporary prosperity. It also seems probable that they did not object to the expansion of the Pharaoh Necho, who ruled over the entire Syro-Palestinian region between 609 and 605. Of course, Nebuchadnezzar's victory over the Egyptians at the battle of Karkemish (605) marked the beginning of a new crisis for the Phoenicians. Nebuchadnezzar (605–562) attacked the Phoenician cities and besieged Tyre, which resisted for thirteen years (586–573), but had finally to surrender, as did Sidon and other localities. Information about Tyre is again provided by Josephus, who quotes the annals of the city from c. 590 to 530.[65] Nebuchadnezzar replaced the defeated king, Ittobaal II, by his faithful Baal, who reigned from 574 to 564. The king ruled together with a Babylonian minister.

With Baal the succession of kings was temporarily interrupted. For seven years, according to Josephus, there was a succession of 'judges' (suffetes): Eknibal, Chelbes, Abbar, Myttyn, and Gerastratus. A king, Balator, reigned for a year, however; and after the judges the succession of kings resumed with Merbal, who returned from Babylon in 556,

23

maybe as a result of a milder policy on the part of Nebuchadnezzar's successors. Merbal reigned for four years and was succeeded by his brother Hiram (552–532).[66]

There is no direct information on the Phoenician cities' reactions to the destruction of the Babylonian empire and the rise to power of the Persians. They can hardly have opposed and may even have approved of an historical event which liberated them from an oppressive rule. The Bible[67] says that Cyrus permitted the Jews, returned from their exile in Babylon, to obtain cedar wood for their new temple from the Sidonians and Tyrians, but this does not give us much idea of the state of the Phoenician towns. We know more about Cambyses, at whose disposal the Phoenician cities placed their fleet for the expedition against Egypt. According to Herodotus, however, they refused to participate in the expedition against Carthage which Cambyses had also planned, thereby displaying a persistent attachment to their old colonies.

The division of the Persian empire into satrapies, effected by Darius I in 515–514, assigned the Phoenician cities to the fifth satrapy, but left the kings and local autonomies (under the control of ministers and strategists who ensured payment of tributes and military loyalty). The cities must have been content with this state of affairs, since no mention is made of a rebellion for a considerable time. Greek sources emphasize the valuable help given by the Phoenician fleet to Darius I (541–486) and to Xerxes (485–465) in the war against the Greeks. Under Artaxerxes I (465–424) and Darius II (425–404), too, there are references to the loyalty of the Phoenician cities to the Persians, in return for which the Persians must have favoured local expansion of the cities. The Periplus of Pseudo-Scylax, written c. 350, but referring to a previous period, attributes the control of the coast from Sarepta to Mount Carmel to Tyre, in addition to a port on the southern slopes of Mount Carmel and Askalon;[68] Aradus extended her influence to the coastal region across the sea; Sidon appropriated Dor and Jaffa, or rather was presented with these possessions by the Persian emperor c. 450, as is stated in the inscription on Eshmunazar's coffin.[69] Furthermore, classical sources tell us that the three cities combined to found or refound Tripoli, each city establishing its own quarter there,[70] and thus proving both the autonomy and political co-ordination existing between the large Phoenician towns.

Various indications suggest the predominance of Sidon. The sovereign of Persia had a residence there, as was proved by the discovery of remains of columns and capitals in the form of bull protomai (of typical Achaemenidian appearance). There are also inscriptions containing information about the local dynasty: one of Tabnit, one of Eshmunazar, and three of Bodashtart.[71] The inscriptions of Tabnit and Eshmunazar on the coffins are intended to commemorate the two sovereigns and safeguard the tombs from violation. The first inscription adds that the father of Tabnit was also called Eshmunazar; the second is more informative and commemorates the building of temples to the gods, explicitly stating that the 'lord of kings', that is the Persian emperor, enlarged the territory of Sidon: 'The lord of kings also gave us Dor and Jaffa, the powerful lands of Dagon which are in the plain of Sharon, in proportion to my mighty deeds. And to the boundaries of our land we added them, so that they shall for ever belong to Sidon.'[72]

Bodashtart, who calls himself 'grandson of Eshmunazar, king of the Sidonians',[73] drew up his inscriptions to commemorate the building of temples. It is not certain which Eshmunazar his grandfather was, so we cannot consolidate the two lines of succession:

Eshmunazar I	Eshmunazar ?
Tabnit	×
Eshmunazar II	Bodashtart
	Yatonmilk

We do not know whether Yatonmilk, crown prince under Bodashtart, actually reigned, and the inscription of Eshmunazar II suggests a long regency under his mother, Ummiashtart. The same Eshmunazar declares that he was 'an orphan, son of a widow';[74] and says that he died in the fourteenth year of his reign: 'I was taken off before my time, son of a limited number of days.'[75] In all probability Eshmunazar became king after his father's death, when he was still a child, and the government was exercised by his mother.

The style of the coffins and the writing suggest that these sovereigns reigned in the fifth century. If, as has been supposed by K. Galling, the gifts from the king of Persia to the king of Sidon were in return for the aid of the Phoenician fleet in the wars against the Greeks, Eshmunazar II can be dated c. 450 B C.

A long inscription from Byblos seems of about the same time. The author claims to be the king Yehaumilk, son of Yeharbaal, son of Urimilk, and declares that he built a temple to Baalat of Byblos.[76] A little later we have two more inscriptions from Byblos on the coffins, one by the son of the king Shipitbaal, which can be ascribed to c. 400 B C,[77] and one of Batnoam, mother of the king Ozbaal, which can be dated c. 340.[78]

In the fourth century B C we notice a certain evolution in the Phoenician cities' Persian policy. In 392, when the Greek Evagoras occupied Cyprus and attacked Phoenicia, Tyre and other cities submitted to him temporarily. In 362 king Straton of Sidon (Abdashtart on the coins) was on such good terms with the Greeks that he was nicknamed the Philhellene, and welcomed an Egyptian army. But the revolt of the satraps was subdued and the hopes of independence from Persia were shattered. Tennes, king of Sidon from 354 to 344, rebelled again in 346, destroying the satrap's palace and sacking the royal park. This time Artaxerxes Ochus intervened and quelled the revolt with much bloodshed. Sidon was burnt to the ground, over forty thousand inhabitants were killed, and not even Tennes was spared, in spite of his treachery. He was succeeded by another Straton, who ultimately submitted to Alexander. A few of the names of the kings of this period are recorded on coins of Byblos: Elpaal *c.* 360, Adramelek *c.* 350, Ozbaal *c.* 340, Ainel *c.* 335.[79]

Persian rule in Phoenicia came to an end with the conquest of Alexander. After the battle of Issus (333) the main Phoenician towns (Aradus, Byblos, and Sidon) opened their gates to the conqueror. In Tyre a princess representing the king Azemilkos, still in the service of the Persians, went to meet him on the mainland to pay homage to him herself. Alexander, however, wanted to go on to the island and sacrifice in the shrine of Heracles-Melqart. The princess countered with the suggestion that he should sacrifice in the more ancient temple of the god on the mainland. Tyre was obviously following her traditional policy, intending to retain her independence as best she could, while an embassy from Carthage encouraged her to resist. Alexander was not prepared to give up the island, however, since it was a military base of great importance, and decided to invade it. He started to build a siege-mole joining the island to the mainland, and, to protect himself during this operation, he obtained the assistance of the fleet of the other Phoenician cities. The other Phoenician towns had abandoned the Persians after the battle of Issus and their ships had gathered in the port of Sidon, while the Tyrian fleet under Azemilkos had returned to Tyre. Tyre did not even receive the aid promised by Carthage, which was involved in other wars, so, several months later, the mole was completed and the island occupied after much bloodshed. The king, the leading citizens, and the Carthaginian envoys who had sought refuge in the temple of Melqart, were pardoned. The town was rebuilt as a Macedonian fortress and colonized by the Macedonians.

Even if the history of the Phoenician cities does not end here, it underwent a serious crisis. As political instruments of the successive rulers, the cities were profoundly penetrated by Hellenistic culture which gradually destroyed the tradition of independence, while the Phoenician language gradually disappeared and made way for Greek.

And yet it is precisely the language that proves that the decline of the Phoenician cities was a slow process with sporadic revivals of independence. Phoenician inscriptions appear at the end of the second century BC, and it was in this period that Tyre and Sidon, which had each had their own dynasties, temporarily regained independence and enjoyed brief spells of city-statehood, Tyre from 120 and Sidon from 111 BC. Even after the Roman conquest in 64 BC Tyre, Sidon, and Tripoli enjoyed partial independence, and, although this was merely a tenacious survival owing to tradition and geographical situation, it was no less incongruous in the context of general historical development.

6 Political organization

Each Phoenician city constituted an autonomous political entity ruling over the inhabited area and the surrounding countryside. As we have seen, there were undoubtedly periods when one or other of the large cities reigned supreme over the others, but this supremacy was never politically defined, except by the title 'King of the Sidonians', which suggests dominion beyond the city limits. As far as we know there were no confederations of cities, apart from the alliances (like the one against Tyre), which were occasional and had no unity of command. And here it is interesting to note that when the fleets of the Phoenician cities offered their services to Xerxes in 480 BC Herodotus mentions three leaders instead of one (Tetramnestos of Sidon, Mattan of Tyre, and Marbal of Aradus).[80]

The cities were governed by kings who usually succeeded each other hereditarily, and from their records we can reconstruct the succession of various dynasties, although they were frequently confused by palace revolts and wars. The records also prove the importance which the kings attached to dynastic succession, and so we have the inscription of Shipitbaal declaring the dynasty and invoking divine protection: 'Wall built by Shipitbaal king of Byblos, son of Elibaal king of Byblos, son of Yehimilk king of Byblos, for Baalat of Byblos, his lady. May Baalat of Byblos prolong the days of Shipitbaal and his years over Byblos.'[81]

The concept of royalty is illustrated in Yehimilk's inscription by the association of the title of king with the attributes of 'just' and 'righteous' in connexion with the building of a temple. This, together with the erection of statues, seems to have been a typical activity of the kings or, rather, an activity to which the inscriptions refer:

Temple built by Yehimilk king of Byblos. He it is who restored all these temples. May Baal Shamim, Baalat of Byblos, and all the holy gods of Byblos prolong the days of Yehimilk and his years over Byblos, he is a just king and a righteous king towards the holy gods of Byblos.[82]

The attributes 'just' and 'righteous' are not coincidental. It is interesting, too, that the nouns 'justice' and 'righteousness' should appear as Phoenician deities in Philo of Byblos.[83] The term 'just king' recurs throughout the ages and is to be found in the Persian era in the inscription of Yehaumilk.[84]

We also find the qualification 'just son', which appears in the second inscription of Bodashtart in reference to the crown prince, and can also be interpreted as 'legitimate' son: 'The king of Bodashtart and the "just son" Yatonmilk, king of the Sidonians, grandson of the king Eshmunazar, king of the Sidonians, has built this temple for his god Eshmun, holy prince.'[85]

An interesting connexion between the royal and priestly functions, already suggested by the dedication of religious buildings, is confirmed by the texts from Byblos and Sidon in the Persian era. Ozbaal, king of Byblos, was of priestly descent, as we see from the inscription of his mother Batnoam: 'In this coffin lie I, Batnoam, mother of the king Ozbaal king of Byblos, son of Paltibaal priest of Baalat, in the garments and attire with the gold mouth-plate of the women of royal descent who came before me.'[86]

In Sidon Tabnit calls himself 'priest of Astarte, king of the Sidonians, son of Eshmunazar, priest of Astarte, king of the Sidonians'.[87] The analogous position of the queen is also illustrated by the inscription of Eshmunazar, whose mother was Ummiashtart, 'priestess of Astarte our lady, the queen, daughter of the king Eshmunazar king of the Sidonians'.[88]

The same inscription of Eshmunazar is of particular interest because of the importance it attributes to the position of the queen: Ummiashtart reigned as regent many years and uses the plural in reference to herself and her son, when she writes of the events of the reign: 'It is we who built the temple of Eshmun, the holy prince . . . The king of kings gave us Dor and Jaffa . . .'[89]

Besides the terms used to describe royalty we are informed about the duties of state in as early an inscription as that of Ahiram. It mentions an official, the 'governor', and a military commander. Although we know nothing more about the latter, the 'governor' is already known to us from the texts of Ugarit and El Amarna as an official who supervises the administration of the court and city. He is mentioned again in Cyprus, in the inscription of a 'governor of Qart-hadasht, servant of Hiram king of Sidonians'.[90]

In the performance of his duties the king was assisted by a council of ancients. It is not known when the council came into being in the individual cities nor whether it exercised its activity continuously, but we do find it in the treaty of Asarhaddon with Baal of Tyre. Part of the text is unfortunately missing, but it definitely mentions 'the ancients of thy land in council'.[91] The classical sources give further information: in Tyre these councils could take decisions in the king's absence;[92] in Sidon, where Diodorus mentions one hundred members of the council,[93] they could even act against the king. Finally the existence of 'ancients' in

Byblos is referred to in Ezekiel.[94] In view of the activities of the Phoenician cities it is reasonable to assume that the ancients were the leading merchants or members of the leading families who controlled trade.

The annals of Tyre inform us of a particular development in the government of this city. In the Neo-Babylonian period, after the reign of Baal, a republic ruled by 'judges' was instituted: there were usually two 'judges' who ruled together for several years.[95] The suffetes of Carthage must, at least in name, have been a continuation of this system. In any case, the 'judges' of Tyre only appear for a brief period.

After the conquest, as we have seen, an Assyrian governor was placed next to the king in certain Phoenician towns in order to supervise his policy. There is a significant passage concerning the governor's functions in the treaty of Asarhaddon with Baal of Tyre: 'Any letter I send thee thou shalt not open without the governor. If the governor is not there thou shalt await him and then open it.'[96]

In other words the governor was the sole interpreter of the king of Assyria's order, and supervised the political activity of the Phoenician state.

The Assyrian governor's main function was obviously to report to his king. Mention has already been made of a letter from Itti-Shamash-balatu, an Assyrian official in the time of Assurbanipal, who resided in Simira and was responsible, as far as we can see, for relations with Aradus. Itti-Shamash-balatu complains that the king of Aradus was warding off all shipping from other ports and directing it to his own city, going as far as to intercept and destroy ships making for ports in Assyrian territory. He also alludes to the interest of high Assyrian officials:

The king my master must know. Many are the courtiers of the king my master to have paid money to this house. But I have trust in the king my master. I give to no one either a shekel or half a shekel; I give all to the king my master.[97]

It is worth noting that while the Assyrian governor exercised his control over a local king in Tyre, Simira had no king and the governor ruled directly.

CHAPTER 3

RELIGION

1 Introduction

The direct sources of information about Phoenician religion are the numerous inscriptions from the Phoenician cities. The nature of these inscriptions, however, as well as their brevity, tend to limit the data almost solely to the names of deities: they tell us little about the cults and religious life, and nothing about mythology.

One source which must originally have been direct, but which has been transmitted to us indirectly is the work of Sanchuniathon, a Phoenician priest from Berytus who, it is thought, lived around the eleventh century BC. Sanchuniathon exposed the Phoenician concepts of the creation of the world, we are told by Philo of Byblos, who wrote in Greek and was born, according to Suidas, c. AD 42 and was still alive in 117, under the Emperor Hadrian. Philo claims to quote in translation the writings of the ancient Phoenician priest. Unfortunately the work of Philo has not been handed down to us directly, but in fragments quoted by various historians, of whom the most famous is Eusebius, the fourth-century author of the *Praeparatio Evangelica*. Eusebius quotes the fragments in order to contest the doctrine, so that a dispute understandably ensued about the authenticity of the traditions which passed through so many complex channels. In the past there were serious doubts about Sanchuniathon's existence; more recently, however, the discoveries at Ugarit proved the likelihood of many accounts, so that it is now believed that Sanchuniathon's work can be considered authentic, even if there were obvious misunderstandings, omissions, and alterations in its transmission.

Further information about Phoenician cosmogony is provided by the Neo-Platonist Damascius, born c. AD 480, who quotes a cosmogony by Mochus, a writer also mentioned in other sources as the author of a Phoenician history. Apart from the cosmogony, other classical writers, Plutarch and Lucian in particular, provide information about the beliefs of the Phoenicians which must be accepted with reservations, especially when it remains unconfirmed elsewhere.

Another problem is the information contained in the Old Testament about a people the Hebrews call the Canaanites, in other words their predecessors in the Syro-Palestinian region. Everything referred to in the Old Testament as Canaanite heredity can undoubtedly be largely applied to the Phoenician cities, but about the independent beliefs of the cities the Old Testament tells us little.

Yet another problem is presented by the texts from Ugarit which contain ample information on the religion and mythology of a city on the north Syrian coast at a time immediately preceding our particular period. The religion of Ugarit can undoubtedly be defined as Canaanite and must have a certain amount in common with the religion of other coastal towns of the Iron Age. It is therefore a useful means of comparison and verification, but it cannot be considered a direct source, since the city is geographically and chronologically just outside the Phoenician area.

For very different reasons Punic religion is in a similar situation. The overseas colonies of the Phoenicians did, of course, largely retain the beliefs and religious customs of their homeland, and the information on the colonies is considerably greater than on the Phoenician cities. There must, however, have been secondary developments and substantial changes in the colonies which prevent us from considering Punic beliefs as purely Phoenician. So here again we have material useful as far as comparison and verifications are concerned, but which cannot be used directly.

These considerations on the sources prove the complexity of the problem of Phoenician religion. It seems to be the chronological continuation, retaining and acquiring independent elements, of the religion which can generically be termed Canaanite in the second millennium B C. The arrival of the Hebrews and Aramaeans in the interior restricted both the cultural and political area of the Canaanites to the coast, thereby allowing them to retain a continuity and traditionalism which would have been impossible elsewhere. It is precisely this continuity and traditionalism, so peculiar to the Phoenician religion, which must be the object of our study.

2 *The gods*

In Byblos the principal deities were El, Baalat, and Adonis. El is a Semitic deity of especial importance in the Canaanite religion and appears in a leading but rarely active position in the pantheon in the texts of Ugarit. The word, meaning 'god', can serve both as a generic term and as a special name. In Byblos, on the other hand, El appears as the leading deity, but not the most active one – a fact which is confirmed

31

by the identification with Kronos suggested by Philo of Byblos and other classical authors. Independently from El, Philo mentions Eliun (Hypsistos), placing him at the head of the divine hierarchy. Eliun reappears, still differentiated from El, in the Aramaic inscriptions of Sephire, but is combined with El in the Bible (El Elyon, 'the most high God').[1]

Baalat, whose name means 'lady' and who reappears as the dominant deity of the city (Baalat Gebal, 'Baalat of Byblos') is considerably more active. The pre-eminence of this goddess is evident in the earliest inscriptions with recurrent dedications to her. The formula begging Baalat to prolong the days and the years of kings of Byblos is repeated in the inscriptions of Yehimilk (where Baalat is mentioned together with Baal Shamim and all the holy gods of Byblos), Abibaal, Elibaal, and Shipitbaal.[2] Later, in the Persian era, the entire inscription of Yehaumilk was dedicated to Baalat and gives some idea of the authority of the goddess:

I am Yehaumilk king of Byblos, son of Yeharbaal, grandson of Urimilk king of Byblos, whom the lady Baalat of Byblos made king over Byblos. I have invoked my lady Baalat of Byblos, and she has heard my voice. I have made for my lady Baalat of Byblos this altar of bronze that is in this courtyard, and this gate of gold that is facing this gate of mine, and the winged disk (?) of gold that is on the stone above this gate of gold, and this portico with its pillars and the capitals that are on them and its roof: this have I done, Yehaumilk king of Byblos, for my lady Baalat of Byblos, and she has heard my voice and has done good to me. May Baalat of Byblos bless Yehaumilk king of Byblos and let him live and prolong his days and his years over Byblos for he is a just king. And may the lady Baalat of Byblos grant him favour in the eyes of the gods and in the eyes of the people of this earth, and may the favour of the people of this earth be with him. Whosoever thou shalt be, each king and each man who continues to perform works on this altar, or on this gate of gold, or on this portico, my name 'I am Yehaumilk king of Byblos' shalt thou add to thine own on that work; and if thou dost not add my name to thine own, or if thou removest this work and movest . . . its base in this place . . . may the lady Baalat of Byblos destroy this man and his seed before all the gods of Byblos.[3]

Baalat, of course, corresponds basically to the earth mother who symbolizes fertility and is consequently regarded as the genetrix of the gods and men as well as the plants. As we know, this is a common and very ancient deity in the whole of the Near East: Innin of the Sumarians, Ishtar of the Babylonians and Assyrians, Isis of the Egyptians.

The third god of Byblos, Adonis, is only given this name by the Greek authors. The name, however, is obviously Semitic – *ādōn* 'master', and the pronominal suffix *-i*, 'my master'. The same Greek sources present the figure of the young god who dies and is resurrected. He expresses the annual death and rebirth of earthly vegetation and is thereby connected with the figure of the mother goddess in the cult and the myth. In its Greek form the myth is as follows: Adonis was a young hunter whom the goddess Aphrodite loved and tried to lure away from his dangerous sport. She failed and Adonis was killed by a boar. He descended into Hades and Persephone refused to return him to Aphrodite. Finally, after a contest between the two goddesses, Adonis could come back to earth. The Greek myth is an obvious repetition of the ancient Oriental myth of the Sumerian god Dumuzi, the Babylonian and Assyrian Tammuz, the Egyptian Osiris, the Hittite Telipinu and the Ugaritic Baal; Aphrodite replaces the Oriental mother goddess. Recent studies have, however, revealed certain differences between the various accounts of the myth: the functions of the young god are not always the same, and, above all, his death or descent into Hades is not always followed by resurrection.

We can conclude the picture of the deities of Byblos with a few secondary elements which show that the formulation of the pantheon was not invariable. Apart from the few names of deities on seals there is Baal Shamim, the 'master of the heavens', who appears both in ancient times (inscription of Yehimilk) and in the Persian era (inscription of Shipitbaal). In this latter inscription Baal Addir is also mentioned, the 'powerful lord', a deity who reappears in the Punic and Neo-Punic inscriptions in Africa and may have been interpreted in Latin as Iupiter Valens, the god worshipped by the African troops. Finally, in the inscription of Yehimilk, the term 'the congregation of the gods of Byblos' appears for the first time to indicate the assembly of deities, and in the Persian era both the inscription of Yehaumilk and Shipitbaal mention 'all the gods of Byblos'. It is worth noting that this term accompanies, but does not include, the names of the leading deities. So Yehimilk says: 'May Baal Shamim and Baalat of Byblos and the assembly of the holy gods of Byblos prolong the days of Yehimilk and his years over Byblos';[4] and Yehaumilk: 'May the lady Baalat of Byblos destroy this man and his seed before all the gods of Byblos';[5] and Shipitbaal: 'Baal Addir and Baalat and all (the gods).'[6]

In Sidon, El corresponds to Baal. This name, too, which is obviously the masculine of Baalat, is known from the texts of Ugarit, where it designates the most active Canaanite god. Its common meaning is 'lord', and it can therefore be applied to various localities and later become specific. Like El in Byblos, Baal was not particularly active in Sidon. Eshmunazar, however, claims in his inscription to have dedicated a temple to him, and the term itself, 'name of Baal', borne by the leading female deity, Astarte, denotes its importance.

Astarte is clearly predominant in the Sidonian pantheon, as is proved by the repeated dedications of inscriptions, the building of temples in her honour, and the fact that kings and queens call themselves her priests. We have already mentioned the term 'name of Baal' which may have resulted from theological speculations now unknown to us; but it is worth noting that the title reappears in the Ugaritic texts. Astarte is also a general Canaanite deity, stemming from the goddess who symbolizes the earth mother throughout the ancient East and therefore corresponds to Baalat of Byblos. In Semitic sources we get the name Ashtart, and the biblical Ashtoret comes from a contamination of the vowels of *bōšet* 'disgrace' – an intentional condemnation of the cult. This cult, however, was notoriously widespread. The Bible mentions Ashtoret on various occasions as a 'deity of the Sidonians', which not only implies the town of Sidon but the Phoenicians in general.

Together with Baal and Astarte, the third god of Sidon is Eshmun. Unlike the other gods, this deity is neither mentioned in previous periods nor outside the Phoenician-Punic area. He appears for the first time in the seventh century, in the treaty of Asarhaddon with Baal of Tyre,[7] and is subsequently referred to continually in the Sidonian inscriptions of the Persian era: Eshmunazar builds him a temple at the 'spring of Yidlal on the mount',[8] and Bodashtart builds him another temple.[9] In each case the designation 'holy prince' which follows the divine name is worth noting. Eshmun undoubtedly corresponds to Adonis in character and functions. The etymology of the name is uncertain, but it may well be connected with *šēm*, meaning 'name', and therefore primarily the divine name. In Greek sources he is identified with Asklepios, which implies a tendency to worship him as the god of healing; and, in his turn, Asklepios, by assuming the functions of Adonis, exemplifies the combination of all these figures in the young god who dies and rises from the dead.

The city-god of Tyre is Melqart – another obvious meaning, since the name means 'king of the city'. In this respect Melqart corresponds to El of Byblos and Baal of Sidon, and is probably the Baal mentioned in the Bible with reference to the sins of King Ahab:

And it came to pass, as if it had been a light thing for him to walk in the sins of Jeroboam the son of Nebat, that he took to wife Jezebel the daughter of Ethbaal king of the Sidonians, and went and served Baal, and worshipped him. And he reared up an altar for Baal in the house of Baal, which he had built in Samaria.[10]

Melqart, therefore, is none other than the Baal of Tyre. Since Josephus tells us that Hiram built a temple to him (as he had done for Astarte),[11] Comte du Mesnil du Buisson recently suggested that Melqart's ascent to the head of the pantheon must be ascribed to the tenth century BC. Another reason for identifying Melqart with Baal is the fact that Baal appears in the proper names of Tyre.[12]

If Melqart corresponds to El and Baal, and can even be identified with Baal, the celebration of an annual feast of resurrection in his honour suggests the convergence and prevalence of the functions of Adonis and Eshmun in his personality. And curiously enough, despite the current intersections and syncretisms of deities, Eshmun also appears on his own, as in Asarhaddon's treaty with Baal, while mythology of Greek origin relates that Iolaus-Eshmun resurrected Heracles-Melqart, son of Asteria (Astarte) and Zeus, killed by Typhon. The continuous importance of Melqart is proved by his temple in Tyre, where Alexander wished to sacrifice, and above all by the cult devoted to him in the colonies founded by Tyre (Carthage in particular). In Greece he was identified with Heracles and his cult was widespread, and later, in the Christian era, Heracles-Melqart, like many other Oriental deities, assumed an increasing amount of solar features.

Together with Melqart, Astarte, to whom Hiram dedicated a temple, was worshipped as the main female deity in Tyre. According to the Bible, one of the sins of Solomon was to have gone 'after Ashtoret the goddess of the Sidonians';[13] and later, about the reforms of Josiah, we are told:

And the high places that were before Jerusalem, which were on the right hand of the mount of corruption, which Solomon the king of Israel had builded for Ashtoreth the abomination of the Sidonians, and for Chemosh the abomination of the Moabites, and for Milcom the abomination of the children of Ammon, did the king defile.[14]

Astarte recurs in the treaty between Asarhaddon and Baal, and later becomes Asteria-Aphrodite, mother of Melqart in the traditional Greek myth.

The treaty between Asarhaddon and Baal is of great interest with regard to the Tyrian pantheon. The fourth column of the treaty invokes the divine protectors of the agreement, Assyrian (in the text they remain Ishtar and Gula) as well as Phoenician.[15] These deities include Melqart and Astarte; Bait-ili, corresponding to the Baitylos in Philo of Byblos, probably the deification of the stelae or the shrines which were regarded as the home of the gods; Anat-bait-ili, composed from the Syrian deity Anat (pre-eminent in the Ugaritic texts) and Bait-ili, which here seems a title or definition of Anat; Baal-samem, obviously Baal-Shamim, subsequently assimilated to Zeus Olympus as god of heaven; Baal-malage, corresponding to the Zeus Meilikios of Philo of Byblos, probably interpretable as 'lord of the sailors'; Baal-sapuni, corresponding to the Baal-Saphon ('lord of Mount Saphon') known from the texts of Ugarit and the Old Testament; and finally Iesumunu, evidently Eshmun.

35

Little is known about the deities of the other Phoenician cities. In Berytus Baalat of Berytus was worshipped. The poet Nonnus, of the fifth century AD, says that Adonis wished to conquer the nymph Berytus and that the contest was won by a sea *ba'al*.[16] In the following century Damascius attributes the myth of Adonis to Asklepios of Berytus, so on the whole the religious characteristics of the leading cities seem relatively similar, and we can proceed to a comparative analysis.

It seems evident that a triad of deities is common to all Phoenicia. This triad is composed of a protective god of the city; a goddess, often his wife or companion, who symbolized the fertile earth; and a young god, somehow connected with the goddess (usually her son), whose resurrection expressed the annual cycle of the vegetation. Within these limits the names and functions of these gods vary, and the fluidity of this pantheon, where the common name often prevails over the proper name, and the function over the personality, is characteristic. All these characteristics appear already in the Canaanite religion in general, and certain aspects of them appear in the earlier forms of Semitic religion. The assumption of well-defined personalities, complex and concrete functions, and a mythology suggests the development of the Semitic religions in the areas of an advanced sedentary culture rather than their primitive structure.

Another characteristic of the Phoenician triad is its flexibility from town to town, so that independent figures, like Melqart, come on to the scene. Here the personality assumes increasing consistency, while the functions are subordinated.

On this basis it seems obvious that the complex Greek interpretation of the Phoenician religion is fundamentally correct. The main or most ancient god becomes identified with Kronos or even Zeus. The goddess corresponds to Aphrodite. The young god, when no longer called Adonis, appears as Asklepios or Dionysius or Heracles. Even the mythological tales told about the gods by the Greeks suit their personality when they are not actually, as in the case of Adonis, Oriental myths in Greek clothing.

The triad of which we have spoken so far is characteristic of the Phoenician religion, but it is not exclusive. To begin with, the functional rather than personal nature of the gods favours numerous different specifications. So Baal appears as Baal Shamim ('lord of heaven'), Baal Saphon ('lord of Mount Saphon'), Baal Lebanon ('lord of the Lebanon'), Baal Rosh ('lord of the promontory'); the Zeus Kasios of Philo of Byblos is probably the same as Baal Saphon. In these specific forms of Baal, which sometimes even suggest substantially autonomous deities, the mountain regions, where there was an evident tendency to localize the *numina loci*, play an interesting part.

Another god, lacking the Baal element and therefore alien to the triad, but of eastern origin, is Reshef, god of lightning and fire, whom the Greeks identified with Apollo. The same applies to Dagon, god of wheat, whose origins are very remote. In Phoenicia he is mentioned by Philo of Byblos as inventor of wheat and the plough.

Finally, the brief inscription on a stele from Amrit, dated to the fifth or sixth century, is dedicated by the offerer 'to his lord, to Shadrapa, because he heard the voice of his words'.[17] This is the earliest mention of Shadrapa, who subsequently recurs in Punic, Palmyrene, and Greek inscriptions from Syria (Satrapes). The name seems composed of two elements, to be translated as 'spirit of healing'. In the Palmyrene representations he is accompanied by serpents and scorpions and is characterized as an autochthonian deity. In Punic Tripolitania he was to be identified with *Liber pater*, of the type of Dionysus.

Astral cults must have been rare in the ancient Phoenician religion. It was only in the Hellenistic era, and under the Babylonian influence which spread throughout the Near East, that astral developments took place in Phoenicia, and they were always of secondary importance. El of Byblos was then assimilated to Kronos, Baalat of Byblos and Astarte of Sidon to Aphrodite.

Finally there are certain deities personifying qualities and functions mentioned by Philo of Byblos and shown to be of great antiquity by interesting Ugaritic precedents. As far as we know these deities were neither widespread nor the objects of large cults, but seem rather to be the result of a theological speculation. They are of considerable interest, however, on account of the general conception of divinity which they reveal. Among these deities Chusor,[18] emerges as inventor of iron and ironwork, a series of manual and industrial activities, charms, and wise proverbs. Philo of Byblos compares him to Hephaestus, but the Ugaritic texts confirm his antiquity. Moral qualities are personified by Sydyk and Misor,[19] whose names mean 'justice' and 'righteousness'.

We have seen that an ample description of the acts of the gods, or of mythology, is given by Philo of Byblos, whose account can be divided into three parts: the origin of the cosmos, the origin of the culture and the genealogy of the gods. Since there are undoubtedly later elements in Philo's work and since the facts about the individual deities have already been dealt with, there seems no point in analysing his account. On the other hand, it is worth mentioning a few general points in which he presumably really did express the ancient concepts of the Phoenician religion. To begin with he claims that the universe originates from wind and chaos, which corresponds partially to what we know about Mesopotamian and Hebrew cosmogonies. He also expounds the theory of a cosmic egg, and of the stars and the separation of the waters from heaven which came into being when the egg was opened – a theory which recalls the Babylonian tale of creation. It is doubtful, however, whether the name of the egg, Mot, corresponds to the god of Ugarit of the same name who reigned over the underworld. At the beginning of the culture the figure of Usoos,[20] the inventor of garments made of animal skins and rival of his brother, Hypsuranios, is reminiscent in name and certain features of the biblical Esau, while the general procedure of attributing the genesis of arts and crafts to individuals, organized genealogically, suggests Oriental methods, particularly as they appear in the Bible. The genealogy of the gods is headed by Eliun and Berut, probably (Baalat of) Berytus. The descendants include El, Baitylos (– betyl, the stone idol), Dagon (called Siton, or 'wheat'), Astarte, Baaltis (Baalat), and Melqart. Among the descendants of El is a Mot (Thanatos) who can probably be identified with the god of Ugarit with the same functions.

As for the cosmogonic traditions, variants are given by Damascius,[21] taken partly from Mochus, whose accounts are of great interest for comparative purposes. The primary nature of Ether and Air is confirmed. El generates Ulomos, whose name is undoubtedly Semitic, corresponding to the Hebrew *'ōlām*, 'world'. From Ulomos comes Chusor, and then the Egg.

The extreme complexity of all these facts makes it seemingly difficult to reconstruct a coherent Phoenician cosmogony from them. On the other hand, the environmental connexions as well as certain facts contained in the inscriptions indicate the existence of mythological traditions concerning the origin of the universe. To these traditions were added others concerning arts and crafts; and finally genealogies of the gods were elaborated by the priests so as to organize the relationships of the pantheon, giving certain gods special priority, probably for political reasons, as happened elsewhere in the ancient Near East.

3 The cult

From the divine epithets and the etymology of the proper names, as well as the divine names themselves, we get a fairly clear idea of the relationship between the human and the divine elements in Phoenician religion. On the whole the epithets accentuate the difference between the human and the divine elements; and while designations of relationship, like 'son' and 'daughter', are rare, attributes like 'slave' are frequent. The gods are termed high, sovereign, powerful, protectors, judges, sages, liberators, and so on.

The cult was usually practised in the mountains, near the waters, trees, and rocks which were considered sacred. We have seen how the specification of divine names with further qualifications (Baal in particular) suggests the concentration of the cult in mountain regions. This is confirmed by the ruins of shrines and sometimes by Christian chapels which have been built on the sites of former pagan sanctuaries. The main cities had their sanctuaries on the neighbouring hills – Aradus at Baetocea and Byblos at Aphka. Lucian visited the temple of Aphka and declared it to be very ancient.[22] In Sidon various temples must have stood on the heights dominating the city – the temple of Eshmun was on the slope of the hill at the foot of which runs the river Asklepios.

The waters were also held in great veneration. The sanctuary of Aphka was in the Lebanese mountains at the source of the river Adonis, now Nahr Ibrahim. Offerings to Astarte were cast into a bowl: it was thought that if the gifts were well received they sank, and if not, they floated on the surface. As it neared the sea the river water occasionally turned a reddish hue. Lucian relates that according to the faithful the red was the blood of Adonis, thereby casting an interesting light on Phoenician mythology, which has unfortunately not been preserved in any other way:

There is, too, another marvellous portent in the region of the Byblians. A river, flowing from Mount Libanus, discharges itself into the sea: this river bears the name of Adonis. Every year regularly it is tinged with blood, and loses its proper colour before it falls into the sea: it dyes the sea, to a large space, red: and thus announces their time of mourning to the Byblians. Their story is that during these days Adonis is wounded, and that the river's nature is changed by the blood which flows into its waters; and that it takes its name from this blood.[23]

Lucian goes on to say that not everybody believed in this mythological interpretation. A man from Byblos told him that the phenomenon depended on natural elements, such as the red soil of the Lebanon which the seasonal winds swept into the river. But, adds Lucian, even if the man had told the truth, there was a supernatural element in the regular coincidence of the wind and the colour of the river. Nor was the veneration of the Phoenicians restricted to the Adonis; it was also accorded to the river Asklepios (Nahr el-Awali), which flowed past the temple of Eshmun in Sidon.

The trees, as well as the waters, were the object of a cult. Sacred groves grew near the sanctuaries, and the Old Testament condemns the cults which took place 'under the green and shady trees'. One of these groves was close to the shrine of Astarte, at Aphka.

In the lithic cult the conical stones placed on the altars were called betyls. The word means 'home of the god' and provides an adequate explanation of the concept of the cult. The most famous betyl in Phoenicia was in the temple of Byblos, and we find it depicted on coins of the Roman epoch. The *ăšērāh*, a small votive column probably of wood, was similar.

The temples usually consisted of sacred precincts in the open air. In the centre was a small chapel, or a betyl, or a chapel containing a betyl, in front of which was a sacrificial altar. A sacred fountain or bowl and a grove usually completed the sanctuary, and the archaeological remains suggest that the sanctuaries of Eshmun in Sidon and in Baetocea near Aradus were of this type. The representations on coins confirm the similarity of the temple of Baalat at Byblos. The Phoenicians also had covered temple buildings, of course, as is proved by other remains and the biblical description of the temple of Solomon built by Phoenician craftsmen.

With regard to the temple staff, the inscriptions often mention priests as well as their 'chiefs'. Mention is also made of priestesses,[24] while the Bible informs us of the prophets of Baal.[25] There were obviously other members of this category, including the sacred prostitutes typical of the cult of Astarte. As we have seen, the priesthood was frequently connected with the royal family in the Persian era. In Byblos the inscription of Batnoam says that Ozbaal, king of the city, was son of the priest of Baalat;[26] in Sidon Tabnit calls himself 'priest of Astarte, king of the Sidonians'[27] while Eshmunazar refers to his mother Ummiashtart as 'priestess of Astarte our lady'.[28] These last references are particularly significant, since they suggest that the royal and priestly duties were contained in the same persons.

The sacrifices were performed with animal and vegetable offerings. Philo of Byblos, however, mentions human sacrifices on occasions of great disaster.[29] This information is confirmed both by the Bible and by the Phoenician colonies in the West, and therefore seems authentic. More will be said about the place of human sacrifice, the *topheth*, in the chapter on art.

The most frequent Phoenician feasts were in honour of Adonis. Citizens from Byblos and probably from other cities flocked to Aphka for these events, and if there was more documentation this could be taken as one of the characteristics of the religion of the Phoenician cities. From an indirect source – Theocritus's account of the *Adoniae* in Alexandria in the second century BC[30] – we gather that the feast was of a mainly funereal nature, repeating the funeral of the god, the offerings, and the banquets.

There is no doubt that the Phoenicians believed in an after-life: besides the usual funerary offerings this is proved by the rich coffins and the embalming process, of which traces have come to light. But above all, the inscriptions are dominated by an invocation not to disturb the

40

deceased, condemning the violator of the tomb to the curse of the gods. Ahiram says:

If a king among kings, or a governor among governors, or a commander of armies attacks Byblos and uncovers this coffin may the sceptre of his rule be shattered, may the throne of his royalty be overturned.[31]

Still more explicit are the inscriptions of Sidon. Tabnit says:

Whosoever thou be, each man who finds this coffin, open not the lid and disturb me not, because with me there is no money, with me there is no gold, nor anything worth plundering, except myself who lie in this coffin. Open not my lid and disturb me not, because this is an abuse of Astarte. And if thou dost open my lid and disturb me there will be no descendants for thee in thy life under the sun, nor rest with the dead.[32]

And similarly, Eshmunazar says:

Whosoever thou be, neither king nor man must open this coffin, nor must he seek anything because nothing is in it, nor must he take the chest from my coffin nor take me from this to another coffin. Even if men say this to thee listen not to their words, because no king or man who opens the lid of this coffin, who takes the chest from my coffin, who takes me from this coffin will have rest with the dead or be buried in any tomb, and there will be no son for him or seed after him, and the holy gods will abandon him to a powerful king who shall reign over him, and kill this king or man who opened the lid of my coffin or took this chest. And the seed of this king or this man shall have no root below or fruit above, nor any form of life under the sun.[33]

The inscriptions mention beings from the other world, which they call rĕphā'îm, 'shades', and confirm a belief both in an underworld and in the souls that inhabit it.

CHAPTER 4

ART

1 Introduction

The Phoenician area in the Iron Age provides remarkably little material. Numerous remnants from the Bronze Age have come to light, particularly after the discoveries at Byblos and Ugarit, as well as objects from the Graeco-Roman era, but few monuments have yet been unearthed from the period of Phoenician independence dealt with in this book. A certain amount of hitherto unpublished information has been provided by recent excavations in Byblos and Sidon, while the excavations at Tyre have so far brought to light nothing earlier than the Roman epoch. Some of the smaller localities, Tell Suqas and Amrit in the north and Akziv in the south, have started to provide interesting finds, while in recent excavations at Khirbet Selm, Qerayé, and Kaldé, Maurice Chéhab has unearthed pottery of the early Iron Age and will probably make further discoveries. The same applies to the necropolis which Chéhab has discovered near the airport of Beirut.

Although material from within this area is rare, more material has come to light outside it, and, as we shall see, there are sound reasons to believe that much of what has been found in the surrounding territory originated from Phoenicia. It is strange, however, that there are often no definite proofs of the origin of the material, and the doubts that arise, even if not applicable to the general production of the discoveries, concern many single works.

The question of indirect information is equally complex and curious. If there are no adequate remains of Phoenician temples, the temple of Solomon in Jerusalem, built by Phoenician workmen, is described in detail in the Old Testament – and the Phoenician temples must have resembled each other. If there are no palaces or city walls, the Assyrian representations depict both, and however simplified the depictions, numerous elements can be deduced from them. On the whole, therefore, the contribution of indirect data is considerable.

This material, and a comparison with what the Phoenician area produced before and since, present the same problems as Phoenician history and religion. What is the relationship between this art and the art of the interior? Are there any characteristics, and if so, what are they?

In 1895 de Vogüé wrote that the Phoenicians had no originality, and this opinion has been frequently repeated. Indeed, Phoenician art is largely included in Syrian art, and stands at the junction of numerous influences, from Egyptian to Mesopotamian, from Aegean to Anatolian. Owing to these conditions, as well as the political and economic situation, there appear to be few aspirations to great art, while the craftsmanship displays a combination of influences and often lacks coherence and stylistic tradition. We notice repeated attempts to establish a characteristic style, but this popular streak does not develop and is really more apparent in the Bronze Age than later.

This being assumed, we can, however, consider in Phoenicia, first of all, the degree of the various influences. It is evident, as proved by Frankfort and other authors, that Egyptian influence is more powerful here than anywhere else, and results from the direct communications by sea and the continuous commercial ties which constituted one of the essential purposes of artistic production.

If this assessment applies generally, however, it must be modified according to the types of art. It certainly applies to the ivories, but applies less to glyptography, which was primarily in the Mesopotamian tradition; to pottery, where Aegean motifs frequently occur; and to metal objects which are strongly influenced by Mesopotamia and Anatolia.

Having considered all these points, we can see that the question of the autonomy and the special characteristics of Phoenician art is a good deal more complex than it might seem; it is not enough simply to affirm or deny originality. There is no doubt that the types and the iconography are widely influenced by the surrounding regions, which we can enumerate, if we wish. But this does not tell us what choices and reactions may have responded to these influences. The first point to make here, recalling what has already been said, is that Phoenician work of the Iron Age represents a lingering on of a culture formerly characteristic of the Bronze Age – a culture historically broken up by the arrival of the Israelites and the Aramaic people. While the new populations brought no artistic tradition of their own, and slowly assimilated that of the region, the Phoenicians kept and continued that tradition.

A remarkable continuity is shown by the difficulty of dating works not found in archeological strata: do the small bronzes, for example, belong to the late Bronze Age or the early Iron Age? With the ivories there is less of a problem, because the ease with which certain groups (particularly those of Nimrud) can be dated gives us a chronological scale. So a line of development can be traced in the iconography. This takes us beyond the area of the Phoenician cities; but if the ivories came from these cities, and there are many indications that they did (and not only the ivories but also the metal bowls and the architecture itself, as the history of Solomon's temple shows), then we may conclude, almost paradoxically, that wherever Phoenician art is the same as that of the interior, particularly at the beginning of the Iron Age, this is because both are, in fact, Phoenician.

Here we should observe that Phoenician art may also be classified in terms of its types and in terms of the forms of work. In the first millennium the Phoenicians were without doubt the great producers in the ancient Middle East of ornamental objects: ivory plaques, metal bowls, jewels, seals. Seen in these terms, Phoenician work takes on its own distinct character, even if this has little to do with the nature of the art itself.

A study of the intrinsic nature of Phoenician work must be taken one piece at a time, either to distinguish its autonomy and its stylistic peculiarities or to follow the undeniable emergence of popular developments, alongside the more stereotyped work of the craftsmen's workshops. Such a study, which has not yet been pursued beyond a few hints, would certainly be fruitful. Yet no less fruitful would be a study aimed at picking out and distinguishing the different centres of production: not theoretically, however necessary that research would be, but simply on the basis of certain examples, since we lack adequate points of reference, which would help classification.

2 *Architecture*

The fullest information concerning the religious architecture is the biblical description of the temple of Solomon, which was built in Israel, but by artists explicitly described as Phoenician.[1]

In front of the temple was a courtyard, in which were the altar for sacrifices and the so-called 'sea of bronze', a great bowl containing lustral water. The temple door was flanked by two columns, also of bronze. The building was in three parts, each following the other: a square vestibule; a rectangular central room, with the golden altar and the cedar table for offerings of bread; then the 'holy of holies', a dark square room reached by a door covered by a curtain. Here was kept the Ark of the Covenant. A few steps in front of the entrance, and others at the entrance of the 'holy of holies', made the level of the building rise from front to back. All around the sanctuary were rooms, on three floors (fig 1).

A comparison of the biblical information with archaeological evidence of the Syrian temples, particularly that of the thirteenth century at Hazor and that of the ninth century at Tell Tainat, shows that the structure of Solomon's temple has all the characteristics of the area. These characteristics seem closer to those of Egyptian temple construction, with its progression of sacred rooms towards the inside, than to the Mesopotamian, with its alternation of courtyards and rooms overlooking them; so we may trace a dominantly Egyptian influence on Phoenician art.

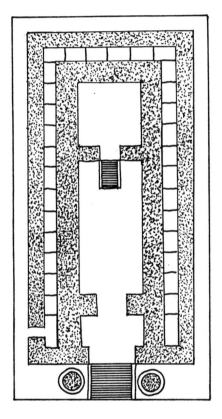

1   Plan of the temple of Solomon

The two columns or pilasters at the entrance to the temple at Jerusalem tally with clay models of chapels at the beginning of the first millennium and are alluded to in a passage from Herodotus, according to whom the temple of Melqart in Tyre had similar pillars, one of gold and one of emerald.[2] With regard to the capitals, the discovery in Cyprus and various Israelite cities (Samaria, Megiddo, Hazor, Ramat Rahel) of so-called Proto-Aeolic examples suggests that these may also have originated in Phoenicia (plate 6). The basic components of these capitals are the two volutes on either side of a triangle; but other elements of Egyptian origin, such as palmettes, sphinxes, and lotus leaves, which have also been known to appear, are a further indication of preponderantly Egyptian iconographical inspiration.

There are remains of Phoenician shrines at Tell Suqas, Sidon, Amrit, and Ain El Hayat. At Tell Suqas the recent excavations of the Danish expedition have brought to light the ruins of two apparently sacred buildings, the structure of which is not yet clear. In Sidon the shrine dedicated to Eshmun and mentioned in the inscriptions of Bodashtart found in the shrine itself was excavated first by Macridy Bey and then by G. Contenau and M. Dunand. It is in a place called Bostan Esh Sheikh, four kilometres north of the present Saida, on the left bank of the Nahr El Awali watercourse. The remains are surrounded by an enclosure about fifty-seven metres wide and thirty-seven metres long. It consisted of at least two terraces sloping down the hill towards the river, perhaps followed by successive terraces in the valley. It can be dated around the fifth century or shortly before. Apart from the inscriptions of Bodashtart, which provide a definite point of chronological reference, not far from the temple, amongst fragments of Greek sculpture, a fragment of a capital of Achaemenidian type with bull protomai, confirming the Persian epoch, has been found.

2   Aedicule of Amrit

As far as the plan and architectural structure are concerned the temple of Amrit excavated by Dunand is in better condition. It consists of a large precinct containing a sacred bowl originally filled with water, forty-eight metres long and thirty-eight metres wide. On three sides of the enclosure was a portico of rectangular pillars. In the centre of the bowl stood a cube-shaped chapel open in front, probably intended to contain the object of the cult, erected on a platform five metres square and surmounted by a cornice of Egyptian type (fig 2). In front of the chapel, close to the east and west sides, the bases of two columns have been found. The shrine of Amrit can in all likelihood be ascribed to the fifth century BC.

The group of sacred buildings identified by E. Renan at Ain El Hayat and originally composed of a pond with low vegetation on each side and two confronted chapels of the same type as the one found at Amrit, is a little later. One of the two chapels, found in good condition, bore a close resemblance to the one of Amrit and had an Egyptian type of ornamentation on the entablature, with a row of uraei surmounted by a solar disk (fig 3).

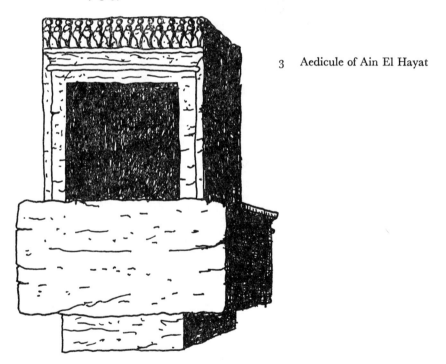

3   Aedicule of Ain El Hayat

So we can see that all the Phoenician sanctuaries that have been discovered, however badly preserved they may be, contain a large fortified precinct surrounding the sacred chapel. An interesting example of this type of temple is shown on a coin from Byblos of the emperor Macrinus (AD 217–18) which evidently reproduces a shrine several centuries old (fig 4). The shrine bears a strong resemblance to the temple *in antis*, preceded by a flight of steps and composed of a sacred enclosure, surrounded by a colonnade and containing a betyl. A terracotta model from Idalion and two representations of the shrine of Cyprus on a golden plaque and a coin respectively bear an even closer resemblance to the chapel of Amrit. The building has been elaborated, but the columns in front and the object of the cult in the centre remain. The motifs of these small shrines are also to be repeated, as we shall see, on many stelae and altars of the Phoenician colonies in the West.

4   Coin of Macrinus

The 'high places' mentioned in the Bible were a further type of sanctuary, consisting simply of stelae or cippi in the open air, usually erected on the heights where the deity was worshipped. In view of the nature of these 'high places' the archaeological remains are insignificant, but it is worth noting the literary tradition, from which we learn, for example, that the Roman emperor Vespasian went to Mount Carmel to consult the oracle and simply found an altar in the open air. The stelae and cippi of these shrines are similar to those of the Bronze Age in Byblos and of the Iron Age in Hazor, in the Palestinian interior. There are also numerous later examples in the West.

48

Finally, another type of sacred place mentioned in the Bible, although outside the Phoenician area, in the vicinity of Jerusalem, is the *topheth*, where child sacrifices were performed.[3] Once again there is no evidence of these sacred places actually in Phoenicia, but there is no doubt that they existed, if we add to the biblical evidence the ample proof provided by excavations in the western colonies. In Carthage, Sousse, Motya, Nora, S. Antioco, and Monte Sirai urns containing the cremated bones of children, and sometimes of birds or other small animals instead of human beings, were found in the remains of large precincts. Of course, the biblical reference to the 'sacrifices to Moloch' and the mention of a *topheth* near Jerusalem suggest the possibility of a general Canaanite rite continued by the Phoenicians during the Iron Age.

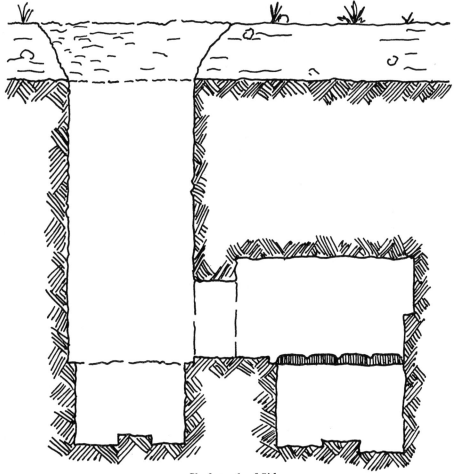

5   Shaft-tomb of Sidon

As for the tombs, there is ample archaeological documentation of large chambers dug in the rock and accessible through a corridor or *dromos*. The tombs of Akziv, recently excavated by an Italo-Israeli mission, are of this type. At Byblos the tomb of Ahiram, containing the famous coffin, has the same basic features: shaft, gallery, and funerary chamber. In the Persian era the tombs of Sidon opened on to the vertical walls of the shaft (fig 5). The presence of similar types at Carthage proves how widespread they were. The tomb is sometimes simply an embrasure cut into the rock, covered by a stone chamber above ground-level, as in the sepulchre of Eshmunazar at Sidon, and in many of the ancient tombs in Carthage. Again in the Persian era, Amrit has subterranean tombs with *dromos*, above which appear interesting funerary monuments known as *meghazils* – a cylindrical one on two levels with lions flanking the base and a cupola (fig 6); a second one shaped like a truncated cone surmounted by a five-faced pyramid; and a third one with a quadrangular base also surmounted by a pyramid. The date of

6   *Meghazil* of Amrit

the *meghazils* is questionable. The first may be slightly earlier than the Persian epoch, while the second and third suggest Greek influence. The western equivalent of the *meghazils* is the mausoleum of Dougga in Tunisia. Finally, some Phoenician tombs were probably cut directly into the slopes of the rocky mountains, as in North Africa.

The civil buildings are depicted by the Assyrian representations, even though these depictions tend to be generic and schematized. The towns were surrounded by turreted and embattlemented walls. An example of this is the representation of Tyre on the bronze gates of Salmanassar III (859–824) at Balawat. Later, in the reliefs of Sennacherib (705–681) the walls of Tyre reappear together with the houses placed artificially above the walls themselves: the walls have elaborate battlements and the houses have small pillars on either side of the front door, as in the temple of Solomon. Other reliefs of Sennacherib show the sack of what seems to be a Phoenician town: besides the walls, the houses of two stories with the top floor narrower than the ground floor are in a prominent position (fig 7). The top-story windows, with balustrades supported by miniature palm-shaped columns, are equally remarkable – they are

7   Phoenician city in the reliefs of Sennacherib

the typical windows reproduced on the ivories, and authentic examples have been discovered in 1962 at Ramat Rahel. Another depiction of Phoenician walls is to be found on a fourth century BC coin from Sidon which shows the towers and battlements of the town. Finally, Strabo's account,[4] according to which the houses of Tyre and Aradus had many stories and those of Tyre were higher than the houses of Rome, confirms the fact that there was more than one floor. This is, as usual, supplemented in the West, where, according to Appian,[5] the houses of Carthage between the forum and Byrsa had no less than six stories.

Phoenician engineers were extremely good at building dams and bridges. Colossal blocks of stone were used, which utilized all the assets of the natural rock. The remains of dams at Aradus, Sidon, and Tyre (the latter discovered by Poidebard) give ample proof of these feats of engineering. There were also artificial harbours (*cothons*), which have hitherto only been found in the colonies at Carthage and Motya. Here, as we shall see, a canal at least seven metres wide led to a rectangular dock of fifty-one by thirty-seven metres, where small ships could take refuge and shelter.

3 Sculpture

The torso from Sarafand, ancient Sarepta, is a monumental piece of sculpture in stone which seems to belong to our period (fig 8). It can be ascribed to the sixth or fifth century BC and is the central part of a male bust, clad in a belted, pleated skirt, ornamented on the front by two large uraei. All that remains of the legs is a well-modelled knee. On the upper part of the chest is a large necklace composed of oblong objects surmounting a pendant consisting of a crescent moon pointing downwards and the solar disk. The statue probably represents a sovereign, or maybe even a god. There are numerous fragments from Amrit, but they seem to belong to a later period, between the fourth and third century. They are mainly heads and male busts clad in lion skins and tight-fitting tunics. Finally, on a smaller scale, a few fragments of sandstone statuettes have recently been found in Tell Suqas, including the head and shoulders of a lion of about the sixth century.

Small bronze sculptures are better documented than stone statuary though less well than in the preceding period. But although the pieces are of Syrian origin they are not necessarily Phoenician. A female figure with a low circular head-dress, a tight necklace, a long plait down her back and two short side plaits, a long tunic with a belt with two tassels in front, now at the Ashmolean Museum, was obtained in Aleppo and ascribed to the eighth or seventh century (plate 44). Also from Aleppo we have another bronze female figure clad in triple-flounced skirt and dated theoretically in the ninth century (plate 42). A third female figure, seated and clad in a long tunic, is from Baalbek and is ascribed to the ninth or eighth century (plate 45). It is hard to distinguish the male bronzes of this epoch from those of the preceding period, which are far more numerous. A probable example of the ninth or eighth century is a small seated idol with a short conical cap, holding a patera and sitting on a throne flanked by lions (plate 43). On the whole, the workmanship is extremely crude, the features of the faces accentuated and almost deformed. They seem to represent either a popular taste or a vivacious sense of observation which distinguishes them from the stereotypes. Because of this these bronzes retain a certain individuality even with respect to the preceding local tradition.

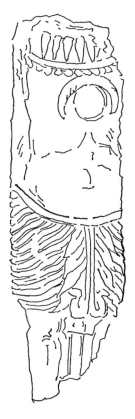

8   Torso from Sarafend

Passing on to stone relief, we must first mention a small monument of great importance for subsequent developments in Punic art: an aedicule from Sidon which is a smaller repetition of the typology of the chapel of Amrit and the antecedent of widespread production in

Carthage and the West (plate 2). The base bears Egyptian mouldings sur-mounted by an aedicule between two plain pillars. In the aedicule two animals, probably sphinxes, support a throne. The aedicule is sur-mounted by a lintel composed of a large winged solar disk and above it is a row of large disk-bearing uraei in relief. Giron, who published this monument, mentions other similar ones in Sidon in a more or less fragmentary condition, which proves that the typology is not isolated. It must be dated in a period before Hellenic influence. Another antecedent of a typology which was to be subsequently widespread in the West is a rectangular stele from Burj Esh Shemali published by Emir Chéhab (plate 26). On a base the niche holds two slightly tapering betyls sur-mounted by a lintel with Egyptian mouldings in the centre of which are the disk and the crescent surmounted by the usual row of uraei. This must also precede Hellenic influence.

The earliest stele seems to be from Amrit and depicts a figure standing on a lion (plate 13). The figure wears a head-dress similar to the white crown of Upper Egypt, with a uraeus on the frontal part of the cap and a tassel suspended from the top hanging behind, and is clad in a typical Egyptian skirt. The right arm, raised, flourishes a small club, while the left arm is folded downwards and the hand holds a lion cub by its hind legs. Above the figure the curve of the stele is moulded with a solar disk with large wings pointing down, under which are a disk and a crescent moon, their points joining upwards. The lion beneath the figure is walking on the stones of a mountain represented symbolically in Assyrian fashion. This relief is particularly interesting. While the icono-graphy of the Bronze Age at Ugarit in the stele of the god of lightning continues, the bull is replaced by the lion and the lightning by the cub held by its hind legs – this is more suggestive of the Anatolian environ-ment, while the Egyptian imprint is considerably stronger in this stele than in any other monument. The date is between the ninth and sixth century.

Another remarkable stele, discovered in 1964 by the Italo-Israeli mission at Akziv (plate 22), is of uncertain epoch. It depicts a door with successive panels, one inside the other, in the centre of which is the schematized figure of the so-called 'bottle-idol', previously only known in the Punic world, and enables us to identify the Phoenician prototype of this particular iconographical motif in the West.

The stele of Yehaumilk is of the Persian epoch. The inscription in the upper field records the restoration performed and the ornaments pre-sented by the king in the temple of Byblos (plate 23). The upper field of the stele ends with the same moulding as the stele of Amrit, with a solar disk with wings outspread. Below this stands the king offering a patera to the goddess seated on a throne. The king has a low cylindrical cap typical of the Persian era, a beard and long hair, a robe reaching down to his feet covered by a cloak. The goddess, who is seated on a cubical throne with a low back and rests her feet on a stool, has the Hathoresque symbol of the double-horned disk on her head, a long close-fitting robe, a long sceptre shaped like a papyrus stem in her left hand, and her right hand raised. The Egyptian influence is even more obvious in this monument than in the preceding one.

The Hathoresque iconography found in the stele of Yehaumilk re-appears in certain fragments which Ronzevalle ascribes to the Hellenistic age, but which, according to Dussaud, are more probably of the Persian period. The first of these, found in Tir Dibba in 1913, shows a female bust with solar disk and horns on her head, an uraeus on her forehead, her hair hanging down in bands, and a papyrus stem in one hand. The figure is facing right (plate 17). Another fragment discovered later in the same locality is very similar to this, except that the figure is facing left. Ronzevalle also published a relief with a female figure in a long

9   Relief from Beirut

garment, facing left, with no symbols on her head, but holding a lotus flower – it seems a variation of the preceding iconography. Finally, a female figure on a throne flanked by lions and with a high back, wearing a small cylindrical crown and holding a lotus and papyrus flower (fig 9) ends the series of these reliefs on stelae which very probably belong to this period.

Further stone reliefs, but not on stelae, complete this particular production: they are especially interesting because they contain certain motifs which we shall find on the ivories and paterae. An alabaster relief from Aradus, ascribed to the eighth-seventh century, shows a panel of palmettes with *guilloche* borders surmounting a winged sphinx squatting on a low podium (plate 7). Particular attention should be paid to the palmettes, because they reappear on other monuments: they consist of two lateral volutes turning inwards at the centre, which is occupied by four vertical elements. The sphinx wears the Egyptian double crown; the low podium has Egypticizing mouldings and bulls.

As we have said, the palmettes reappear in other reliefs. One of them, from the Museum of Geneva, bears a sacred plant stylized by two almost

10   Relief from the Museum
        of Geneva

56

component palmettes flanked by two rampant winged gryphons in the central field (fig 10). A band with fish-bone decoration borders the central field above and below, while the upper field (only little of the lower field is visible) is occupied by rows of palmettes. Another relief from Aradus presents the same scene in the centre field. The lower edge is missing, while the upper one has a *guilloche* border; the lower field is missing and the upper one shows palmettes. Finally, the palmettes reappear on a vertical band on the right of a fragment of relief from Adlun, near Tyre, of which the head of a sphinx remains as part of a throne on which was seated a deity whose knee is visible as well as a hand holding a stele in front of a sort of incense-burner (plate 1).

The motif of the throne flanked by sphinxes is very ancient, although the specimens discovered in Phoenicia are usually later than this period. There is, however, an interesting depiction of a goddess seated on a throne from Fi, south of Tripoli, to be ascribed rather to the Persian epoch (Dussaud) than to the Hellenistic epoch (Ronzevalle) (fig 11).

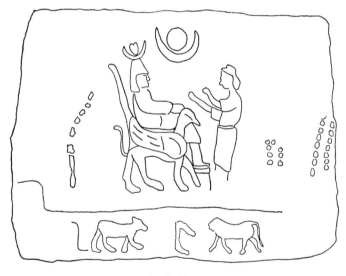

11   Relief from Fi

The throne has a high back and is flanked in front by a small stool on which the deity rests her feet. On her head she bears the solar disk between the Hathoresque horns and wears a long garment on which she rests one hand while she raises the other towards a figure facing her in the act of prayer. In the top centre field the solar disk surmounts the crescent moon. The base has an interesting ornamentation of two confronted bulls on either side of the sacred plant.

57

A typical relief of the Phoenician area and its overseas territories, even if it does not actually originate in the area, is that carved on the stone sarcophagi. The earliest is probably Ahiram's. The sarcophagus can be ascribed to the thirteenth or twelfth century, while the inscription is probably of the tenth (plate 11). It is rectangular and based on figures of squatting lions whose bodies are carved in relief on the long sides, while their heads jut out. On each side of the coffin a depiction is carved in relief, surmounted by a continuous frieze of buds and lotus flowers pointing down. On the long sides the depiction represents processional scenes: the main one shows the sovereign, or, according to some, a god, with a withered lotus flower in his hand, seated on the usual throne flanked by winged sphinxes before a table laid for a feast, towards which (and towards the sovereign) advance seven figures of worshippers and offerers. The other long side shows worshippers and offerers and each of the short sides shows four female figures beating their chests or tearing their hair. The lid has two lion heads in high relief overlapping the short sides. The bodies of the lions are carved in low relief along the centre line of the lid and on the sides two figures hold lotus flowers, one fresh and the other withered. On the whole, the scene of the offering has definite similarities with Syrian iconography of the second millennium, as we see from a famous ivory from Megiddo, but the general depictions and the use of the sarcophagus are original.

After Ahiram new sarcophagi are only found in the fifth century, if this is, as it seems, the date of the sarcophagi of Tabnit and his son Eshmunazar (plate 8). Both the sarcophagi, of black basalt, are of wholly Egyptian type, and were probably imported from Egypt. The sarcophagus of Tabnit was even used again and still bears the hieroglyphic incisions with the name of its first occupant. Together with these two examples a third was found, containing the body of a woman, but it was unfinished and maybe intentionally disfigured.

Between the fifth and fourth century the production of sarcophagi began to spread. Most of them are from Sidon, where recent discoveries have added to the earlier ones, but there are also many from other localities both in the East and the West. An analytical study of these sarcophagi has been made by Kukahn on the basis of examples from Sidon, and we can trace both the obvious Egyptian inspiration and the dominant Greek influence in the appearance of the head and the headdress, that being the only part of the body represented. In view of the prevalent Greek influence we shall not analyse the sarcophagi in question; but it is worth noting that this influence is not necessarily the result of Alexander the Great's conquest, but almost certainly preceded it by a few decades at least.

4 Ivories

For the reasons already mentioned Phoenician production developed widely in the minor arts. The origin of the production, however, can only be found through a critical examination of the objects, since the material has nearly all been discovered outside the Phoenician area.

One fundamental category of these 'minor arts' is ivory relief. The main groups are from Nimrud, Samaria, Zincirli, Arslan Tash, and Khorsabad. Others have also been found in Samos, Crete and Ialisos, and in Etruria in the Bernardini tomb at Praeneste. Phoenicia herself has only provided a few examples from Sidon: this fact, however, is accompanied by the incision of Phoenician letters on many ivories, which does, in certain cases, suggest their origin.

It seems reasonable to connect the spread of this craft in numerous localities of the Syro-Palestinian and Mediterranean area with the maritime expansion of the Phoenicians and the trade in ornamental objects so characteristic of them. But the situation is different in the Assyrian interior, where the ivories evidently either arrived as war booty or tribute, or were made by Phoenician craftsmen employed at the courts.

Ivory work in the Phoenician and Syro-Palestinian area originated a few centuries before the beginning of the Phoenician era. Reliefs in ivory are found in the late Bronze Age, in other words from the sixteenth century, at Alalakh, Ugarit, Byblos, Megiddo, Lakish, and other localities. This type of production, however, begins to develop at the beginning of the Phoenician period, and therefore with the Iron Age, when the span of the production stretches from the ninth to the seventh century.

The ivories can be considered to have served a primarily ornamental purpose, since they were used to decorate sacred or royal objects like altars, incense-burners, thrones, stools, beds, tables, and other furniture. The biblical references to the temple of Solomon and Ahab's 'ivory house'[6] suggest that the ivories were also used to adorn the walls of the temples and royal palaces, but there is no definite proof.

The most comprehensive and accurate study of ivories has been made by Barnett. On the basis of abundant material from Nimrud he has distinguished a group which he claims to be of Phoenician origin from another group which, for stylistic reasons, he believes to be of Syrian origin, in other words from the politically Aramaic cities of the interior. A further group of ivories can be considered of Assyrian inspiration if not actually made by Assyrian artists.

In view of the accuracy of Barnett's study we shall outline his presentation of the material and then formulate certain general observations. The ivories from Nimrud are divided into two groups named after the discoverers: the 'Layard group' from NW palace, and the 'Loftus group' from the SE palace.

The Layard group is actually considered Phoenician. The NW palace, from which the group comes, was built by Assurnasipal II (883–859 BC), but the objects it contains belong to the period of Sargon II (721–705). This does not, of course, imply that the ivories were produced in this epoch, but simply that it was Sargon II who brought them to Assyria. For more accurate chronology Barnett resorted to a hieroglyphic inscription on an ivory which reads *'iwbnre*, and suggested that this name is the same as Ia'u-bi'di, king of Hama, whom Sargon defeated in the battle of Qarqar. In this case at least the majority of the group would be from furniture originally made for this king and carried off by Sargon as war booty. The ivories of the Layard group, then, would belong to the end of the eighth century BC. Their provenance from Hama has been fully confirmed by the discovery in 1961 of two ivories, one bearing the name of Hama and the other the name of Laash, the second city of the kingdom. Furthermore, in 1962, fragments of shell were found with the name 'Urkhilina, great king' in hieroglyphic Hittite (Urkhilina was king of Hama and was defeated by Salmanassar III *c.* 850 BC). Finally fragments of ivory from a workshop were traced back to Hama by the Danish expedition.

The ivories themselves mainly consist of rectangular plaques, in more or less high relief. There are also, however, 'open' reliefs and round pieces. The subjects are as follows: two boys binding a papyrus plant; a boy holding a lotus stem in one hand and raising the other in greeting or blessing (plate 80); two winged goddesses holding a lotus flower on either side of a figure of Horus seated on a lotus flower; the sacred plant flanked by gryphons, which can also be among the branches; the *jed* pillar and sphinxes; winged sphinxes walking (plate 81); a cow giving milk to her calf, her head turned back; a woman at the window (plate 79); two seated figures flanking a cartouche (plate 82); a buck or deer drinking or grazing; a lion walking; a lion devouring a negro in a papyrus field.

It is immediately obvious that this group of ivories is dominated by Egyptian influence. In certain cases the religious values of the motifs may have been retained, while in others they may have been adapted in Phoenician garb or developed for ornamental purposes. The motif of the 'woman at the window' occupies a place to itself. Barnett studied its origins and saw the female figure as Astarte-Aphrodite, connected with the myth including a male god of the type of Adonis, and symbolizing the religious sacrifice of virginity. Here, therefore, we are confronted by a motif based on local religious tradition which will continue until the classical era in the cults of Aphrodite *parakyptousa* or 'Venus prospiciens' witnessed at Salamis in Cyprus.

Not all the ivories of the NW palace are of what Barnett calls 'Phoenician style'. One group is clearly distinguished by Mesopotamian motifs: confronted figures in wholly Assyrian garb (plate 83) sometimes flanking a winged solar disk, as well as confronted animals before a rosette or a stylized tree.

We now come to the Loftus group, which Barnett has characterized as Syrian, but which has close ties with Phoenicia. The group is represented in Nimrud in the SE palace, which was in use between 824 and 703 BC. In all likelihood the ivories were imported from a Syrian locality which, according to Barnett, was Hama. Indeed, on the level F of this city fragments have been found bearing a strong resemblance to those of the Loftus group, and there are various analogies between this group and different types of pieces originating from the zone of Hama. Further details can be derived from the inscription 'to Malkiram' cut on an ivory. If, as Barnett supposes, this is the Malki-rammu of Edom, defeated by Sennacherib, the date of the group goes back to the end of the eighth century. It must also be mentioned that according to Mallowan the SE palace of Nimrud was destroyed at the death of Sargon. Barnett's theory is that the ivories were made in Hama, a great centre of this type of craft, for Malki-rammu, king of Edom. They would have been captured as booty by Sargon during the sack of Hama in 720 before being given to the king of Edom. Finally both the Layard and Loftus groups would have been brought to Assyria at the same time and originate from Hama, although they represent different schools and styles.

Most of the Loftus ivories are fragments of small boxes, cups, vases, brushes, combs, and flat objects similar to the Layard group. With regard to the subject-matter, Barnett distinguishes between pieces with few or no Egyptian characteristics, of almost definite Syrian make, and pieces in which certain Egyptian characteristics suggest that they were either made in part by Phoenician craftsmen or are simply Phoenician imitations by Syrian artists. The themes are: men fighting with lions or sphinxes; real or fantastic animals (lions, bulls, gryphons) fighting; frontal views of nude or clothed female deities sometimes holding flowers or lions; processions; sphinxes walking and confronting the sacred tree; ornamentations of foliage or rosettes.

According to Barnett's study, the ivories of this group are connected both iconographically and stylistically to the artistic tradition of the Syrian interior. As an example we can compare the Layard and the Loftus version of the sphinx by the sacred tree: the different treatment of the Loftus group, which bears a strong similarity to Syrian motifs found on other works, is immediately obvious. Finally, Barnett considers the Loftus group to be as obviously Syrian as the Layard group is Phoenician, and to contain very different artistic traditions.

Barnett's grouping of the ivories based on the examples from Nimrud is confirmed by further examples from the Near East and the Mediterranean area. We shall start with a survey of the ivories found at Arslan Tash, which constitute a fairly homogeneous group, similar to the Layard one, and therefore worth considering as further documentation of supposedly direct Phoenician production. As for the dates, one of these ivories bears an inscription mentioning 'our lord Hazael', who is probably the king of Damascus known both from the Bible and the Assyrian sources of the time of Salmanassar III (858–824 BC). Phoenician craftsmen would therefore have worked these ivories for the king of Damascus about the middle of the ninth century; the ivories would then have been transported to Assyria either as part of the tribute of Bar Hadad III, son of Hazael, to Adad-nirari (809–782 BC) or as part of the

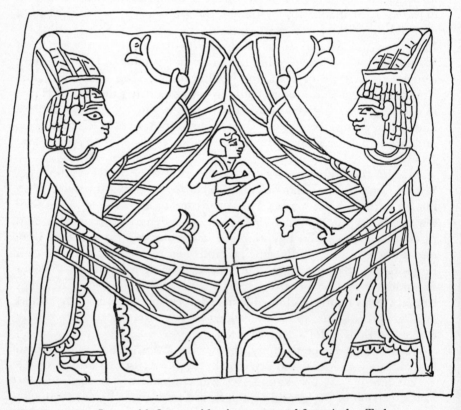

12   Ivory with figures with wings outspread from Arslan Tash

13 Ivory depicting youths binding a papyrus plant from Arslan Tash

booty captured by Tiglatpileser III in the sack of Damascus in 732 B C. This second theory is supported by the fact that Arslan Tash (ancient Khadatu) was definitely an Assyrian residence under Tiglatpileser III, while it is not certain that it was before.

The ivories of Arslan Tash depict the following subjects: two apparently female figures with wings outspread and the double crown of Upper and Lower Egypt, holding lotus flowers and flanking a small Horus on a lotus flower; two female figures with wings outspread on either side of a sacred plant of the type with volutes (fig 12); two boys with a double crown binding a papyrus plant bearing a small goddess Maat (fig 13); two confronted rams on either side of a sacred plant with volutes (fig 14); winged sphinxes advancing or seated with faces frontal;

14 Ivory with confronted rams from Arslan Tash

processions of offerers which must have formed part of a complex frieze with symbolical elements; a woman at the window; a deer lowering its head to drink or eat (plate 86); a cow giving milk with its head turned back towards the calf (plate 87); friezes with palmettes of sacred plants (plate 23), buds and lotus flowers, and buds and papyrus flowers plaited. Apart from these two panels showing strong Syrian influence there is one with the frontal view of a bearded figure, his hands folded on his stomach, and a long tunic, and two plant stems entwined on either side; and another with a bearded figure with long curls and short skirt, advancing on a base with mouldings and bulls.

Apart from the marginal problem presented by these last two figures, which are anyhow fairly close to the Egyptian iconography of the Asiatics, the basic Egyptian inspiration of the ivories of Arslan Tash is evident, as well as their strong similarity to the Phoenician group of

Nimrud. It is equally interesting that the king of Damascus should have applied to Phoenician craftsmen for this production.

The same applies to the kings of Israel. In Samaria another collection of ivories was found in the ruins of the residence of Omri (879–869 B C) and Ahab (869–850 B C). There have been controversies about the date, some maintaining that it should be ascribed to the ninth century and others to the eighth. The first theory is supported by the notable similarities with the Arslan Tash group, which is of the ninth century, the epigraphic characteristics of the letters cut on certain pieces, and the biblical reference to the 'house of ivory' of king Ahab.

15   Ivory with fighting animals from Samaria

From the typological point of view we find here, as in the Layard group, pieces in more or less high relief, 'open' relief, and round pieces. The motifs are: Horus on a lotus flower (plate 85); two winged female figures with a solar disk on their heads and lotus flowers in their hands flanking the *jed* pillars (plate 84); Egypticizing sphinxes walking (plate 78); confronted winged rams flanking a sacred plant with volutes; scenes of animals fighting (fig 15); rampant bucks on either side of a shrub; a frieze of buds and lotus flowers (fig 16), superimposed palmettes, large

16   Ivory with friezes with buds and lotus flowers from Samaria

palm flowers with curved petals widening at the base, rosettes, plaits, and other geometrical designs. The woman at the window is rare, but exists.

On the whole, the iconography of the ivories of Samaria seems of completely Egyptian inspiration, like the Layard group of Nimrud and the ivories from Arslan Tash. These three groups are the most numerous and of the best quality, but to complete this study we must also mention the ivories of Khorsabad, which share Phoenician characteristics and come from the residence of Sargon II (721–705 BC). The motif of the woman at the window is prevalent, together with the winged female figures flanking the sacred plant, sphinxes walking with faces frontal (fig 17), and ornamentations of stems and lotus flowers. We must also record a few ivories from Assur which contain the theme of the buck lowering its head to drink or eat. The ivories of Zincirli, on the other hand, go back to the ninth or eighth centuries, and the style of the figures usually bears a closer resemblance to the group considered Syrian; the same could possibly be said about the ivories of Tell Halaf, were the documentation not so scarce.

On the whole, the division of the ivories into groups and the establishment of a Phoenician series as opposed to a Syrian series seems well founded. The Egyptian influence seems predominant in the Phoenician series, owing as much to the choice of themes as to the stylistic treatment. Furthermore, the Phoenician ivories prefer linear designs, in contrast to the markedly volumetric nature of the Syrian tradition. Finally, the Phoenician ivories display a definite sense of the decorative which leads to antithetic schemes and sometimes to the neglect of subject-matter. In this respect, however, there has been much exaggeration: even if certain concepts have been evolved, altered, and attenuated, it is unlikely that such elements as the sphinx or Horus have lost all religious value.

It is also true to say that a division into schools can sometimes appear questionable. If we consider the general progress of history and Syro-Palestinian culture in the Phoenician area, we will see that the Phoenician region is the centre of artistic production. The question therefore remains whether the specialization of schools in the Syrian interior, however influenced by the traditions of this area, is not frequently a secondary development of the centre of production which remained in the coastal area.

5 Bowls

Another 'minor' product which has appeared in countries where Phoenician activity spread, but not in Phoenicia herself (and in this case there are no exceptions), is the decorated metal bowls (of bronze,

17   Ivory with a sphinx from Khorsabad

silver, and gold). The bowls continue a tradition originating in Ugarit
and, as with the ivories, since they develop the type and link very
different themes, they undoubtedly and eminently show characteristics
of the Iron Age. The bowls come from Assyria (Nimrud), Cyprus,
Greece (Athens, Delphi, Olympia), Crete, and Italy (Praeneste, Cerveteri, Salerno); their date can be placed between the eighth and seventh

67

century B C. In all the bowls there is a decorative convergence of Egyptian (chiefly), Mesopotamian, and Aegean iconographical elements. In view of the absence of finds in Phoenicia it has been sustained that the original place of production was Cyprus: but the presence of Phoenician inscriptions must be kept in mind, one of which (on the bowl of the Bernardini tomb in Praeneste) has long been known, while others have recently been identified by Barnett, who is preparing a comprehensive study on the subject. The definite prevalence of Egyptian motifs also suggests that Phoenicia rather than Cyprus is the centre of production. This does not, of course, exclude the fact that some of the bowls have actually been worked in Cyprus, and we must remember that some of the ones found in Italy differ from the Phoenician style and, like many Orientalizing works of art, cannot be given a definite date or place of origin.

Starting our study with the paterae of Nimrud, it must be pointed out that they are from the NW palace, where the ivories were found and were also discovered by Layard. The palace contained objects ascribed to the time of Sargon II and the paterae cannot be much later, and are therefore probably of the eighth century.

Certain general characteristics can be identified in the bowls: the presence of a central medallion; the ornamentation of concentric bands; geometrical motifs next to the human and animal ones in the dividing zone of the bands as well as in the bands themselves. Passing from the simpler types to the more complex, we have a patera with a large medallion consisting of a central medallion and a triple circuit of joined rings interposed with dots: in this patera the medallion is evidently the main part (plate 109). On the whole the friezes of the plainer bowls consist of series of geometrical elements, or floral elements such as palmettes, buds, and papyrus flowers, or animals like winged sphinxes, winged scarabs, fantastic birds, deer, and bucks. The metopes contain four winged scarabs, rosettes, eyes of Horus, and globular elements.

Of the more complex types we can examine a cup which has a central medallion formed by numerous internal rosettes; round it is a large star forming triangular metopes each containing a rosette; the remaining surface of the cup consists of a series of narrow concentric friezes with series of animals, and is divided by rays formed by single two-faced figures (fig 18).

In the more complex types there are numerous bowls with a geometrical decoration in the centre zone and in the outer or partly outer band larger and more elaborate depictions of animals and humans. The examples are as follows: a bowl with an outer frieze representing confronted rams flanking the sacred tree (plate 50); a bowl with a centre frieze showing large birds of prey confronted and devouring a reclining

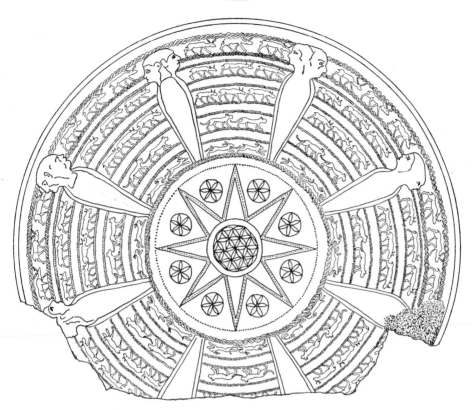

18   Bronze bowl with medallion and concentric friezes from Nimrud

hare; a bowl with an outer frieze with aedicules showing two winged
gryphons with a double Egyptian crown facing a narrow platform bearing a winged scarab; a bowl with a centre frieze representing men
spearing a lion; a bowl with an outer frieze showing a lion hunted by an
archer in a chariot, looking back (a motif which, as Breasted proved,
originated in Egypt and passed on to Assyria through Phoenicia).

A decoration of human figures in the central medallion appears in
a bowl with two concentric friezes with animal and human figures; the
medallion shows a scene typical of the Syro-Anatolian repertory: two
confronted figures holding a central figure by his crossed arms and
striking him on the head. Another interesting bowl marks a typological
passage to the examples with decorated surface and no medallions, or a
deformed medallion. It has four female faces in the centre, including a
lenticular motif surrounded by schematic representations of mountains.
On the outside, but with no circular dividing bands, is a series of
probably divine figures (plate 110).

Coming finally to the bowls with an all-decorated surface and no medallion, or a deformed medallion, we have one with a lenticular oval in the centre and round it a series of schematized protruberances in a star shape, in the cavities of which are figures of goats and trees in low relief (plate 51). Another bowl, with no centre zone, is entirely composed of an entanglement of gryphons and lions fighting.

Passing on to the bowls from Cyprus, a detailed study has been made by Gjerstad, who has classified them into various groups and periods. The bowls that Gjerstad defined as Cypro-Phoenician are divided into three groups: I (800–700 BC); II (700–600); III (600–550). It is likely that these bowls, which present certain peculiarities and independent developments, are to be attributed to Phoenician artists in Cyprus rather than to importation from Phoenician cities.

To the first Cypro-Phoenician period belongs a silver bowl from Amathus which contains a small medallion in the centre, surrounded by three bands of concentric decorations (fig 19). Of these the first is composed of a series of sphinxes with wings outspread bearing a solar disk with uraeus on their heads; the second has Egyptian deities and a winged solar scarab on altars also of Egyptian type, a figure of Horus on the lotus flower and a stylized palm from which two figures of Phoenician, or anyhow Asiatic type, are picking flowers; the third shows

19   Bronze bowl of Cypro-Phoenician group I

warriors of Assyrian type attacking a turreted city from the right, while on the left figures of Egyptian type scale the walls on ladders and others cut trees with axes of Aegean type. This bowl is an excellent example of the confluence of the most varied motifs, which have a greater possibility of expanding in a free ornamentation on a bowl than on ivory.

In the second Cypro-Phoenician group are three bowls, two of which are in the Cesnola collection and one in the Louvre. Cup no 4554 of the Cesnola collection (fig 20) is the only one with a centre decorated with a motif of probable Assyrian origin, if it is not a Syrian inheritance of the second millennium: a spirit with four wings outspread spearing a lion standing on its hind legs. Of the two friezes divided by a border of

20   Bronze bowl of Cypro-Phoenician group II

71

plait-work the inner one shows cows, sphinxes, and horses walking and an archer among small trees; the outer one presents various juxtaposed motifs, rampant gryphons, sphinxes, and goats flanking sacred plants, the pharaoh slaying his enemies, the hero spearing a gryphon. The other bowl in the Cesnola collection (no 4556) is in fragments, but shows various friezes with scenes of war, while the centre represents the massacre of his enemies by the pharaoh. The third bowl of the second Cypro-Phoenician group, found in Idalion and now in the Louvre, has a large central area with a geometric frieze consisting of a series of small rosettes with six petals surrounded by two narrow bands with floral motifs; on the centre frieze the motif of the hero spearing a monster alternates with the sacred plant with volutes; the outer frieze has a continuous scene of

21   Bronze bowl of Cypro-Phoenician group III

horsemen, archers, soldiers, camels, and chariots, completed by floral fillings.

The third group of Cypro-Phoenician bowls contains two examples, one with animal figures in the centre and on the concentric friezes, the other with the pharaoh slaying his enemies in the centre, a centre frieze with a succession of gryphons and sphinxes with a paw on the head of a reclining man, and an outer frieze with repeated scenes of combat – heroes with lions or gryphons (fig 21).

In order to get some idea of the bowls outside the Near Eastern and Cypriot area we should examine a bowl from Olympia which shows a large eight-pointed star in the centre with six petalled rosettes in the voids (fig 22). A thin plaited band borders the large circular frieze

22   Bronze bowl from Olympia

subdivided into panels; four corresponding panels show deities surmounted by winged solar disks, two clothed and two nude, while, of the
others, two corresponding ones show a banquet scene and the two
remaining ones contain a scene of musicians and the slaughter of the
gryphon respectively.

Passing on to Etruria, the two silver bowls from the Bernardini tomb
at Praeneste, of the late seventh century, are of special interest. One,
almost completely Egyptian, shows in the centre the familiar motif of
the pharaoh slaying his enemies and round it four papyrus boats carrying deities and winged scarabs; other figures, among lotus leaves, stand
between the boats while above and below the frieze is bordered by
inscriptions in imitation hieroglyphs making no sense, while there is an

23   Bronze bowl from Praeneste, Egypticizing style

inscription in Phoenician giving the name of the owner, Eshmunazar ben Ashto (fig 23). The other bowl shows, in the central medallion, Egyptian warriors and an Asiatic prisoner; the inner frieze has a succession of horses and birds, and the outer frieze shows Assyrian-looking warriors and chariots in scenes of war and country life surmounted by the Egyptian winged solar disk.

These examples are a good illustration of the basic significance of the bowls in the history of Phoenician art: they show maximum assimilation of iconographical motifs from the neighbouring regions, maximum ornamentalization of these motifs, and maximum spread of these motifs in the Mediterranean world. It is equally true that a certain artistic independence, which seems distinctive and original, corresponds to this multiplicity of components. Egyptian influence is evident, but so is a typical tendency towards ornamentalization as well as the assembly of Syrian, and eventually Assyrian, themes. It is interesting to note that this type of product, unlike others, was to have no developments in the Punic West.

6 Glyptic Art

Phoenician glyptic art consists of seals in the shape of scarabs or more rarely scaraboids, bearing on the lower face the incision of the mould of the seal. The fact that certain seals of the cylinder type should have been found inscribed with Phoenician names does not constitute a proof of the Phoenician origin of the seals themselves: the obviously Assyrian or Persian iconography suggests Mesopotamian and Iranian origin, while the addition of the name is merely a secondary indication of ownership.

The predominance of the stamp over the cylinder-seal characterizes the Iron Age in Syria and Palestine after the spread of the alphabet. With the alphabet, clay was replaced by papyrus as a writing material, so that the cylinder rolled on clay went out of use and was succeeded by the Egyptian type of scarab. These scarabs, on the other hand, were frequently used not only as seals but also as rings and components of necklaces, and always retained a magical and apotropaic value which partially accounts for the iconography.

The spread of the seal in the Iron Age covered the whole of the Syro-Palestinian area: in other words, numerous examples of these products are found both in the Phoenician localities and the Israelite and Aramaic area. The problem is therefore to distinguish the actual Phoenician products and to establish the similarities between them and the others. When we realize that the examples from the ancient Phoenician cities are few we shall see that the problem is not easy to solve although the inscriptions are a great help: the names of gods are in all probability an indication of the origin of the proprietor. Furthermore, here as in the rest of the 'minor' arts, the iconography and the general situation of the centres of artistic production play a significant part.

With regard to the iconography of the seals a comprehensive study by Galling enables us to identify the following motifs: a winged sphinx walking (fig 24); confronted lions squatting on podiums; goats running

24 Phoenician seal with walking sphinx

(fig 25); a sort of goat giving milk to its kid; a falcon with four wings outspread; a deity walking with four wings outspread and holding a shrub; a scene with animal-headed deities; a figure with tall crown and sceptre facing an incense-burner; a figure walking with double crown and short loin-cloth, holding in one hand a stick with a crescent moon on the end and the other hand raised in greeting or blessing (fig 26). These basic themes are usually accompanied by the winged solar disk, the solar disk, or a crescent moon, and the uraeus acting as fillings.

In addition to the iconographical motifs on the seals bearing inscriptions, there are others on seals with no inscriptions: the four-winged scarab; the god Horus naked kneeling on a lotus flower flanked by two uraei; the small Horus on a *jed* pillar flanked by two figures in Syrian garb; a frontal view of the god Bes; the human figure kneeling with four wings outspread; two winged sphinxes squatting on either side of a sacred plant; Isis suckling Horus standing; the falcon-headed deity under a solar disk and uraeus; two rampant winged gryphons on each

25 Phoenician seal with running goat

26 Phoenician seal with advancing figure

side of a sacred plant with volutes. While all these themes are the results of Egyptian influence, certain seals, probably of the Persian era, can be attributed to Phoenicia; they represent a bearded male deity on a throne, sometimes flanked by sphinxes in front of an incense-burner. It has recently been suggested that these seals, of which a few, apparently later, examples have been found in the West, represent the image of the god Melqart.

Apart from this last case both the predominant influence of Egypt and the themes already found in the Phoenician ivories and bowls are evident in the complex iconographical tradition. It therefore seems reasonable to assume that this production was mainly centred in the Phoenician cities, and that the seals to appear in the Israelite and Aramaic cities were of Phoenician origin or the work of emigrated Phoenician craftsmen, if they were not imitations of their work by artists in the interior.

7 Other minor arts

Similar considerations, although the motifs are often less complex (according to the different form of product), can be applied to the jewellery found occasionally in Phoenicia and mainly in Cyprus, Carthage, Sardinia, Etruria, and Spain. We have necklaces, bracelets, ear-rings, every sort of pin, pectorals, medallions, mainly of gold with repoussé ornamentation (plate 99). The themes are humans, like the nude female figure symbolizing fertility; animals, like scarabs, heads of sphinxes, lions, goats, birds; floral designs, of palmettes in particular; and geometrical designs. As always, the Egyptian iconographical influence prevails.

A typical Phoenician craft was glasswork. Although it must not be thought that the Phoenicians actually invented this product, as some ancient authors affirm, they certainly propagated it. And besides the opaque glass used in Egypt, they propagated the transparent, frequently iridescent type, which was of particular value. Pliny's praise[7] of the Sidonian glassworks is justified: bowls, bottles, and flasks have appeared in quantity in the tombs; and later, in the Roman epoch, there is an abundant export to the West.

The first coins were struck in the Persian era. The earliest coins seem to be from Tyre, going back to about the middle of the fifth century. On one side we get a dolphin in the waves and a murex shell, and on the other an owl. Between the end of the fifth century and the fourth there are further coins from Tyre, and also from Aradus, Sidon, and Byblos. In Tyre again we have an owl on one side and a dolphin and murex shell or Melqart with a bow on a sea-horse on the other (fig 27). At

Aradus we get a fish-tailed deity on the obverse (fig 28) or a bearded
male and on the reverse a galley or a sea-horse on waves. At Sidon the
types are more varied: on the obverse a galley before a fortress or a
galley on the waves, or even a bearded male head in a cap; on the reverse
the king of Persia in a trap together with his groom, followed on foot

27   Coin from Tyre

by a figure who may be the king of Sidon, or even the king of Persia,
shooting a bow or slaying a lion. Finally, at Byblos, we see a galley and
sea-horse on the obverse, and a vulture or lion attacking a bull on the
reverse. The striking of coins, however unique, is a late activity, and
develops considerably in the Hellenistic age.

28   Coin from Aradus

We now come to terracotta. There is a large series of figurines from
the tombs, comprising, particularly, female images, of which some are
remarkably original (the Akziv image of a woman raising her child to
her chin (plate 71)). Contenau found a group of figurines with prevalently male heads at Sidon in which the Egyptian wigs and Osirian

79

beards of a few copies and the tall pointed Syrian caps of others are particularly remarkable. Certain amulets found in the tombs are also of terracotta, or sometimes of glass paste; they are of wholly Egyptian type (cf. a figurine with the head of a dog found at Akziv).

An interesting group of terracottas discovered at Kherayeb in 1946 and studied by Emir Chéhab consists mainly of figurines of the Hellenistic age. A small proportion of them, in which Egyptian influences prevail, are slightly earlier than this period: they consist of certain heads, figures wearing caps of Egyptian type; figures of Harpocrates, Bes, and Apis. In some cases, on the other hand, the influence is Persian, as is shown by certain bearded figures with characteristic caps.

Coming to the vases, there is a notable sort of fine, red-burnished pottery which recurs in numerous places on the coast, such as Akziv, Beth Peleth, Dor, and even Er Retabeh (in the Egyptian Delta). There are three main types: the mushroom-lipped jug, the trefoil-lipped jug with a long neck, and the biconical jug. The earliest examples of the three types can be dated around the ninth-eighth century B C, although the shapes continue to be widespread, above all in the seventh century

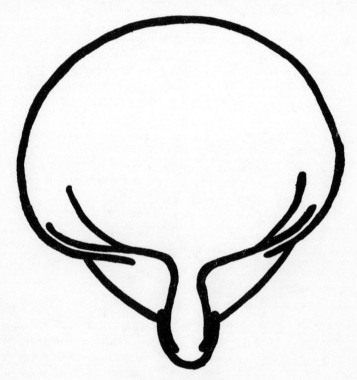

29   Phoenician lamp with one beak

and in some regions as late as the sixth or fifth century. The forms are usually of metallic derivation, as is seen, for example, from the foliated aspect of the mushroom lips and the ring half-way up the neck. Together with this category of fine pottery, the Phoenician sites have also yielded much unglazed crockery of common use, like the typical plates with large central umbilications and a band round the rim; the equally typical lamps with open saucers and one beak (fig 29); the ovoid amphorae with square shoulders; and the pots with one handle.

CHAPTER 5

ECONOMY AND TRADE

1 Economy

We possess little direct information about the economy of the Phoenician cities, but with the help of indirect material and archaeological evidence we will try to identify the specific nature of Phoenician society characterized by its environment, as a premiss for understanding certain later cultural and historical developments peculiar to it. Far more information is provided, however, by the Mediterranean colonies, above all by Carthage, and in most cases it reflects economic and commercial forms originating in the homeland.

There is no doubt that the Phoenicians exploited the small extent of arable land as much as they could, forcing cultivation right up to the slopes of the Lebanese mountains and using the watercourses for irrigation. The terrain which it was possible to flood enabled them to cultivate cereals, while the rocky land was restricted to plantations.

The system of cultivation of the cereals, in particular of grain, must have remained in use until recently. The Punic stelae show a very simple plough which, according to Mago, was drawn by oxen and bears a close resemblance to the modern Berber and Syrian plough. It would seem, therefore, that the Phoenician plough was similar. Stone wheels, found in more or less good condition, must have been used for grinding.

Vines, olives, figs, and date-palms were the commonest plantations. Certain large stones with holes, found in Phoenicia, may have been olive and grape presses, and it is likely that the systems of vine-dressing described by Mago and Columella in the West were imported from the homeland. Another widespread plantation in Carthage, the pomegranate, was also probably imported from Phoenicia.

Finally, the drinking water in the Phoenician cities, and above all on the islands, was obtained through large cisterns which gathered the rain. Archaeologists have brought their remains to light, and Strabo gives an interesting account of the way in which the inhabitants of Aradus used a spring which gushed out in the sea: they apparently let a funnel of lead into the spring, attached to a leather tube which carried the water straight to the island.[1]

The most important factor in Phoenician economy was the exploitation of the cedar and fir forests, which provided the neighbouring countries with valuable wood. Egyptian sources mention this trade from the beginning of history, particularly with Byblos. And in the period with which we are concerned both the Bible and Mesopotamian sources provide us with the information mentioned in the chapter on history. Furthermore, a relief of Sargon II depicts ships carrying large tree-trunks. Trade with Egypt was, of course, all done by sea, while for Mesopotamia caravans were used as far as the Euphrates and the trunks were then transported along the river. An interesting account of this means of transport is given by an inscription of Nebuchadnezar which records an expedition accomplished in 'Lebanon, mountain of cedars, green forest with fragrant air':

With the force of Nabu and Marduk, my lords, I armed my troops for an expedition in Lebanon. I drove out the enemy above and below, I brought happiness to the heart of the earth. The scattered population I gathered and brought back to their home. That which no king had done before, I did: I cleft high mountains, I cut blocks of stone from the mountains, I opened paths, prepared roads for the transport of the cedars. On the canal Avakhtu, as though they were reeds of the river, I floated large cedars, tall and strong, of great beauty, of imposing aspect, rich product of Lebanon, and brought them before Marduk, the king.[2]

Stone was also used by the Phoenicians. The custom of cutting tombs in the rock is a proof of their use and large blocks were taken from the quarries to build the city walls. In many cases the method of building with rough blocks was probably earlier than the use of square blocks, although the technique cannot be considered a definite proof. The stone coffins are an additional indication of the workability of the stone.

The main Phoenician industry was textiles. Homer refers on several occasions to the many-coloured garments of the Sidonians, and the Asiatics depicted on Egyptian monuments wear equally colourful garbs. The Phoenicians were famous for dying their textiles with the *murex trunculus* or *murex brandaris*, shells once very common in the sea just off the Phoenician coast, but which gradually disappeared through intensive exploitation. The dead murex secretes a liquid which, when applied to white material, colours it violet, and this is the purple colour connected with the name of the Phoenicians. According to the intensity of the liquid and the length of its exposure to the sun the colour could vary from pink to dark violet. Besides the vast literary evidence, the Phoenician purple industry is attested by the immense deposits of shells found near Sidon and Tyre. South of Sidon there is a hill close to the sea composed literally of layers of shells several metres thick: presumably the receptacles in which the fish were exposed until they putrefied and secreted their liquid were placed at a considerable distance from the city because of the pungent smell. Deposits of shells have also been discovered in the West, thereby proving the spread of this industry in the colonial area.

Glass was another notable industry of the Phoenician cities after the seventh century. As we have already seen, we cannot accept Pliny's claim[3] that the Phoenicians invented this industry, since it undoubtedly existed in Egypt some time earlier. It is true, however, that the Phoenicians developed it, because they also used transparent glass, while Egyptian glass had been opaque. Only in the first century BC was a further invention developed: that of blowing glass.

The metal and ivory work mentioned in the chapter on art indicates wide commercial activity: copper came from Cyprus, silver and gold from Ethiopia and maybe from Anatolia (although there were copper- and iron-mines in Wadi Araba, which Solomon exploited amply), ivory from India or Punt. All this shows the importance of the Red Sea route, which gave access both to the African coast and India. We therefore have a clear general picture of a mercantile economy based on the exploitation of local resources and goods which could be shipped from distant lands and exported once more over the sea routes.

2 Trade

Phoenician trade is probably best described by the Hebrew prophets, who condemned the Phoenician cities and contrasted their past splendour to their future ruin. With regard to Sidon, and especially to Tyre, we have the prophecies of Isaiah, Jeremiah, and, most comprehensive of all, Ezekiel:

O Tyre, thou hast said, I am of perfect beauty. Thy borders are in the midst of the seas, thy builders have perfected thy beauty. They have made all thy ship boards of fir trees of Senir: they have taken cedars from Lebanon to make masts for thee. Of the oaks of Bashan have they made thine oars; the company of the Ashurites have made thy benches of ivory, brought of the isles of Chittim. Fine linen with broidered work from Egypt was that which thou spreadest forth to be thy sail; blue and purple from the isles of Elishash was that which covered thee. The inhabitants of Sidon and Aradus were thy mariners: thy wise men, O Tyre, that were in thee, were thy pilots. The ancients of Gebal and the wise men thereof were in thee thy calkers: all the ships of the sea with their mariners were in thee to occupy thy merchandise. They of Persia and of Lud and of Phut were in thine army, thy men of war: they hanged the shield and helmet in thee; they set forth thy comeliness. The men of Aradus with thine army were upon thy walls round about, and the Gammadims were in thy towers: they hanged their shields upon thy walls round about; they have made thy beauty perfect. Tarshish was thy merchant by reason of the multitude of all kind of riches; with silver, iron, tin, and lead they traded in thy fairs. Javan, Tubal, and Meshech, were thy merchants: they traded the persons of men and vessels of brass in thy market. They of the house of Togarmah traded in thy fairs with horses and horsemen and mules. The men of Dedan were thy merchants; many isles were the merchandise of thine hand: they brought thee for a present horns of ivory and ebony. Syria was thy merchant by reason of the multitude of the wares of thy making: they occupied in thy fairs with emeralds, purple, and broidered work, and fine linen, and coral, and agate. Judah, and the land of Israel, they were thy merchants: they traded in thy market wheat of Minnith, and Pannag, and honey, and oil, and balm. Damascus was thy merchant in the multitude of the wares of thy making, for the multitude of all riches; in the wine of Helbon, and white wool. Dan also and Javan going to and fro occupied in thy fairs: bright iron, cassia, and calamus were in thy market. Dedan was thy merchant in precious clothes for chariots. Arabia, and all the princes of Kedar, they occupied with thee, in lambs, in rams, and goats: in these were they thy merchants. The merchants of Sheba and Raamah, they were thy merchants: they occupied in thy fairs with chief of all spices, and with all precious stones and gold. Haran, and Canneh and Eden the merchants of Sheba, Asshur, and Chilmad were thy merchants. These were thy merchants in all sorts of things, in blue clothes, and broidered work, and in chests of rich apparel, bound with cords, and made of cedar, among thy merchandise. The ships of Tarshish did sing of thee in thy market: and thou wast replenished, and made very glorious in the midst of the seas.[4]

The prophecy is of great importance, since it reconstructs in unique detail the commercial activity of a Phoenician city. There may be some doubt about the identification of the localities mentioned and the exact nature of the goods, but the general picture is most impressive and shows the incredible abundance and intensity of Tyrian trade.

In the first part of the passage the allegorical image of Tyre as a great ship suggests the goods she traded by mentioning the materials used to build the ship, and the people taken as sailors. The wood implies Mount Hermon (of which Senir is a peak), the Lebanon, Bashan (north-east of Lake Tiberias) and Cyprus (Chittim, from the name of the Phoenician colony Kition). The linen is from Egypt, the purple and violet again from Cyprus (Elishash or Alashiya is the name of this island currently used in the second millennium). The reference to the inhabitants of Sidon, Aradus, and Byblos among the sailors indicates the close co-operation among the Phoenician cities and suggests a certain predominance of Tyre over the others. As for the army, some believe Persia to be an anachronism, so Kush should be read instead (the textual variant is possible); Lud may not be Lydia, but a Libyan or at any rate an African people. Phut is obviously Nubia.

In the second part of the passage the picture of the commercial relations starts with the mention of Tarshish, which probably means Spain, and it is stated that metals like silver, iron, tin, and lead came from there. Then we have Anatolia: Javan is Ionia, Tubal northern Cilicia; Meshech Phrygia, Togarmah southern Armenia. Of these regions the first three again provide metals (brass) and slaves, while the fourth gives horses and mules. We now come to Arabia with Dedan and the 'many isles': it provides ivory and ebony (maybe only as a place of transit from India and Africa: in fact, Dedan breaks the geographical order of the account and Arabia is mentioned later, but the change to Rhodes, which is geographically possible, does not suit the products mentioned). This is followed by the Syro-Palestinian region: Syria provides cloth and precious stones, Judah and Israel agricultural products and perfumes, Damascus wine and wool. Dan and Javan bring us back to Anatolia: Dan implies the Danunas of central Cilicia, while Javan we already know, and both regions appear here as producers of iron (as Cilicia had already been in the Hittite period). Returning to Arabia, Dedan is mentioned for its leather saddles, Kedar for its sheep, Sheba and Raamah for perfumes and precious stones. Finally Mesopotamia trades garments, embroidery, and cord with Phoenicia.

This impressive picture may be inaccurate in certain details, owing mainly to misunderstandings and errors in the transcription of the text, but on the whole it remains valid. To complete it there are accounts by other prophets, such as Isaiah, who speaks of Sidon's overseas commerce in Egyptian grain,[5] and the historical facts about the fleet of Hiram which imported gold, precious stones, and wood from the region of Ophir (probably southern Arabia), while from Tarshish it brought back wood, silver, ivory, monkeys, and peacocks.[6]

The Phoenicians traded in ships depicted by the Assyrians. There were two main types which both appear on the Assyrian reliefs from Nineveh showing the flight of Luli from Tyre. The first type, used purely for war, has a convex stern and a ram on the surface of the water; there are two banks of oars under a deck on which warriors' shields are hung; the mast rises above the ship. The second type, probably for trade, but also defended by soldiers, has convex prow and stern; the sailors sit on two banks, as in the preceding model, but there are no masts. A third, smaller type of ship is depicted on the bronze gate of Balawat and in the reliefs of Sargon II at Khorsabad, with convex stern and horsehead prow. There is a single bank of oars, and no warriors or shields. It is obvious from the shape of these ships that their function was purely commercial, for transporting cargo of secondary importance, not deemed worthy of military protection (at least not on the ship itself).

For lack of compass, navigation was performed under the guidance of Ursa Minor, which the Greeks called 'Phoenician'. The ships did not go far out to sea: the Phoenicians, as we shall see in the chapter on their Mediterranean expansion, probably founded their landing-stages at a day's voyage apart, so as to be able to shelter on the mainland at night. Nevertheless, they were not deterred by the most distant destinations and made special use of the islands as anchorages in the open sea.

According to Herodotus,[7] the furthest voyage the Phoenician sailors ever undertook was the circumnavigation of the African continent, accomplished on the orders of the Pharaoh Necho c. 600 B C. The journey is supposed to have taken three years and the navigators sailed westwards from the Red Sea. The fact that the sun was to their right as they passed Libya is considered a positive element in favour of the veracity of this tradition. Two subsequent voyages were undertaken from Carthage: c. 450 by Himilco, who sailed round Spain to the British Isles, and c. 425 by Hanno, who seems to have sailed through the Pillars of Hercules to the Gulf of Guinea. These voyages, undertaken not from Phoenicia but from Carthage, appear to be the natural continuation of an expansion and naval art of which the Phoenicians were masters.

During their voyages the Phoenicians seem to have sometimes resorted to piracy, and specialized in kidnapping boys and girls to be sold as slaves in other countries. Thus, in the *Odyssey*,[8] Eumeus tells that 'Phoenicians, men famed for their ships, greedy knaves, bringing countless trinkets in their black ship', arrived in his country when he was a child. They arranged with the Phoenician nurse of the palace to carry off both the nurse and the child so as to sell them into slavery. Again in the *Odyssey*,[9] Ulysses tells that a Phoenician took him to his land under the pretext of shipping the cargo as far as Libya with him, but actually to sell him as a slave. Further evidence is provided by Herodotus: Io, daughter of Inacus, was kidnapped by the Phoenicians, who took her to Egypt;[10] Theban priestesses were kidnapped in Egypt to be shipped to Libya.[11] On the whole, however, piratical activities must have been fairly limited, otherwise they would have jeopardized trade relations to which the Phoenicians attached great importance, and there was also a difference between piracy and organized slave traffic which was legal and considered part of normal commercial activity.

CHAPTER 6

SCRIPT AND LANGUAGE

1 Script

One of the greatest, if not the greatest, glory of the Phoenicians was the spread of the alphabet in the Mediterranean area. There is no doubt that the Phoenicians taught the alphabet to the Greeks, nor that the Phoenicians and the Greeks were responsible for spreading it in the West.

Although this is certain, and gives the Phoenicians an important role in the history of civilization, the origin of this alphabet is not so clear. That the Phoenicians should have spread it does not necessarily mean that they invented it, and the nature and limitations of the Phoenician contribution must be examined apart from the origin of alphabetic script.

It was a common theory in ancient times that the Phoenicians invented the alphabet. Some authors, however, do not speak so much about invention as about diffusion. So, in a much quoted passage from Herodotus, we read:

These Phoenicians who came with Cadmus . . . among other kinds of learning, brought into Hellas the alphabet, which had hitherto been unknown, as I think, to the Greeks.[1]

And Diodorus Siculus:

And in reply to those who say that the Syrians are the discoverers of the letters, the Phoenicians having learned them from the Syrians and then passed them on to the Greeks . . . men tell us, on the other hand, that the Phoenicians were not the first to make this discovery, but that they did no more than to change the forms of the letters.[2]

Even the Latin authors frequently mention other inventors of the alphabet. Pliny, who on one side claims that the invention of letters is a Phoenician feat,[3] speaks elsewhere of Mesopotamian origin.[4] Tacitus maintains that it is of Egyptian origin, adding that the Phoenicians took all the credit for what they received before passing it on to others.[5]

So the classical evidence is by no means univocal and shows an awareness of the problem in question.

While the attitude of ancient authors to the origin of the alphabet is of documentary interest, there is no point in dwelling on more recent opinions. The defenders of a Mesopotamian origin are outnumbered by the champions of an Egyptian origin, usually assumed on account of the Palaeo-Sinaitic inscriptions. Numerous attempts have been made to decipher these inscriptions, dated *c.* 1800 or 1500 BC, by alphabetical values (Albright, van den Branden), but the results are still uncertain. Others maintain that the solution to the problem is contained by the 'pseudo-hieroglyphic' inscriptions of Byblos, ascribed to the second millennium, but, despite the attempts of Dhorme to decipher them, interpretations are dubious. Certain small inscriptions, known as Proto-Cananaitic, found mainly in Palestine (Bet Shemesh, Lakish, Gezer, Tell El Ajjul, etc) and ascribed to about the middle of the second millennium, have also been studied, but have proved equally indecipherable. Finally, the discovery at Ugarit of a wholly alphabetic script of at least the fourteenth century puts the problem back and complicates it, since the script contains cuneiform signs.

The search for the origin of the alphabet cannot be purely and simply identified with a search for the type of script on which the alphabet is based. The Ugaritic alphabet proves the cuneiform inspiration of the script, but does not imply in any way that the idea of the alphabet comes from Mesopotamia, where it, in fact, never existed in any form. On the other hand, the acrophonic principle in Egyptian – the possibility of using a sign for its initial consonantal value alone – suggests that the alphabetical idea is of Egyptian origin, but does not diminish the truly revolutionary value of the invention.

If an Egyptian origin seems likely, the Sinaitic, pseudo-hieroglyphic and Proto-Cananaitic scripts seem to be the first attempts at a process which led to the origin of the alphabet. This applies, at least, to the Sinaitic and Proto-Cananaitic scripts, since the pseudo-hieroglyphic script has such a number of signs that it must be considered syllabic. On the other hand, when we try to trace a passage from Sinaitic and Proto-Cananaitic forms to the Phoenician forms we see at once that the signs are very different (and sometimes vary more in the early than in the later stages). Now, if for many centuries of its history the Phoenician alphabet remained substantially unchanged, why should it have undergone such radical changes in the alleged phase of its origins?

There is another possibility: whatever the preceding attempts, the alphabet could have been invented, in all its characteristics, at Ugarit, around the fifteenth–fourteenth century. The Phoenician alphabet, the first examples of which are inscriptions on arrowheads of the twelfth century, would have based itself on the Ugaritic alphabet, and altered and simplified the shape of the signs (which is quite an achievement). Were this hypothesis correct, on one side the credit of inventing the alphabet as such would go to Ugarit, but on the other side the Phoenicians would get the credit for inventing simplified alphabetical forms which are the predecessors of our own, as well as having spread them in the Mediterranean area.

The connexion between the Phoenician and Ugaritic alphabets has in recent years been accentuated by certain new facts. The discovery of a Ugaritic spelling-book – the list of the letters of the alphabet in the order assigned to them – has shown that this order corresponds, on the whole, to that of the Phoenician alphabet, which we know from certain biblical psalms. Moreover, the variations of the order correspond to the phonetic evolutions which have come about through the ages, and the dropping of certain signs in Phoenician corresponds to evolutionary facts, such as the dropping of the relative consonants. We must mention one more point: the simplification of the alphabet from thirty to twenty-two signs also started in Ugarit, as is proved by certain hitherto unpublished texts which lack the signs of subsequently dropping consonants. So the Ugaritic alphabet appears to be an antecedent of that of the Phoenician cities, and is either the first phase in the formation of the alphabetic principle or the phase first to appear clearly. Earlier evidence is still uncertain.

From the origin of the alphabetic principle we come to the problem of the origin of the Phoenician signs. The opinion is widespread that the names of the signs correspond to the objects usually reproduced by the signs themselves: *aleph* would correspond to an ox, *beth* to a house, *daleth* to a door, etc. But, however widespread, the theory is dubious, both because there appears no formal resemblance in certain cases, and because certain signs have names which do not correspond to any object. It must be supposed, therefore, that the names of the letters followed the invention of the letters themselves, and were introduced for mnemonic purposes. It is possible that certain formal associations existed in the choice of the names, but this does not seem to apply generally.

The origins of the forms themselves, on the other hand, could indeed stem from invention – an invention which may well contain associations. But these associations, if they exist, are not necessarily univocal, and may involve Egyptian, Sinaitic, pseudo-hieroglyphic, and Cretan signs.

In conclusion, the alphabetic principle as such was certainly invented earlier than the Phoenician period as we have defined it, but the invention of the alphabetic principle was followed by another invention – that of simple, convenient signs which spread over the Mediterranean. This second invention seems unquestionably to be the work of the

Phoenicians, and even seems to be one of the distinctive facts which mark the beginning of their epoch. We can say nothing definite, on the other hand, about the place where the new signs appear for the first time. The long tradition that attributes the origin of the alphabet to Byblos, however, is definitely possible, and the invention of the forms we know may well have taken place in this city.

Passing on to the development of the alphabet in the Syro-Palestinian area, we must say that according to all evidence, the other forms found in this area go back to one source, which is Phoenician. The earliest Hebrew inscriptions present no major graphic distinction from Phoenician, and it is extremely interesting to note that the earliest known Hebrew inscription, the 'calender' of Gezer of the tenth century, is directly paralleled by the graphic forms of the Phoenician inscription of Ahiram and not by any Palestinian variant on the arrowheads. This proves that these variants are secondary aberrations destined to fade with the predominance of the centre of expansion, Byblos. As far as Aramaic is concerned the variants of the earliest inscriptions are minimal. These variants do not indicate an independent source or branch, and certain incomplete correspondences between signs and consonants (in ancient Aramaic the Protosemitic interdentals were still phonetically independent, although this does not seem to be so in the script of Phoenician type) prove the continuity of an already existing graphic system, the Phoenician one.

2 Language

The language presented by the Phoenician inscriptions is undoubtedly closely connected to the other Semitic languages of the Syro-Palestinian area, both previous and contemporary, and it is certainly divided into dialects just as Phoenician history and culture is divided. But in spite of this we can say that the Phoenician language has an independence and individuality which adds the collective consciousness of the speaker to the definition of the people as a whole.

Recent studies have profoundly altered opinions on the history of North Western Semitic, and although the linguistic situation of the middle and late Bronze Age (chiefly manifested in Amorite, Ugaritic, and the glosses of Tell Amarna) is very coherent and cannot be classified with the languages of the Iron Age, the Iron Age languages (mainly Phoenician, Hebrew, and Aramaic) emerge in a remarkably independent form resulting from progressively divergent innovations and the consequent formation of autonomous isoglosses. This new linguistic picture confirms the independent emergence of Phoenician culture after the Iron Age.

We can now proceed to a more detailed examination of the nature and characteristics of this emergence of Phoenician as an autonomous language. In the first place the phenomenon is gradual, not immediate: the earliest inscriptions from Byblos preserve numerous archaic elements which subsequently vanish and present isoglosses which cannot yet favour a division into Phoenician, Hebrew, and Aramaic. So, there is no article in Ahiram's inscription or the Hebrew inscription from Gezer, while it exists in later Phoenician. The verbal stem with affixed t appears in the inscription of Ahiram and in Moabitic, but not later. The pronominal suffixes of Byblos (third person masculine singular –h, pl. –hm) are paralleled by the Hebrew and earlier Aramaic forms, while they change in later Phoenician (–y, –nm); the demonstrative and relative pronouns of Byblos (zn, z) are paralleled in Aramaic, while they differ from the later Phoenician forms. Similar phenomena also occur in the subsequent development of the languages, but to a lesser extent, according to the areas.

In the second place Phoenician, as presented in the first millennium, contains dialectal variants. Besides the variants of Byblos in general and the inscription of Ahiram in particular, there are further sporadic examples in Cyprus, Karatepe, and Ur, not to mention the development of Punic. In this respect we must emphasize the limitation of our knowledge, especially as far as Phoenician of the homeland is concerned. However, in view of the fact that in many cases the variants depend on different phases of development and conservation of archaic elements, or on a remarkable geographical dispersion, the general impression is of an extraordinarily coherent language. So, generally speaking, the documentation confirms the division of the area, but also its basic autonomy.

With regard to Syro-Palestinian Semitic of the second millennium, Phoenicia presents both continuity and intense development. The continuity is proved both by archaic elements evolved elsewhere (such as the pronoun of the third person masculine plural hmt, the indefinite pronoun mnm, the feminine suffix –t, the unevolved nominal schemes $qatl$, $qitl$, $qutl$) and the innovations derived from the forms found in the second millennium. The intense development is shown by the quantity of innovations (crises of consonants, dropping of the nominal inflexion, appearance of the article, reduction of verbal stems, semantic arrangement of perfect and imperfect 'tenses', etc.). The result of these phenomena is a highly developed language compared to the preceding one, from which it obviously stems, and the linguistic distinction of Phoenician becomes perfectly clear.

The affinity with other languages of the first millennium is considerable and seems to suggest a strictly parallel development, particularly as far as Hebrew is concerned. Most of the Phoenician innovations are common to Hebrew, with two differences: the conservation of archaic elements in one language and not the other (for example, the Phoenician archaisms already mentioned) and divergent innovations (for example, the Phoenician pronominal suffix of the third person singular *–y*, the causative verbal stem *y–*, the change from *ā* to *ō*, even in the case of secondary *ā*, the assimilation of *n* in the verbs in which it is the third radical, etc). A general evaluation of Phoenician is conditioned by the old problem of the actual nature of Hebrew. If, as it seems, it was adopted on the spot, this would provide yet another indication of the Phoenician area as a zone of continuity of the culture of the preceding age, which would have been assimilated by the populations recently moved into the interior. The comparison between Phoenician and Hebrew does indeed show the reciprocal autonomy, but above all the concomitance and parallel development. This parallel development, which also took place in the Israelite area, produced no major differences.

CHAPTER 7

PHOENICIAN EXPANSION

1 The problem

The dates of Phoenician colonization constitute a problem which scholars have been trying to solve for decades. When did this colonization begin? It is primarily a question of dates, but beyond the dates lie complex historical queries which ultimately cover the whole of early Mediterranean history.

According to the classical authors Phoenician colonization in the Mediterranean preceded Greek colonization and goes back, with its first settlements, towards the end of the twelfth century. The foundation of Cadiz is ascribed to 1110,[1] of Utica to 1101[2] and, if we are to believe an account by Pliny,[3] the settlement of Lixus on the Atlantic coast of Morocco would be earlier; Diodorus also mentions Phoenician colonies in Africa before the foundation of Cadiz.[4]

The Phoenicians also preceded the Greeks in Sicily, according to Thucydides.[5] So the spread of the Phoenicians in the West was to follow the arrival of the 'peoples of the sea' and precede the Greeks who are unanimously attested from the eighth century. This was to be succeeded by the long struggle between the Phoenicians and the Greeks for the control of the maritime routes.

In the last century the archaeological and literary discoveries concerning the Phoenicians seemed to confirm this theory and even led some authors to exaggerate the Phoenician contribution to the history of civilization. Subsequently, however, a strong reaction set in against this tendency, and its first and greatest exponent, Beloch, submitted the classical tradition to radical criticism, finally concluding that Phoenician expansion in the Mediterranean did not begin before the eighth century, and therefore competed with the Greeks; the traditional dates for the foundation not only of Cadiz and Utica but also of Carthage (814) could not be considered of any historical value. The greatest supporters of Beloch's theory were the archaeologists of the successive decades: emphasis was laid on the absence of any archaeological evidence which could be termed Punic before the eighth century.

In recent times flaws have been found in this attitude. Even archaeologists are beginning to place Phoenician expansion in the Mediterranean at an earlier period. They claim that lack of evidence is no argument and refer to the information contained in archaeological findings and in inscriptions which has so far been neglected.

2 Archaeology

From the point of view of archaeological documentation we have no Punic material which we can definitely date before the eighth century BC, but what does this prove?

We have already said that arguments based on lack of evidence are relatively tenuous, and this has been proved by the discovery in the sea just off Selinunte of a bronze statuette published by Chiappisi in 1961, representing a walking deity of a type widespread in Phoenicia. As far as we can judge from Phoenician art the statuette can be ascribed to the end of the second millennium BC. It can, of course, be claimed that the bronze figurine was not brought by the Phoenicians, but by other peoples; certain scholars have even suggested Mycenaean merchants. But this theory is unnecessary, and there is no reason why the Phoenician piece should not be attributed to the passage of Phoenician ships.

Furthermore, the archaeological ascriptions are not always certain. As far as the Corinthian pottery in Carthage is concerned, for instance, the claim that it could be ascribed to the end of the eighth century and its attribution to the earliest stratum of the precinct of Tanit seems to deny the traditional date of the foundation of the city. But the excavator of the sanctuary, Donald Harden, clearly indicated right from the beginning that the pottery in question was only from the second stratum of the precinct, not the first, so that it can in no way be taken as a chronological criterion. Another example is the red pottery found in Mogador, very similar to the more ancient pieces from Carthage. Thinking it unlikely to be of the seventh century, Cintas claimed that it was not from Carthage, but from Cyprus or Phoenicia, and should be ascribed to the fourth century. But some Greek pottery, later found together with the material in question, is undoubtedly of the seventh century, so the earlier date seems indispensable.

The reservations formulated so far, however, are generic if isolated. To judge their actual value we must add certain literary and historical information, and, above all, one general consideration: the beginning of archaeological documentation does not necessarily imply the beginning of Phoenician colonization, but the beginning of stable and sufficiently developed settlements. In the first phases of the settlements the Phoenicians probably limited themselves to founding landing-stages and occasionally installing small groups of settlers, living in the simplest conditions, with no architecture or remains appreciable through archaeological research. So it is quite natural to expect archaeology to indicate the consolidation rather than the first foundation of the colonies, and there might be decades, if not centuries, between the two phases.

3 Epigraphy

Passing from archaeology to epigraphy, it is certain that the Phoenician alphabet was handed on to the Greeks no later than the eighth century. Now, such a phenomenon was certainly not instantaneous, but must have been the culmination of a process of diffusion and assertion on both a commercial and cultural level. In other words, if the West inherited the alphabet from the Phoenicians no later than the eighth century, it is likely that relations with the Phoenician world would have already been going on for some time. Here, too, the phenomenon with which we are faced is the end rather than the beginning of a long process of diffusion.

But going straight to the Phoenician texts, a funerary inscription from Cyprus[6] is ascribed, according to all evidence, to the ninth century BC. Less certain, but still probable, is the ascription to the same century of the inscription from Nora in Sardinia.[7] Now, if the Phoenicians left this evidence in such an early period, it seems reasonable to assume that their arrival in the islands of the East and West must be still earlier. The inscription of Nora is particularly significant in this respect, because it suggests a development in Sardinia of Phoenician colonies which had progressed far enough in the ninth century to leave an inscription which was certainly not the first manifestation of the Phoenician landing-stages on the island.

4 History

Passing on to the historical sources, we must record a remark made by Albright: why should all the classical authors have affirmed that the Phoenicians preceded the Greeks in the Mediterranean if this precedence bore no relation to reality? The classical authors might, of course, have based themselves on inaccurate information, but, since they wrote so close to the time, this does not seem very likely.

Furthermore, at the time of Solomon, the Bible mentions the merchant fleet of Tyre, capable of undertaking long and difficult crossings. It mentions specifically a 'navy of Tarshish',[8] and, in all likelihood, Tarshish must be identified with the south of Spain. Now, it is quite possible that in this case the expression may mean 'ocean-going navy', but nevertheless the reference exists and so, since we have no reason to doubt the veracity of biblical sources in this respect, it seems probable that Phoenician navigators had penetrated to the far West as early as the tenth century and obviously had to make use of numerous landing-stages.

The annals of Tyre also provide us with information about King Hiram, the contemporary of Solomon and protagonist of the vast naval enterprises described in the Bible. They include one account of particular interest. Hiram, say the annals, dispatched an expedition against the inhabitants of a colony which had refused to pay tribute.[9] According to some the name of the inhabitants should read 'Uticans', and in this case it would confirm the foundation of Utica in the tenth century and the close relations between the colonies and the homeland. As we have said, however, it is more likely that in this case reference is made to the closer Kition (Cyprus).

Historical sources, at any rate, suggest that Phoenician colonization starts before the tenth century. But in addition to these sources, the circumstances themselves favour this dating. The Mycenaean peoples controlled the Mediterranean routes until *c.* 1200. At this time the invasion of the 'peoples of the sea' provoked a general crisis in the eastern Mediterranean, as a result of which the power of the Mycenaeans declined and the Phoenicians emerged in vigorous independence. Now, three centuries, the eleventh, tenth, and ninth, certainly elapsed before the beginning of Greek expansion. It is natural that Phoenician expansion should profit from this historical movement and be basically facilitated by it, while it would be difficult to imagine a prolonged commercial inactivity followed by fierce competition between the Phoenicians and the Greeks.

Finally, the accounts provided by the classical tradition have been reassessed by the most recent critics. But although they may contain inaccuracies or misunderstandings, we can probably conclude that Mediterranean expansion by the Phoenicians started *c.* 1100 BC or even earlier. This would fit in with an historical plan placing the beginning of the actual history of the Phoenician cities after the invasion by the peoples of the sea. We can therefore consider overseas colonization, virtually non-existent before this period, as a further characteristic element of Phoenician civilization.

5 Chronology

The historical results of Phoenician expansion will be analysed and documented in the remaining chapters of this book. But we can give some idea of the general chronology here, and it must be kept in mind that the Phoenicians did not only settle in places where colonies subsequently developed, but that small groups founded trading-posts in regions ethnically and politically different, and either remained there as small settlements or dissolved.

Considering the region north and south of the actual Phoenician area, to the north the inscriptions of Zincirli and Karatepe show, in the ninth and eighth centuries respectively, the spread of Phoenician language and culture as far as southern Anatolia. However, this was not necessarily a colonial expansion. The same can be said for the typical red Phoenician pottery of the ninth and eighth centuries discovered in several places in southern Palestine, such as Beth Beleth and Regeish. It may imply the use of landing-stages on the route to Egypt, but it does not seem to suggest colonization.

In Cyprus, Phoenician settlements were probably in existence from the second millennium and certainly existed from the beginning of the first. We have already mentioned the inscription of the ninth century, as well as the account by Elissa (ninth century) and Luli (eighth century). The main Phoenician city must have been Kition, in the vicinity of which numerous inscriptions have been found and where Myres brought to light a settlement which may correspond to the Qartihadashti of Assyrian sources, whose king paid homage to Sargon II in 709–8. Golgoi, Idalion, Tamassos, Marion, and Lapethos were probably other Phoenician centres in Cyprus.

In the Aegean archipelago it seems evident that the Phoenicians settled in Rhodes, especially in the two principal cities of Camiros and Ialysos. Greek tradition has it that this took place under the guidance of a certain Phalas about the time of the Trojan war (1190) and that the Phoenicians were subsequently driven out by the Greeks or the Carians. Again from Greek tradition we learn that Phoenician cities had been established in other Aegean islands (Thasos, Kythera, Melos, Thera) and in Crete (Itanos).

On the African coast landing-stages probably existed in Egypt, where Herodotus refers to a quarter of the city of Memphis called the 'Tyrian field', and adds that a temple to Astarte ('Aphrodite the Stranger') was supposedly founded there at the arrival of Helen after the Trojan war.[10] This last part of the story is obviously legendary, but the legend concerns the origins and not the existence of the quarter. Moreover, red Phoenician pottery has been found at Er Retabeh and other places in the Delta, and probably suggests quarters of cities or landing-stages. On the whole, the colonies flourished in areas which were politically relatively weak, while in solid and centralized states like Egypt Phoenician penetration never amounted to occupation or autonomy.

Proceeding farther along the African coast of the Mediterranean, the earliest colony, traditionally, is Utica. Velleius Paterculus says that the Phoenician fleet which controlled the seas founded Cadiz about eighty years after the fall of Troy, and Utica a little later.[11] Since he ascribes the fall of Troy elsewhere to *c.* 1190 BC, Cadiz appears to have been founded *c.* 1110 and Utica *c.* 1100. Pliny confirms Velleius Paterculus's assertion, saying that the cedar beams in the temple of Apollo in Utica were 1,178 years old.[12] Since he was writing in AD 77, this would date the foundation of Utica in 1101. Finally, a pseudo-Aristotelian text quotes Phoenician historians according to whom Utica was founded 287 years before Carthage,[13] which makes the date of the foundation of Utica 1101 and Carthage 814. In Carthage, as we have said, the archaeological finds are slightly later, but not excessively so. The other Phoenician colonies in North Africa are Auza (not identified), which the annals of Tyre say was founded by Ittobaal in the ninth century;[14] Leptis Magna, which Sallust claims to be a colony of Sidonian refugees[15] and which others attribute to the Tyrians;[16] Hippo, which Sallust again attributes to the Phoenicians;[17] and Hadrumetum (Sousse), attributed to the Tyrians.[18] We cannot, of course, be sure of any of these traditions, since the foundations are, in fact, Carthaginian. The problem is that Carthage rapidly rose to power and started to found her own colonies, and this so-called secondary movement is not always distinguishable from the main Phoenician one. The other colonies of probable Punic foundation in North Africa are Oea, Sabratha, Acholla, Thapsus, Leptis Parva, Hermacon (Cape Bon), Philippeville, Constantine, Chullu, Djidjelli, Tipasa, Gouraya, Melilla, Emsa, Sidi Abdselam, and Tamouda.

In the Mediterranean islands we have said that the bronze figurine of Melqart found in the sea near Selinunte may suggest the presence of Phoenicians in Sicily from the end of the second millennium, and we have recorded Thucydides's claim that the Phoenicians preceded the Greeks in the island and only withdrew later, before the Greeks, to the far western regions. In any case, the settlement of Motya goes back to the eighty–seventh century, and was followed by Palermo and Solunto. Donald Harden emphasizes close affinities between the earliest pottery of Motya and that of Carthage, concluding that Carthage must have played a large part in the foundation of the settlement.

Of the islands south of Sicily, Malta was certainly a Phoenician base and, from the archaeological data, can be ascribed to the eighth century. Gozo, Pantelleria, and Lampedusa were occupied at the same time or soon after.

Passing on to Sardinia, we have said that the inscription of Nora suggests the presence of Phoenicians on the island as early as the ninth century. The other ancient cities were Cagliari, Bythia, S. Antioco (Sulcis), Carloforte, and Tharros. Recent excavations by G. Pesce and

F. Barreca have brought to light pre-Carthaginian settlements in these latter localities and have confirmed the Phoenician presence at Carloforte, already mentioned in an inscription as 'the island of Hawks'.[19] Of the Balearic Islands, Diodorus Siculus ascribes the foundation of Ibiza to 654/3,[20] attributing it to the Carthaginians, and there is no archaeological indication of an earlier date; the name of Port Mahon in Minorca also suggests Punic foundation.

Beyond the Pillars of Hercules the Phoenician or Punic colonies were Tangier, Lixus, and Mogador. About Lixus there is a tradition recorded by Pliny[21] according to which the local shrine of Heracles-Melqart was earlier than the one in Cadiz. Were this tradition correct Lixus would be the earliest Phoenician colony we know. The archaeological material from the Moroccan colonies, and the pottery in particular, goes back to the seventh century BC. This period leaves some doubt as to whether the foundations were Carthaginian, unless the theory that they were founded by the earliest colonies in Spain proves true.

Finally the most controversial point about Phoenician colonization concerns Spain. The colony of Cadiz goes back traditionally to the end of the twelfth century. The material from it is far later (fifth century) and the earlier remains of other localities, which can probably be ascribed to the eighth century, are still far from the traditional date. Tarshish (Tartessus) was probably to the north of Cadiz, at the source of the Guadalquivir. The most likely opinions place it on the site of Asta Regia. The identification of Tarshish with Tartessus leads us to believe that we can ascribe Phoenician settlement in Spain to the tenth century, if not to the traditional date. Another reason for earlier ascriptions of the archaeological data is provided by Mazar's mission in Spain in 1957, the results of which have not yet been published. Mazar asserts that there are archaeological traces of the Phoenicians in Spain going back at least as far as the ninth century.

6 Methods

In a few excellent pages of his book on the Carthaginians in Morocco, Cintas describes the methods of Phoenician-Punic expansion:

We must dismiss all excavations the results of which are purely hypothetical, as well as the excavator in his seven-league boots who scours the Moroccan coast from Cape Spartel to Plage-Blanche in search of Carthaginian treasures on the beach. When I began my study I never asked myself where I should start digging: I simply applied certain principles of scientific archaeology. Neglecting the sites to which the ancient authors supposedly referred, I explored the countryside and the coast in search of a 'landscape', a certain type of landscape – a 'Punic landscape'. A Punic *facies* exists both on the Moroccan coast and in the interior, and we can visualise it if we think of the necessities which regulated the primitive lives of the Carthaginians and which give us the basic principle of their development.[22]

There is indeed a Punic (and Phoenician) type of landscape. We only have to think of the conditions of the Phoenicians' existence and the navigation which was the means of their colonial expansion. We already know that they preferred promontories and islets lying off the coast, because of the possibility of landing and shelter for their ships. But they also required a hinterland, however limited, where they could live, and at least one accessible spring of water. There was no need for deep water for the shallow keels of their ships – shallow water was safer for anchorage. Furthermore, the care the Phoenicians took with their dead induced them to seek places with rocky hills in which they could dig their shaft-tombs. And since slabs were invariably cut out of the rocks to cover the entrance to the tombs, the quarries are still visible to an attentive observer of the landscape.

Above all, the ancient ships had to cast anchor at night and resume their voyage by day, so the distance from one anchorage to the other can be used to locate the landing-stages as yet unknown to us. This is exactly what Cintas has done, with great success (as at Tipasa).

In view of the eminently maritime expansion of the Phoenicians and Carthaginians the settlements of the interior were always of a secondary nature and are usually found on the readily defensible heights which protect the coastal reaches and guard the approaches from the hinterland. Here again water was essential, and Constantine in Algeria and Monte Sirai in Sardinia are good examples of this topography.

Our information about the landing-stages and the means by which trade was practised mainly refers to the Carthaginians, but we can assume that the earliest Phoenician navigators behaved similarly. Herodotus writes:

Hither they come and unload their cargo; then having laid it orderly by the waterline they go aboard their ships and light a smoking fire. The people of the country see the smoke, and coming to the sea they lay down gold to pay for the cargo and withdraw away from the wares. Then the Carthaginians disembark and examine the gold; if it seems to them a fair price for their cargo, they take it and go their ways; but if not, they go aboard again and wait, and the people come back and add more gold till the shipmen are satisfied. Herein neither party (it is said) defrauds the other: the Carthaginians do not lay hands on the gold till it matches the value of their cargo, nor do the people touch the cargo till the shipmen have taken the gold.[23]

The expansion of the Phoenicians and later of the Carthaginians was predominantly commercial, with no intent of conquest, requiring no stable settlements or mass emigration of the population. This does not, of course, infer that stable settlements and emigration, as well as conquest, did not ensue, but that they were in no way dependent on the phenomenon of expansion, and either could not take place at all or could take place later.

CHAPTER 8

THE PHOENICIANS IN CYPRUS

1 History

The only Phoenician colony in the East to undergo any particular development was Cyprus, no less a colony, as far as its origins were concerned, than those in the West. But Cyprus was close to the homeland, and exchanges were so frequent that it is not always easy to distinguish between Phoenician and Cypriot origin, especially in the artistic field.

No great importance can be attached to the poetic and mythological references to the presence of the Phoenicians in Cyprus, particularly since these references are all of a late period. They do, however, undoubtedly reflect the antiquity of Phoenician presence in the island. Alexander of Ephesus[1] says in reference to Lapethos: 'They were from Belos Kition and enchanting Lapethos' – Belos is the Greek adaptation of the Phoenician name Baal and Kition the name of the largest Phoenician colony on the island. Virgil[2] makes Dido say that her father, Belus, ruled Cyprus when Teucer, the son of Telamon, king of Salamis, driven from his homeland, came in search of new kingdoms and sought the help of Belus. Now, Teucer must have arrived immediately after the fall of Troy, and he is also the alleged founder of Salamis in Cyprus, which constituted the border between the area of Greek and Phoenician influence.

We have already referred to the doubt concerning Josephus's account,[3] of Hiram, king of Tyre, in the tenth century BC, who quelled the rebellion of the inhabitants of a colony. However widespread the interpretation which associates it with Utica, it seems far more likely to be Kition, the largest Phoenician settlement in Cyprus. We have both historical and textual reasons to assume this: it is hard to imagine a punitive expedition being sent to Utica in the tenth century, especially since the western colonies resembled trading-posts rather than territorial possessions bound to pay tribute. We can, on the other hand, conceive a rapid mission to the Cypriot coast across the sea, particularly since Kition was later to recognize the political supremacy of the Phoenician homeland.

We have more concrete information on the question of Phoenician settlement in Cyprus from archaeology. The excavations performed by the Swedish mission to Kition, the main Phoenician city on the island, have uncovered an acropolis going back to the eleventh century BC. Admittedly Gjerstad says that Phoenician settlement could not be earlier than the eighth century, but, in fact, there appear to be no marked divisions between the earlier strata, which Gjerstad claims to be pre-Phoenician, and those of the eighth century, which are unanimously ascribed to the Phoenician period. Nor are there any signs of destruction or radical change in the pottery. So it seems likely that the acropolis was built by the first Phoenicians to settle in the island, particularly since the presence of peoples in Cyprus from the Asiatic coast is probably earlier than the independence of the Phoenician city-states. From the middle and late Bronze Age contacts between the two regions (as is shown by the finds at Ugarit) were intensive.

Finally, there is a certain amount of epigraphical information about Phoenician settlement in Cyprus. A funerary inscription[4] of uncertain origin, but which probably came from Kition, has epigraphical traits that suggest it to be of the ninth century BC. So, together with the inscription of Nora in Sardinia, it documents the beginning of colonial expansion or at least of Phoenician presence. Further epigraphical evidence of the Phoenicians in Cyprus goes back to the second half of the eighth century. King Hiram II of Tyre, who paid tribute to the Assyrian king Tiglatpileser III (745–727 BC), is mentioned in a Phoenician inscription of Mouti Sinoas,[5] in which a governor of the city Qart-Hadasht calls himself 'servant of Hiram, king of the Sidonians'. The inscription is particularly interesting, since it provides evidence of the colonial possessions of Tyre in Cyprus, or anyhow of the presence of a small Cypriot state subject to Tyre. As we shall see, the most likely identification for Qart-Hadasht is with Kition.

If Kition was undoubtedly the most important Phoenician city in Cyprus, it was certainly not the only one. Epigraphy and onomatology point to others in Golgoi, Idalion, Tamassos, Marion, and Lapethos. We know of no historical events connected with these cities, but we do know that the independence of the Phoenician colonies generally disappeared after the end of the eighth century or, more exactly, after the reign of Sargon II (721–705 BC), the conqueror of Cyprus, who left an account in his annals of tribute paid to him by the Cypriots, and who erected a basalt stele in Kition in his own honour. Of course, the fact that the subjugation of local princes should be mentioned several times by the Assyrian sources of the period after Sargon II proves that these princes retained a certain autonomy, as did those of the Phoenician region and the Syro-Palestinian area in general. It can be assumed, however, that after the age of Sargon the Cypriot cities looked towards Assyria and no longer towards Phoenicia. This is of special historical interest, because it indicates a basic change in Mediterranean politics as a result of which the Phoenicians were no longer the sole masters of the trade routes, but fell under the aegis of the greater powers of the Near East.

Under Sennacherib (705–681) a Syrian coalition was formed against Assyria and one of the participants was Luli (Elulaeus), king of Tyre and the surrounding region. Defeated in 701 or 700 he fled to Cyprus, where he died.[6] So the ties between Tyre and the island obviously still existed, if Cyprus could serve as a place of refuge.

Asarhaddon (680–669) left us a list of vassal kings[7] which includes certain kings of Cyprus. It is interesting to note that some of these sovereigns have Greek names. The localities, which have not all been identified, include Idalion, Chytros, Paphos, Kurion, Tamassos, and Ledra. The presence of Qart-Hadasht should be identified with either Kition or Amathus, which are not mentioned. In this case the Phoenician name seems to refer to Kition, the main Phoenician colony, rather than to Amathos.

Further mention of Cypriot sovereigns, vassals of Assyria, is made under Assurbanipal (668–626).[8] They include Damasu, king of Kurion, Admesu, king of Tamassos, Damusu of Qart-Hadasht, and Unasagusu of Ledra. Then there is no information, at least as far as the Phoenician colonies are concerned, until 449, when the Persians conquered the island: then a series of cities with relatively independent Phoenician dynasties flourished and were certainly favoured by the Persians as opposed to the Greeks. A vast number of Phoenician inscriptions, between the middle of the fifth century and the third–second century BC, allow us to reconstruct certain events and names of sovereigns of these dynasties.

A sovereign with a typically Phoenician name, Baalmilk, reigned in Kition c. 450 BC. Equally Phoenician was the name of his son, Ozbaal, who extended his rule to Idalion. The successor, Baalmilk II, continued this dominion. The dynasty ended c. 410, but a new one began in 372 with Milkyaton, son of Baalram. Milkyaton, who also governed Idalion, was succeeded in 361 by Pumayyaton, who is referred to as 'king of Kition, Idalion, and Tamassos' in an inscription,[9] and had therefore extended the rule of his dynasty. According to a passage of Athenaeus,[10] Tamassos was sold to Pumayyaton by the king of Amathus. The kingdom of Pumayyaton lasted until 312, when Ptolemy I had him executed and annexed the territory, thereby ending the autonomous Phoenician dynasty.

Certain coins of Lapethos provide information about the sovereigns of this city. At the beginning of the fifth century the name of a king Demonikos appears in Phoenician characters; at the beginning of the fourth century the same name is found in the same characters. Later, in the second half of the fourth century, a Phoenician inscription mentions a king, Barakshemesh: so here the name is Phoenician as well as the language. Barakshemesh is called son of Demonikos, and was either the second member of the dynasty already mentioned or a successor.

The Ptolemaic conquest did not destroy the independence of the city-states, as is proved by local eras in Kition (311) and Lapethos (304). The inscriptions which bear witness to these eras continue for a considerable time to prove the vitality of the Phoenician language, at least in a literary field.

2 Archaeology

In character with the geographical position of the island, Cypriot culture appears to stem from several converging sources. To begin with there is the autochthonous element; then there is the Greek element, widespread in its earliest Mycenaean form and then continuously renewed by contributions throughout the first millennium; finally there is the Phoenician element, evident in the inscriptions and traceable in a series of artistic productions which rarely seem to be free from other components.

On the whole, the Greek component in general and the Mycenaean component in particular are predominant in Cyprus. The Phoenician, or rather Asiatic contributions, however, are undeniable, although no excavations have yet brought to light the early Phoenician phase. As far as we can judge, the Proto-Aeolic capitals, the cult objects, the styles of pottery, and the figurines all indicate the existence of a parallel production on the island and the Asiatic coast.

While Phoenician culture in Cyprus evidently represents a continuation of manifestations peculiar to the homeland, it must be noted that some characteristics of the world of the western colonies owe their origin to Cyprus. So, we have certain temple plans in Sardinia, certain architectural details like capitals with volutes and echinus composed of horizontal elements and iconographical motifs like the male figure with a stiff beard jutting forwards. These specific contacts between Cyprus and the western colonies are not limited to archaeological data, but sometimes also extend to religious matters. So, in the proper name of the king Pumayyaton, one component is the divine name Pumay, which recurs in Cypriot onomatology and in the Sardinian religion documented by the inscription of Nora. Here, therefore, specific contacts seem to emerge which allow Cyprus to assume a particularly significant role in the cadre of Phoenician dispersion.

No architecture that can be defined as typically Phoenician remains in Cyprus. In the field of architectural decoration, however, Cyprus has left us important remains of Proto-Aeolic capitals similar to the Syro-Palestinian type, but chronologically slightly later. A fine example from Golgoi, which can be ascribed to the sixth century, shows the two volutes on either side of a triangle in high relief with several listels, in which reappear two symbols destined to develop in the Punic West: the disk and the crescent moon (plate 3). The capital of Golgoi is remarkably elaborate: above the volutes and the triangle are the curved palmettes enclosing lotus flowers and then a triple echinus. Still more elaborate is another capital from Golgoi, this time in relief on only one side of a stele, ascribable to the fifth century: the palmettes above the volutes and triangle rise high and enclose two small winged sphinxes confronted on either side of a plant: here again a triple echinus surmounts the capital (fig 30). Finally there is an interesting Hathoresque

30   Capital from Golgoi

capital from Kition dated between the end of the sixth and beginning of the fifth century. It represents an Egypticizing aedicule of the type which later became characteristic of the Punic stelae, and also here provides a valuable antecedent.

Although we have no Phoenician religious buildings from Cyprus, we do have a small terracotta model of a shrine, twenty-one centimetres high, found in Idalion and dated in the eighth–seventh century B C. On the façade two small lotus-shaped columns flank the entrance, out of which leans a bird with a human head; on the other sides, heads are peering out of windows. The model recalls the shrine of Amrit and anticipates the motifs of the Punic stelae.

Cypriot plastic art is very interesting. Hundreds of female terracotta figurines with coarse features and a typical cylindrical body with broad base (plate 105) were found in the shrine of Kamelarga, near Kition, and elsewhere. These figurines are connected with the vast Syro-Palestinian production and also anticipate one of the most characteristic products of the Punic world, as we shall see with reference to Bythia in Sardinia. There are also certain equally remarkable male figurines: a priest clad in a long tunic and pointed cap, holding a small animal for a sacrifice, comes from the shrine of Ayia Irini and is dated between the end of the seventh century and the beginning of the sixth (fig 31); the typology and iconography are characteristically Phoenician and re-appear in the Punic world.

Metal bowls were a very important Cypro-Phoenician production. Since we have already dealt with them with reference to the general Phoenician production to which they belong, we shall simply say here that Egyptian, Mesopotamian, and Aegean motifs converge for purely ornamental purposes. The bowls of Cyprus, which Gjerstad has sub-divided into three groups (I: 800–700 BC; II 700–600; III: 600–550), can probably be attributed to Phoenician craftsmen working in Cyprus rather than importation. But we must consider unlikely the theory that all this production originated in Cyprus rather than Phoenicia.

A large amount of metalwork was produced in Cyprus and reveals clear Phoenician and Asiatic influences. One example is a bronze pot-stand or incense-burner (plate 108), with open-work panels on the sides which show a harpist, a man with two fish, a man with a cup and two rolls of cloth, and a man with a rod. They can be dated around the end of the second millennium and originate from Kurion.

Finally Cypriot pottery contains certain forms of Phoenician origin: in particular the mushroom-lipped jugs, usually rather wide and with a ring half-way up the neck. These examples are found from the ninth to eighth century until the fifth century. In a later age a typically local design of stripes and small hoops appears. The single beaked lamps, similar to the Phoenician type, are interesting, while double-beaked lamps prevail in Carthage and the West. Greek influence and native tradition, however, clearly distinguish Cypriot production from the Phoenician style.

31 Terracotta figurine
from Ayia Irini

3 Religion

The Phoenician cults in Cyprus are attested by the inscriptions and onomatology. Thus we find several familiar deities: Astarte, Melqart, Eshmun, Resheph. An inscription of the eighth century is dedicated to Baal, with the equally familiar specification 'Baal of the Lebanon'.[11] Furthermore, the name of this deity appears in proper names like Baalyaton, Azerbaal, etc. It is interesting that these names should anticipate forms which spread throughout the Punic world.

A pre-Phoenician deity found in Cyprus is Anat. And there are also local deities assumed by the Phoenicians, like Pumay (hence the Greek Pygmalion), who was assimilated to the Phoenician Adonis-Eshmun. Then we have Sasm, found in the onomatology of Marion, Lapethos,

Kition, and Tamassos. Mikal, frequently coupled with Resheph (Resheph-Mikal), is also noteworthy: the Greek correspondence with Apollo Amyklaios probably only reflects a Greek assonance of the Semitic form. Reshef and Mikal are in all likelihood of different origin, the former corresponding to Apollo and the latter to Heracles. Furthermore, Resheph does not only appear in combination with Mikal: two bilingual inscriptions of the fourth century are dedicated respectively to Reshef-'*lyyt* (Apollo Heleitas) and Reshef-'*lhyts* (Apollo Alashiotas), the former probably reflecting the place-name Helos of Cyprus, and the second Alasia, or Cyprus. In other words, they are Phoenician adaptations from the Greek and not vice versa.

At a later date Egyptian deities like Osiris and Horus appear in Cyprus as in other Phoenician-Punic localities, and we notice connexions like Eshmun-Melqart which seem the result of later symbioses and are therefore different from the Resheph-Mikal type.

In conclusion, Phoenician religion in Cyprus seems to have retained its original elements, but also adapted certain local deities and, above all, stimulated the Phoenicians to their own interpretation of Cypriot deities through assimilations where the influence moved from Cyprus to Phoenicia and not vice versa.

II

PHOENICIANS AND CARTHAGINIANS IN AFRICA

CHAPTER 9

HISTORY

1 Introduction

We have, in fact, no direct sources for the history of Phoenician expansion in Africa or the history of Carthage. That such sources did exist, and that some of the classical authors whose writings have survived consulted them, is undoubtedly true and has even been proved, as by the inscription of Hanno recorded in his Periplus. These sources, however, are not usually historical in the accepted sense of the term. There is no lack of inscriptions from the Phoenician colonies in North Africa, and above all from Carthage, but they refer to religion and cults, and describe the deities and rites without throwing any relevant light on the social and political activities.

Our knowledge of Phoenician and Carthaginian history in North Africa is therefore based on indirect sources. In this case, moreover, there are no sources from the same geographical environment, as there are with the Phoenicians in the East – there is no historiography which corresponds to that of the Israelites and the Mesopotamians. On the other hand, the classical documentation in the West is far broader and more detailed, because of the decisive importance of Carthage in Mediterranean affairs.

The Greek and Latin authors chiefly concentrated their attention on the wars first between Carthage and Syracuse, and later between Carthage and Rome. Here the accounts are comprehensive, detailed, and written soon after the events. With regard to the rest of Carthaginian history the information is sporadic. Aristotle's observations on the Punic constitution, Polybius's account of the revolt of the mercenaries, the Greek version of Hanno's inscription, the list of Carthage's dominions in Africa in the middle of the fourth century given by Pseudo-Skylax, are examples taken from a scattered and disorganized documentation, full of lacunae and frequently difficult to assemble.

The light which the Greek and Latin historians shed on Carthage was obviously influenced by various factors. There was an instinctive hostility towards such bitter enemies, and the authors naturally tended to give a pejorative account of them, accusing them of cruelty and treachery. Hannibal, however, is an exception. Probably in order to justify the heavy defeats he inflicted on the Romans, historiographers praise his character and skill. Similarly, we often get an exaggerated picture of the power of Carthage: the figures given for the strength of her army and fleet, as well as her population in general, the wealth of the city, and the extent of her rule are sometimes obviously excessive.

So the idea left us of Phoenician and Punic colonization in North Africa and of the affairs of Carthage is distorted by the indirect and fragmentary nature of the documentation. On the other hand, the abundance of data provided by classical authors is such that we know far more about this part of the Phoenician-Punic world than any other.

2 The foundation of Carthage

Classical sources agree in ascribing the foundation of Carthage to 814–813 BC. But we must first consider the problem of whether the city rose from an earlier Phoenician settlement or whether it was an original foundation.

There is a tradition going back to Philistus, a Greek from Syracuse of the fourth century, according to which Carthage was founded by the Tyrians, Azoros (or Zoros) and Karchedon, shortly before the Trojan War.[1] The improbability of this tradition, repeated by Euxodus of Cnidus[2] and Appian,[3] is evident from the two names alone: Zoros is clearly a distortion of Tyre, Karchedon of Carthage. It is true that Carthage, meaning 'new city', could be so called because of a previous foundation or city, but it is more likely that the 'new' is in relation to the homeland. It remains possible, however, that the Phoenicians founded the city on a site already familiar to them.

Passing on to the events of 814–813 BC, we have ample and unanimous accounts from the classical sources, started by Timaeus, amplified by Justin, and subsequently repeated, with minor variations, by numerous other authors.

According to Justin,[4] the founders of Carthage hailed from Tyre. Here Elissa, sister of the king Pygmalion, married her uncle Acharbas, priest of Melqart and a man of great wealth. Pygmalion had Acharbas assassinated, so Elissa, together with a group of citizens loyal to her murdered husband, fled secretly to Cyprus after having paid homage to the god Melqart (Hercules). In Cyprus she was joined by the high priest of Astarte (Juno) on the condition that, in the land they were about to colonize, the priesthood should remain hereditary in his family. Eighty girls destined to religious prostitution were also taken in order to ensure the continuity of the Phoenician religion.

The navigators sailed straight to the place where Carthage was to be founded. In order to obtain a large enough territory Elissa resorted to the trick of bargaining for a plot of land as big as an ox-hide would cover. She then cut the hide into the narrowest strips and wound them round the entire hill which rises on the promontory of Carthage. Here there is an obvious Greek pun: *byrsa*, the Phoenician word for acropolis, means ox-hide in Greek.

The colonizers were given a warm welcome, and envoys from Utica came bearing gifts for their compatriots. However, Hiarbas, the local king who allowed the exiles to settle in his territory, fell in love with Elissa and told one of the notables of the city that he would declare war if she did not marry him. Elissa, wishing to remain faithful to her husband's memory, leapt into a sacrificial pyre. Her subjects then deified her and continued her cult until the destruction of Carthage. It must be noted that in the tradition the name of Elissa was associated with and then substituted by that of Dido, whose tale was subsequently elaborated in Virgil's *Aeneid*.

According to Dionysius of Halicarnassus,[5] Timaeus places the traditional date of the foundation of Carthage thirty-eight years before the first Olympiad, in 814 B C. Velleius Paterculus[6] accords 667 years to the history of Carthage, which would place it in 813 B C. Other authors confirm this date and we can therefore consider it accurate as far as historical tradition is concerned.

Although the account of the classical authors does contain definite legendary elements, the total and indiscriminate scepticism which has accompanied it for so long does not seem justified. Maintaining that there is no archaeological proof of the existence of Carthage before the middle of the eighth century, a critical current to which we have already referred rejects the entire traditional account. Today, however, we see that the earliest pottery – the urns of the first stratum of the precinct of Tanit – goes back to *c.* 800 B C (Harden). And we know that the period of a few generations would quite naturally have elapsed between the disembarkation of the first settlers and the production of works of art destined to survive for centuries.

If we examine the traditional origin of Carthage with a broader and more positive attitude, we will see that elements of unquestionably Greek origin (like the name of Byrsa) are accompanied by others which denote familiarity with the Phoenician environment – the names of the protagonists Pygmalion (Pumayyaton) and Elissa (Elisha); the reference to the cult of Hercules (Melqart) in Tyre; the cult of Juno (Astarte) and the sacred prostitution in Cyprus as well as the hereditary priesthood; and the knowledge of the antiquity and Phoenician origin of Utica.

An interesting confirmation of this tradition is also provided by

Josephus. In one of the fragments from the annals of Tyre which he quotes it is said that a Pygmalion reigned in Tyre and that in the seventh year of his reign his sister fled to Libya and founded the city of Carthage.[7] Admittedly Josephus does not give the exact date, but the period of Pygmalion is about the end of the ninth century and in no way contradicts the traditional date.

The Tyrian origin of Carthage is best confirmed by the annual embassies which the city sent through the ages to Tyre.[8] These embassies constantly carried offerings to the temple of Hercules (Melqart); and if it is true that the offerings constituted one tenth of the government revenue (as Diodorus Siculus claims),[9] the offerings themselves could be considered as a form of tribute. Later, writes Diodorus, the offerings were reduced, but in moments of danger the Carthaginians remembered the god of Tyre and returned to honour him with large sums and tributes.

Coming now to the area of occupation, the geographical position, well protected from the winds, and the archaeological finds, suggest that it must be near Le Kram, south of the Acropolis of Byrsa. If the story of the ox-hide is the result of later etymology, it still seems that control of the hilly area was the first object of the settlers, who realized that it provided protected anchorages.

It has long been observed that the actual name of the city may prove historically indicative of the strategic intention of its founders. Qart-Hadasht means 'new city', but it can also mean 'new capital', thereby revealing a definite political intent accompanying its foundation. In fact, it was necessary to establish a base for the spread of Phoenician activity in the West, which had for some time been developed well beyond the actual zone of Carthage. That this plan should be fulfilled in a place already familiar to the Phoenician navigators is plausible, but the supremacy soon attained by Carthage over every other Phoenician colony was undoubtedly later than 814–813 and probably resulted not from unforeseen circumstances but from a calculated purpose.

On these premises it is also possible to understand why the colonizers did not limit themselves to the near-by base of Utica. In fact, the position of Carthage was exceptional both in itself and for the possibilities of expanding into the interior. Opening like a vast promontory between two lagoons which provided excellent defences for its flanks, Carthage was joined to the mainland by a sandy isthmus easy to guard and defend. The large extent of arable land on the promontory made the whole area isolable and readily defensible.

Finally it is quite possible that the pathetic tale of Elissa, apart from certain clearly legendary components, contains elements of truth and is the result of historical events. We can therefore consider the date of 814–813 for the foundation of Carthage to be accurate and we can also suppose that Carthage was founded by settlers from Tyre with the intention of building a city destined to assume primary importance in West Phoenicia.

3 The formation of the empire

We have little information about the earliest history of Carthage – indeed, until the foundation of a colony in Ibiza (654–653 B C) we have none whatsoever. The historical situation, however, shows that Carthage developed into the main Phoenician city in the West and imposed her authority on all the colonies.

The essential motive for this convergence of the scattered Phoenician world of the West under the aegis of Carthage stems from the Greek penetration of the Mediterranean area. After the eighth century this penetration affirmed itself with increasing vigour, creating competition and a substantial danger for the Phoenician colonies. It is true that the new-comers tended to concentrate on places where there was little resistance: they found no Phoenicians in southern Italy, Corsica, and Gaul, and they did not venture to the African coast between the Syrtes and the Straits of Gibraltar, where the Phoenician colonies had their most secure dominions. But the conflicts in Sicily, where, according to Thucydides,[10] the Phoenicians had to withdraw to the north-western extremity of the island, prove that amicable agreements or divisions of influence were not easy.

The Greeks were not the only danger. The very nature of the Phoenician colonies – small maritime trading-posts a considerable distance apart – exposed them to attacks from the local population, and these attacks developed particularly if the colonies showed signs of weakness or had no means of retaliation. So this was yet another reason for alliance with a large city which naturally arose in the strongest colony.

To these considerations, which account for the progressive creation of links between Carthage and the other Phoenician colonies in the West, can be added the decline of Tyre and East Phoenicia. The decline was slow, with alternate phases, but none the less real, and such as to jeopardize the possibility of effective aid to the far West. This was all the more true since Greek expansion interrupted the lines of communication.

Whether all the Phoenician colonies accepted the supremacy of Carthage with good grace and immediately acknowledged its necessity is another matter. But historical and archaeological data at our disposal are not detailed enough to indicate crises and disjunctions between the Phoenician and Punic phases of the colonies: on the contrary, it is precisely this difficulty of distinguishing between the two phases that constitutes one of the most complex historical problems.

As we have said, the first reference to the activity of Carthage concerns the foundation of a colony at Ibiza in the Baleares. Diodorus Siculus[11] dates the foundation of the colony 160 years after the foundation of Carthage, in 654–653 BC. With Ibiza, Carthage secured herself a port on the route from Sardinia to Spain. We do not know the extent of Carthaginian assertion in the Baleares, but it is remarkable that Port Mahon in Minorca should have a seemingly Carthaginian name (Magon).

It was probably about this time that the Carthaginians also settled in Sardinia and Sicily, or at least intensified their ties with the local Phoenician colonies. The events of the subsequent decades assume Carthaginian settlement in the two islands, and we can therefore say that the Mediterranean expansion of Carthage and her progressive take-over from Tyre as leader of the colonies as well as founder or reoccupier of the colonies themselves took place in the course of the seventh century BC.

According to an account by Thucydides,[12] the Carthaginians tried vainly to prevent the Phocaeans from founding Marseilles and were defeated in a naval battle c. 600 BC. Exactly where this took place we do not know. But it was certainly a heavy blow to Carthage, because it enabled the Greeks to control a key point in Mediterranean navigation – the access to the valley of the Rhône. It also marked the beginning of the increasingly close alliance between the Carthaginians and the Etruscans in the common purpose of opposing Greek expansion. The Carthaginian general, Malchus, won a victory against the Greeks in Sicily c. 550 and, according to Justin,[13] subjugated part of the island: it seems evident that he intervened in order to support the Phoenician colonies on the western extremity of the island. Malchus then went to Sardinia, but was heavily defeated by the local population.

Justin goes on to say that Malchus, together with the remains of the army, was banished from Carthage as a result of this defeat and rebelled and besieged Carthage, finally managing to occupy it.[14] But soon after he was accused of aspiring to tyranny and put to death. He was succeeded by Magon, the founder of the Magonid dynasty, which ruled Carthage for three generations and initiated a series of enterprises destined to develop the power of the city. The most notable members of the family were Magon's sons, Hamilcar and Hasdrubal.

The alliance between the Carthaginians and Etruscans resulted in the defeat of the Phocaeans in 535 BC. Using Alalia in Corsica as a base, the Phocaeans were practising piracy to the detriment of Mediterranean commerce. The Carthaginians and Etruscans encountered them in the naval battle of Alalia and heavily defeated them – an event of great importance, because it prevented Greek expansion in Corsica and

Sardinia. Treaties divided the spheres of influence between the Etruscans and the Carthaginians: to the former, Italy from the Alps to the Campania; to the latter, the vast area which included the zone of Greek occupation in the south-east. The Etruscan material found in Carthage testifies to the close relations between the two peoples in the cultural field as well as the political, just as further evidence of these relations and their continuity at a later date is provided by the Punic inscription found at S. Severa (ancient Pyrgi) in July 1964. This inscription, ascribed to *c.* 500 B C, is accompanied by two very similar Etruscan texts and contains a dedication to the 'lady Astarte' made by Thepharie Velianas or Veliunas, prince of Caere (Cerveteri) in the sanctuary of Pyrgi.

At this point we must note that the alliance between the Etruscans and Carthaginians was of greater significance on a Mediterranean level: it consolidated the anti-Greek chain in the West formed by the Oriental nations under the Persian empire. It is no coincidence that relations between Carthage and Phoenicia should be particularly active at this period. When Cambyses, after having conquered Egypt, wished to send an expedition against Carthage, the Phoenicians refused to participate. And it is also certain that the periodical embassies from Carthage to Tyre not only carried offerings for the sanctuary of Melqart but also discussed the mutual anti-Greek struggle.

The events connected with the expedition which Doriaeus, brother of a king of Sparta, led first to Africa and then to Sicily are a part of this struggle against the Greeks. Towards the end of the sixth century, at a date which we are unable to specify, Doriaeus landed in Africa between the two Syrtes, in a place situated eighteen kilometres south-east of Leptis: it took the Carthaginians three years, with the aid of the natives, to repel him. He went back to the Peloponnese, but soon returned to the West, this time to Sicily, where, near Mount Eryx, he founded a city which he named Heracleia. He was defeated and killed by the Carthaginians and the Elymi, while Heracleia was destroyed.

The first sign of the crisis in the anti-Greek alliance in the West was marked by the decline of the Etruscans and the revolt against the Tarquins in 510, together with the rise of Rome as an independent republic. As early as 509 Rome concluded a treaty with Carthage defining the respective spheres of influence. The text of the treaty, repeated by Polybius, is interesting because it attests the power of Carthage in the western Mediterranean:

'There is to be friendship between the Romans and their allies and the Carthaginians and their allies on these terms: the Romans and their allies not to sail with long ships beyond the Fair Promontory unless forced by storm or by enemies: it is forbidden to anyone carried beyond it by force to buy or carry away anything beyond what is required for the repair of his ship or for sacrifice, and he must depart within five days . . . If any Roman come to the Carthaginian province in Sicily, he shall enjoy equal rights with others. The Carthaginians shall do no wrong to the peoples of Ardea, Antium, Laurentium, Circeii, Terracina, or any other city of the Latins who are subject to Rome. Touching those Latins who are not subjects, they shall keep their hands off their cities, and if they take any city shall deliver it up to the Romans undamaged. They shall build no fort in the Latin territory. If they enter the land in arms, they shall not pass a night therein.'[15]

In the meantime the decisive encounter was about to take place between the Persians and the Greeks – a phenomenon of considerable importance which shows the victorious attempt by the Greeks to break the encirclement and affirm their own supremacy over a large part of the Mediterranean area. Even the ancient authors point out the connexion between the battle of Salamis in the East, where the Persian fleet and particularly the Phoenician contingent, were defeated, and the battle of Himera in the West, where the Carthaginians failed in their attack against the Greek outpost in Sicily.

This was no mere coincidence of time. A Greek historian, Ephorus,[16] tells that the Persian and Phoenician delegates went to Carthage just before the war, requesting the most powerful Carthaginian fleet possible to sail to Sicily and defeat the Greeks, and then to make for the Peloponnese – a request with which the Carthaginians complied. Diodorus[17] says that Xerxes sent delegates to Carthage to arrange a double advance. He agreed to attack Greece while the Carthaginians marched against the Greeks in Sicily and Italy, and an accord was signed.

In any case the situation in Sicily demanded Carthaginian intervention. Gelon, tyrant of Syracuse, had formed a powerful state in eastern Sicily, and had allied himself to Theron, tyrant of Agrigentum, the sovereign of another powerful state. In his turn Theron had acquired Himera and driven out Terillus, ally of Carthage. So, apart from the offence to an ally, Carthage saw herself confronted by a Greek power which was no longer split, but which was uniting and becoming increasingly aggressive: she had no alternative but to intervene.

Hamilcar, son of Magon, took command of the expedition, sailing from Carthage with a large fleet. In spite of a storm which destroyed the ships carrying the horses and chariots, the Carthaginians landed at Palermo and thence made for Himera. In the battle Theron and Gelon were victorious: Hamilcar died in the field, and his soldiers were killed or enslaved, his fleet set on fire. The year 480 was decisive for the success of the Greeks in the Mediterranean, both in the East and the West.

Even if the terms of peace were not as onerous as they might have been (the possessions in Sicily were retained, maybe because Gelon did not wish for too powerful an ally in Agrigentum), the offensive capacity of Carthage in Sicily was temporarily shattered.

4 The colonies

Before concentrating on the encounter between the Carthaginians and Greeks in Sicily we should pause to consider the position of Carthage in Africa, and examine that aggregation of Punic rather than Phoenician settlements which were proof of the expansive force of Carthage, even if it was on a commercial rather than a political level. We will say more later about the actual control which Carthage exercised on these settlements, and now merely list them as such. The evidence is primarily archaeological, and the remains are mainly of necropolises which can usually be dated by the pottery. It is, of course, only necessary to glance at the map in order to see that the points of settlement followed the traditional Phoenician policy of spaced-out coastal bases.

Going from east to west, the first major settlement is Leptis Magna, where a necropolis of the third-second century has been identified, and an important group of undoubtedly Punic sculptures probably of the Hellenistic era has been unearthed. Then comes Oea (present Tripoli), where a necropolis of the third to second century, with chambers dug in the rock, was identified in 1957, while the near-by Bou Setta has provided a large group of amphorae with bowls distinguished by Punic signs like the caduceus and the symbol of Tanit. In Sabratha, the third major city of Tripolitania, a monumental Punic necropolis with a grandiose mausoleum was excavated by Di Vita from 1962 to 1964, while further tombs of the third century B C, previously excavated by Bartoccini, have provided pieces of necklace in glass paste with typical Egypticizing representations of Harpocrates, Apis, small negro heads, bunches of grapes, doves, and so on. From Sabratha we also have important fragments of sandstone statues ascribable to the Punic-Hellenistic era.

In the geographical area of what is now Tunisia the first major Punic city is Acholla, traditionally founded by Phoenician settlers from Malta, where a topheth has been discovered and partially excavated. Thapsos, mentioned several times by classical sources, has been located at Ras Dimasseh and a fourth-century Punic necropolis, subsequently Romanized, has been excavated. Another necropolis, the largest after that of Carthage, is in Mahdia, a Punic city of which we do not know the ancient name. The funerary objects suggest it to be of the fifth century and include clay statuettes of a naked goddess with a crown. All that remains of Leptis Minor, now Lamta, are shaft-tombs with wooden coffins. Hadrumetum, now Sousse, is far more interesting, however: it prospered after the sixth century, and has a *topheth* with particularly important funerary stelae; there is also a necropolis the earliest part of which is under the present city. No less important is the Punic city under the present Kerkouane on the Cape Bon. The excavations begun by Cintas and widely developed by Tunisian archaeologists have brought to light inhabited areas datable to the fourth and third century B C with floors, walls, and well-preserved hygienic installations. In the immediate vicinity the zone of Djebel Mlezza has provided numerous tombs with jewels, amulets, various pieces of pottery, and the remains of paintings. Continuing westwards, Utica is traditionally the earliest Phoenician colony in North Africa. Cintas has unearthed two necropolises of between the eighth and fourth centuries B C full of votive objects, including rings, scarabs, amulets, and polychrome vases.

Little is known about Hippo Acra (Bizerta), Hippo Regius (Bone), and Philippeville (also Punic settlements), which bring us to the present Algerian territory. Cirta (Constantine) is better known and is the place of origin of an abundant production of stelae which are not earlier than the third century, but retain obvious elements of an earlier tradition. The acropolis of Chullu is no earlier than the third century either, while there is some doubt about that of Igilgili (Djidjelli), excavated by M. Astruc, according to whom the tombs go back beyond the third. Little is known about Icosium (Algiers) in view of the vast extent of the modern city. Numerous coins of the Punic period, however, bearing the name *yksm* prove the pre-Roman phase of the locality. At Tipasa the tombs have indicated Punic occupation: the earliest, going back at least as far as the fifth century, are chambers dug in the rock near the sea; others are near the surface of the rock, so that the side walls jut out and enframe them. The Punic tradition is confirmed until the Roman epoch by stelae with the sign of Tanit. Continuing still farther west, we have Iol (Cherchel), where a few sporadic remains suggest the late Punic era; Gunugu (Gouraya), where a necropolis of the second–third century has provided numerous ostrich eggs painted red and black on a white background, with geometrical and vegetable, and sometimes human motifs; Les Andalouses, where an inhabited area and a necropolis have provided pottery of the fourth century; the island Rachgoun, where Vuillemot has brought to light over a hundred tombs, mainly crematory, with votive pottery, lamps, weapons, jewels, amulets, all going back to the seventh–sixth century, and significant on account of special relations with the island of Motya; Mersa Madakh, forty kilometres west of Oran, with walls and a great deal of pottery, perhaps going back to the seventh–sixth century.

Proceeding to the present territory of Morocco, the first Punic city

Relief Sculpture

1 Fragment of a relief, from Adlun

2 Aedicule, from Sidon

3 Proto-Aeolic capital, from Golgoi

4 Sepulchral aedicule, from Marsala

5 Sandstone relief, from Tharros

6 Proto-Aeolic capital, from Ramat Rahel

7 Relief, from Aradus

Sarcophagi

8 Sarcophagus of Eshmunazar, from Sidon

9 Coffin showing winged woman, from Carthage

10 Anthropoid coffin, from Pizzo Cannita

11 Sarcophagus of Ahiram, from Byblos

Stelae

13 Stele, from Amrit

14 Stele with a pillar-shaped
betyl, from Carthage

15 Stele with an engraved rectangle, from Motya

16 Stele depicting male nude, from Motya

17 Fragment of a stele, from Tir Dibba

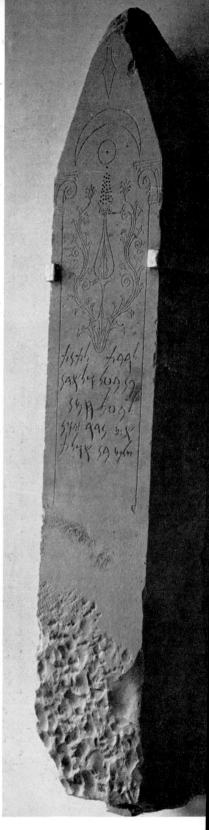

18 Stele with the 'sign of Tanit', from
Constantine

19 Stele with floral and astral
motifs, from Carthage

20 Bottle-idol motif on a stele found in Nora

21 Sculpture showing a woman and child, from Monte Sirai

22 Stele, from Akziv

23 Stele of Yehaumilk, from Byblos

24 Betyls and columns used as
decorative motifs on a stele, from Susa

25 Stele, from the Ghorfa

26 Stele, from Burj Esh Shemali

27 Representation of the
deceased on a stele,
from Carthage

28 Stele with betyls and caducei, from Susa

29 Sulcis, stele with a portrait of a man

30 Bottle-idol decoration on a stele, from Carthage

Statues in stone

31 Statue of a woman seated on a throne, probably from Pizzo Canita

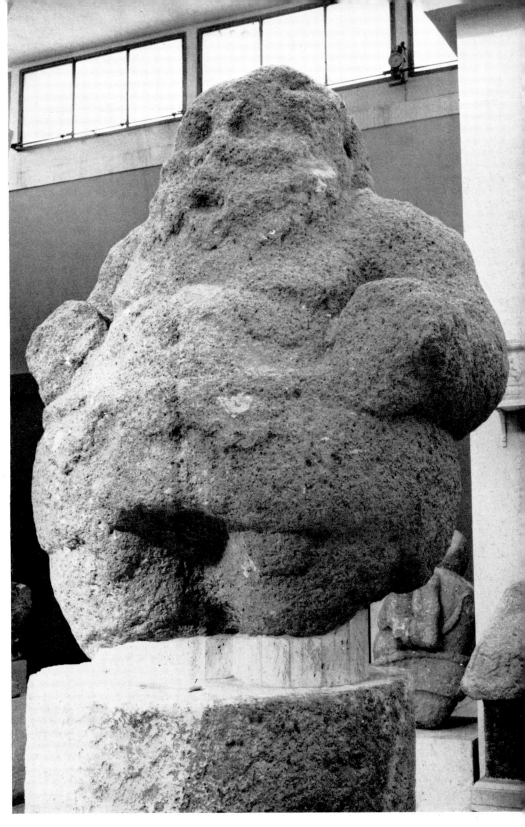

32 Sandstone statue, from Maracalagonis

33 Stone bust, from Tas Silg

34 Stone statue, from Monte Sirai

35 Male statue, from Motya

Religion and the gods

36 Alabaster statue of seated deity, from Galera

37 Stele with the sign of Tanit and other symbols

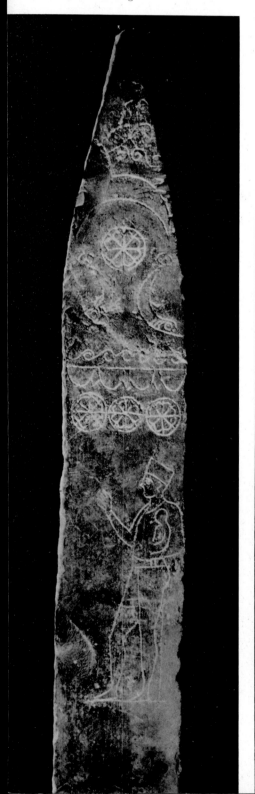

38 Stele depicting a priest, from Carthage

39 Stele depicting a worshipper, from Carthage

40 Stone head of a
demon, from Monte
Sirai

41 Stele depicting a
woman, from Monte
Sirai

Statuettes in bronze

43 Male figurine, probably from Homs

42 Female figurine, from Aleppo

44 Female figurine, from Aleppo

45 Figurine of a woman, from Baalbek

46 Bronze statuette, from the Nurra

47 Figurine, from Cadiz   48 Bronze statuette found in the sea near Selinunte

Animals in art

49 Stele depicting a ram, from Sulcis

50 Bronze bowl showing rams flanking a tree, from Nimrud

51 Landscape showing bucks with trees and mountains

52 Granite sphinx, from Cagliari

53 Duck-shaped vase, from Carthage

54 Group of a lion and a bull, from Alesa

55 Stele depicting a rabbit, from Carthage

56 Sandstone lion, from Tharros

Figures and protomai in terracotta

57 Terracotta figurine, from Ibiza

58 Female protome in terracotta, from Ibiza

59 Female protome in terracotta, from Tharros

60 Female protome, from Motya

61 Hellenizing female protome, from Carthage

62 Egypticizing female protome, from Carthage

63 Male protome, from Monte Sirai

64 Terracotta plaque showing a
woman, from Carthage

65 Female statuette with a disk, from Carthage

66 Vase in terracotta, shaped like a human
head, from Ibiza

67 Terracotta figurine, from Nora

68 Terracotta figurine, from Isla Plana

69 Male statuette, from Carthage

70 Terracotta statuette, from Bythia

71 Figurine, from Akziv

Masks in terracotta

72 Mask, from group I, Carthage

73 Mask, from group II, Carthage

74 Mask, from group III, Carthage

75 Mask, from group IV, Carthage

76 Terracotta mask, from Motya

Terracotta masks, from Ibiza

Ivory work

78 A winged sphinx, carving from Samaria

79 Ivory carving showing a woman at a window, from Nimrud

80 Ivory, from Nimrud, youth with a lotus stem

81 Winged sphinx, from Nimrud

82 Ivory, from Nimrud, showing figures and a cartouche

83 Ivory with figures of an Assyrian type, from Nimrud

84 Ivory, from Samaria, with figures showing Egyptian influence

85 Horus on a lotus flower, carving from Samaria

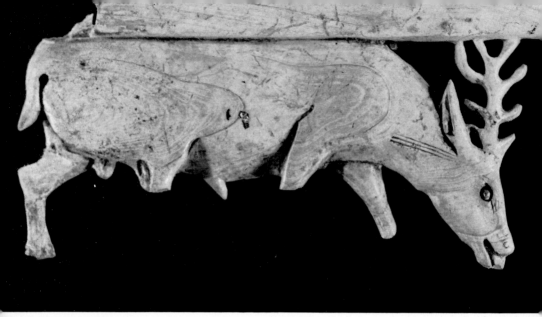

86 Ivory depicting a deer, from Arslan Tash

87 A cow giving milk, from Arslan Tash

88 Engraved ivory head, from
Monte Sirai

89 Frieze of palmettes, ivory
carving from Arslan Tash

Jewels and Amulets

90 Scarab of glass paste, from Carthage

91 Pendant in the form of a mask, in glass paste, from Carthage

92 Gold bracelet, from Tharros

93 Jewels, from Carthage

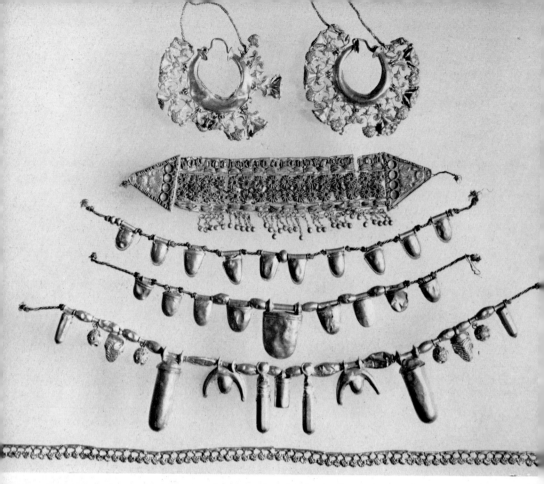

94 Gold diadem, necklaces, and pendants, from Aliseda

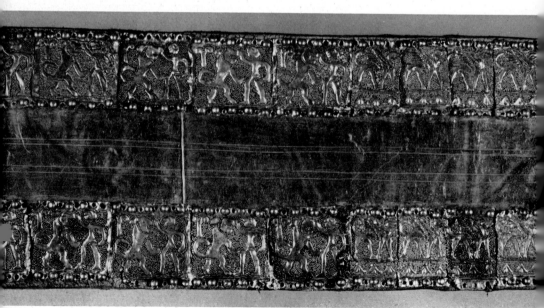

95 Repoussé gold belt, from Aliseda

96 Necklace of glass paste, from Ibiza

97 Amulet of glass paste with *ujat* eye, from Carthage

98 Amulet of glass paste with Ptah-Patechus, from Carthage

99 Phoenician gold pendants in the Louvre Museum

100 Gold amulet case, from Carthage

Coins

101 Gold coin, from Carthage, obverse

102 Gold coin, from Carthage, reverse

Domestic life

103 Punic pottery, from Carthage

104 Perfume-burning vase, from Carthage

105 Earthenware vase in human shape, from Cyprus

106 Two-beaked lamp, from Carthage

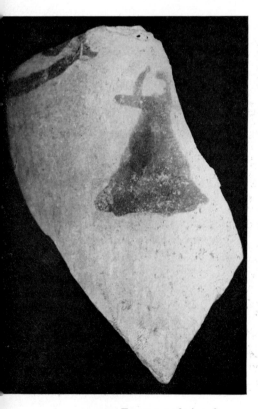

107 Fragment of a jug, from Tas Silg

108 Bronze incense burner, from Kurium

109 Bronze bowl with geometrical design, from Nimrud

110 Bronze bowl with human figures and chematized mountains, from Nimrud

111 Fragment of a decorated ostrich egg, from Carthage

112 Bronze razor, from Carthage

113 Bronze razor, from Ibiza

we find is Rusaddir (Melilla), where a necropolis has revealed simple graves covered by rows of amphorae: an unusual characteristic, which has a parallel at Olbia in Sardinia (as well as a similar date, between the third and first century BC). Farther west is Emsa, where the remains of walls and rooms of houses appeared together with pottery of the third–second century. Then comes Sidi Abdselam, which has provided successive strata of a settlement which would, judging from the pottery, be from about the fifth to first century BC. In Tamuda, owing largely to Tarradell, the ruins of a vast city have emerged, with walls, squares, streets, and numerous houses. But the settlement is late, between the second century BC and the first century AD. In Tangier the discoveries of Ponsich are broadening our knowledge, formerly limited to the Roman era, and especially noteworthy are the coins bearing the name of the city in Phoenician characters, *tng*.

Continuing in Moroccan territory on the Atlantic coast, we have Lixus (Arzila), the most important pre-Roman city in Morocco. While we have already recounted what the sources tell us of the settlement, we should here say that the excavations led by Tarradell have brought to light an urban centre of considerable size of at least the seventh–sixth century, with the remains of walls, a temple, two vast necropolises, inscriptions, coins, and pottery. Between Lixus and Mogador a few Punic remains have come to light, as in Muley Buselham, but the next important city is Mogador, where the typical red pottery places the origin of the settlement in the seventh–sixth century.

Finally there is one reservation. Until now we have spoken of Carthaginian settlements. There is obviously no clear distinction between Phoenician and Punic elements, however. In general the supremacy of Carthage determines its substitution to the homeland in the task of colonizing in the West, but occasional finds suggest an immediately Oriental origin, or anyhow some contact with the Phoenician world. If the power of Phoenicia diminished, therefore, it did not necessarily vanish altogether.

5 Carthaginians and Greeks in Sicily

The defeat at Himera destroyed the basic plan of alliance against the Greeks promoted by Carthage. However, the possessions of the western Mediterranean and the control of this area remained in Carthaginian hands, and a strong reaction avoided a crisis. To begin with, Carthage exiled the principal members of the Magonid family, Hanno and Gisgo, thereby altering the structure of a régime that had for three generations led Carthage through an almost continuous sequence of wars. Moreover, a Court of One Hundred was instituted as an oligarchy intended to protect the state from excessive personal power. It may have been at this time, too, that the title, and presumably the functions, were changed from kings to judges, with the consequent reduction of the length of office. To sum up, the governmental system underwent a process of change which permitted a new political outlook.

Political changes were accompanied by a religious reform clearly indicated in the Punic inscriptions. While the few earliest of these inscriptions only present one god, Baal, the very numerous inscriptions of the later period present Tanit (with the attribute 'face of Baal') and Baal Hammon.

Finally, in the archaeological field, we note a rapid reduction of material of Greek importation – an indication that the government of Carthage gave up all commerce with the Greeks, who had impoverished the city, by depriving it of primary matter in exchange for luxury goods.

Altogether, political changes, religious reforms, and commercial development show a definite desire to break away from the Hellenic world. This undoubtedly entailed a cultural crisis, but it also entailed a more marked cultural independence, and therefore a greater possibility of surviving Greek influence. And this, we must note, did not occur in East Phoenicia.

Again in the cadre of this attempt at independence we have the policy of expansion into the African interior, as well as the agricultural development in the country, which took place in the fifth century. The impulse to consolidate and extend the contacts beyond the national territory was equally strong. It was in the fifth century that the long voyages were made beyond the Pillars of Hercules. Himilco sailed up the Spanish and French coast to Cornwall, evidently with the intention of gaining access to products such as tin which were inaccessible by land, since the Greeks had cut all contacts by occupying Marseilles. And Hanno, as is related in the Greek version of a Punic text in the temple of Baal Hammon in Carthage, sailed round the African coast, probably reaching the Gulf of Guinea and thereby ensuring access to valuable commercial products in this region.

This policy was evidently also intended to obtain solid bases – both military and economic – for the inevitable renewal of the struggle against the Greeks. This resumed in 409, when Segesta, menaced by Selinunte, requested the aid of Carthage, and Carthage sent Sicily an army commanded by Hannibal, a descendant of the Hamilcar who fell at Himera (which either implies a sort of sacred union between the Carthaginian parties against the common enemy or simply that the Magonids, in spite of evidence to the contrary, continued to have considerable influence in the government of the city). The expedition was entirely successful: Selinunte and Himera were destroyed and three thousand prisoners sacrificed where Hamilcar had fallen. Shortly after, in 406, a new Carthaginian expedition, commanded again by Hannibal and by Himilco, son of Hanno, attacked, defeated, and destroyed Agrigentum after a long siege. Hannibal died of the plague, but Himilco continued the venture and destroyed Gela immediately afterwards. The whole of Greek Sicily was now threatened.

The Greek reaction was headed by Dionysius of Syracuse. Elected strategos at the fall of Agrigentum, he concluded an unfavourable peace with Carthage (405), so as to be able to consolidate his position. He then moved to the attack and, winning one victory after the other, conquered and sacked Motya in 398. The war then continued unevenly: the Punic fleet under Himilco intervened and Dionysius was defeated at a naval battle near Catania and blockaded in Syracuse, but he managed to get away owing to a plague which broke out in the Carthaginian army (396). Further encounters in 393 and 392 were concluded by a treaty which, according to Diodorus,[18] led to the restoration of the situation of 405. Subsequent battles between 382 and the death of Dionysius (367) brought the frontier to the river Halycus, where it remained for about a century, extending the rule of Carthage to almost a third of Sicily.

For a long period Carthaginian history is only known because of the battles with the Greeks in Sicily. This is merely a factual circumstance, however, determined by the sources at our disposal, and we must not think that Carthage had no other lines of political development. The second treaty with Rome, in 348 BC, is particularly interesting in this respect. The text, repeated by Polybius, makes it clear that Carthaginian rule had spread considerably, especially in North Africa and Spain (Mastia of Tarseum):

'There is to be friendship on the following conditions between the Romans and their allies and the Carthaginians, Tyrians, and the people of Utica and their respective allies. The Romans shall not maraud or trade or found a city on the farther side of Fair Promontory, and Mastia of Tarseum. If the Carthaginians capture any city in Latium not subject to Rome, they shall keep the valuables and the men, but give up the city. If any Carthaginians take captive any of a people with whom the Romans have a treaty of peace, but who are not subject to Rome, they shall not bring them into Roman harbours, but if one be brought in and a Roman lay hold of him, he shall be set free. The Romans shall not do likewise. If a Roman gets water or provisions from any place over which the Carthaginians rule, he shall not use these provisions to wrong any member of a people with whom the Carthaginians have peace and friendship. The Carthaginians shall not do likewise. If either do so, the aggrieved person shall not take private vengeance, and if he do his wrongdoing shall be public. No Roman shall trade or found a city in Sardinia and

Libya nor remain in a Sardinian or Libyan post longer than is required for taking in provisions or repairing his ship. If he be driven there by stress of weather, he shall depart within five days. In the Carthaginian province of Sicily and at Carthage he may do and sell anything that is permitted to a citizen. A Carthaginian in Rome may do likewise.'[19]

Hostilities resumed between Carthaginians and Greeks at the time of Timoleon the Corinthian, who restored democracy to Syracuse. The Carthaginian attacks induced him to react violently, and in 340 he won a major victory at the river Crimissus. A peace treaty was drawn up in the following year, 339, leaving the frontier at the rivers Himera and Halycus, and the general situation little changed.

In 332, after a long siege, Alexander occupied Tyre, dealing a mortal blow to the power of the Phoenicians in the East. In the city he supposedly[20] found a Carthaginian embassy which he spared. As to his plans for the future, he probably also hoped to extend his empire to Africa: according to certain historians, a document was found at his death containing plans to build a large fleet to conquer Carthage and the African coast as far as the Pillars of Hercules.[21] Another tradition has it that the Carthaginians, anxious about the Macedonian's intentions, employed an envoy, called Hamilcar, to enter his confidence and discover his plans. Hamilcar allegedly transmitted much information, but on his return to Carthage was accused of treachery and put to death.[22] However accurate these traditions, the Carthaginians must have feared for their future, and it is also certain that the sudden death of Alexander put an end to all his plans.

Carthage, however, was soon to be confronted with another unexpected danger. Agathocles, the new tyrant of Syracuse, started his career under the aegis of the Carthaginians, but then turned against them and was defeated and blockaded in his city in 310. At this point, however, he carried out an extremely bold plan – the invasion of Africa. With about fourteen thousand men on sixty warships he departed in secret and, avoiding the Punic fleet, landed near Cape Bon, set fire to his ships, and made resolutely for Carthage.

The blow was quite unexpected. The invaders were not opposed by fortifications and garrisons, but by fertile fields and vineyards. This is how Diodorus describes the advance:

The intervening country through which it was necessary for them to march was divided into gardens and plantations of every kind, since many streams of water were led in small channels and irrigated every part. There were also country houses one after another, constructed in luxurious fashion and covered with stucco, which gave evidence of the wealth of the people who possessed them. The farm buildings were filled with everything that was needful for enjoyment, seeing that the inhabitants in a long period of peace had stored up an abundant variety of products. Part of the land was planted with vines, and part yielded olives and was also planted thickly with other varieties of fruit-bearing trees. On each side herds of cattle and flocks of sheep pastured on the plain, and the neighbouring meadows were filled with grazing horses. In general there was a manifold prosperity in the region, since the leading Carthaginians had laid out there their private estates and with their wealth had beautified them for their enjoyment.[23]

Having sacked the cities of Megalopolis (which we are unable to identify) and Tunis, Agathocles encamped in the vicinity of Carthage. Here, amid the confusion and anxiety, an army was rapidly prepared and sent out against the invader but was heavily defeated. This led to the paradoxical situation of two enemies each besieging the other's city. While Hamilcar was trying vainly to conquer Syracuse, Agathocles extended his area of occupation to the zone east of Carthage and was formulating an ambitious plan of alliance with the successors of Alexander in Egypt.

The plan was contrived as follows. In 322 Ptolemy Lagus of Egypt appointed Ophellas, a former member of Alexander's bodyguard, as governor of the Greek cities in Cyrenaica. Agathocles proposed to Ophellas an alliance against the Carthaginians: Ophellas would have ruled over North Africa, Agathocles over Sicily. So Ophellas advanced with ten thousand men from Cyrene towards the camp of Agathocles, but quarrels soon broke out between the two allies, and Agathocles had Ophellas killed by treachery and appropriated his army.

In the meantime Carthage was subject to an internal crisis. Bomilcar was striving for absolute power, but was assassinated on the verge of success. Taking advantage of this situation, Agathocles captured Utica and Hippo Acra, later Bizerta. Here he started to build a fleet and at the same time sailed for Sicily with a small army to liberate Syracuse. His absence proved disastrous. The Carthaginians attacked and routed his troops, regaining most of their former allies. Swiftly returning to Africa, Agathocles tried vainly to save the situation; he then fled to Sicily, while his troops came to terms with the Carthaginians. Soon after, in 305, a treaty with Agathocles marked the end of the war: Carthage secured all her possessions in Africa and in Sicily as far as the border of the Halycus, while Agathocles received a sum of money as nominal compensation for his abandoned territories.

So Carthage closed one of the most dangerous episodes of her history with moderation and wisdom. In this episode, the first to bring the enemies of Carthage into Africa, the government of Carthage well understood the vital importance of the African territory. No treaty was attempted with Agathocles, even at the hardest moments, as long as he remained on African soil. And this was not because of an imperialist policy, which was never practised by Carthage in the accepted sense of the term, but because of a genuine knowledge of the decisive importance of the limited territory of the homeland. Agathocles's venture, however unsuccessful, showed the way in which the Carthaginians could be defeated – a way which was later followed by Atilius Regulus and Scipio.

On the whole the course of events in the fifth and fourth centuries shows Carthage's affirmation of independence both from her original homeland and the Greek world, and consequently the formation of an autonomous state with a distinctive policy of its own. This policy was in the Phoenician tradition, in its essentially commercial purpose, but also had new phases and a new centre of gravity. As we have just seen, it had no imperialistic aims, and this was later to be the cause of its collapse when confronted with a state such as Rome. But the fact remains that for the first time Carthage brought Africa to the front line of Mediterranean history and became the expression and the symbol of resistance to the Greeks in the West.

6 Carthaginians and Romans

Picard shrewdly pointed out that despite the numerous wars in the fourth century Carthage was in a state of prosperity amply proved by the archaeological remains. To explain this situation – confirmed by ancient historians and in particular by Diodorus's account of the region through which the army of Agathocles advanced, we must keep in mind that with the sole exception of Agathocles's invasion the Carthaginians had managed to fight all their battles abroad. Other lands were laid waste, while the Carthaginians reaped the benefits of the booty; and the use of mercenaries, which was later a cause of crisis, then saved the population from diminution and reduced all military commitments to a purely economic problem.

But at the end of the fourth century Carthage was characterized not only by prosperity but also by the spread of Greek, or rather Hellenistic, culture which, after the period of relative isolation and independence, returned both in artistic and social life. Alexander's death established an entirely novel situation in the Mediterranean area: it ended the peril of an attack in the West, and the division of the empire, together with the consequent internal strife, removed any threat of military occupation of Carthage.

In Egypt, Ptolemy Lagus had formed a state extending to Phoenicia on one side and Cyrenaica on the other. Carthage had every reason to ally herself with this state, which convoyed and regulated trade along the African coast of the Mediterranean without exerting any political pressure, and thereby to secure the ties between the East and West. This situation is obvious in the picture of cultural and social life given us by literary tradition and archaeology.

On the other hand, the political problems in the West were now changing: the power of Rome was gradually increasing and it was therefore with Rome, no longer with the Greek world, that a decisive encounter was brewing. But the decline of Carthage also had other causes, local but no less relevant. These were principally the power of the mercenaries and the progressive independence of the neighbouring peoples leading to the formation of independent African states and their alliance with the great enemy of Carthage.

We will not give a detailed account of the struggle between Carthage and Rome. The first two treaties between the cities have already been mentioned. A third, renewing the preceding pacts, was concluded in 306. A fourth was drawn up in 279–278, confirming the preceding clauses and adding others concerning mutual aid in defence against the common enemy Pyrrhus, king of Epirus, who landed in Sicily with a powerful army in 278 and rapidly subjugated the whole island with the exception of Lilybaeum. This was the last episode of Greek intervention in Sicily, and it was brief: in 276 the combined force of the Carthaginians and Romans, as well as the collapse of the contracted alliances, obliged Pyrrhus to abandon Sicily.

The departure of Pyrrhus left Carthage face to face with Rome. Here are the main phases of the struggle. The First Punic War (264–241) ended with a treaty which took Sicily from Carthage and imposed a long and onerous payment of damages. The defeat was followed by the crisis in Africa: the Libyans were hostile, Utica and other towns wished to free themselves from Carthaginian rule, and finally Carthage (probably because of the economic situation brought on by the heavy fines due to Rome) suspended payment to the mercenaries. A bloody war ensued and enabled Rome, in exchange for neutrality, to obtain Sardinia and a sum of money (238).

By now the only route left to Carthage for expansion was Spain. And Spain was secured by the work of one family, the Barcids, who had in the meantime secured almost absolute authority in Carthage. Immediately after the end of the war of the mercenaries Hamilcar Barca went to Spain with his son Hannibal (237). In 229 he was succeeded by his son-in-law Hasdrubal, who founded Cartagena in 228 and signed a treaty with Rome in 226 in which the spheres of influence were divided by the Ebro. This was the last Punic colonial venture which must really be regarded as a phenomenon of conquest and the constitution of a sort of principality connected with the Barcid family.

Hasdrubal was assassinated in 221 and succeeded by Hannibal, who started the Second Punic War (218–202) at Sagunto in 218. As we know, this war first led to the greatest danger ever to have menaced Rome and then to Roman victory on African soil with the help of the Numidians under Massinissa. Once again the terms of peace were onerous: the Carthaginian fleet was burnt, a huge indemnity had to be paid, and, above all, Carthage had to undertake never to go to war without the consent of Rome. Carthage was thus exposed to the provocations of Massinissa, and when she finally reacted (150) Rome intervened and destroyed the city in the Third Punic War (149–146).

Carthaginian territory became a Roman province. But the heredity of Carthage – in language, religion, and culture – survived for centuries. To explain this phenomenon it must be said that although the Romans destroyed Carthage and her allies, they favoured all other Punic and African cities which had been of assistance to them. In this way seven Punic cities were granted the statute of free cities and became formal allies of the Roman empire, while the Numidian kingdom prospered as a result of the fall of its former rival. In other words, the destruction of Carthage was a military and political event which did not coincide with the end of Punic culture.

So it happened that while the ruling classes posted in Africa by Rome obviously spoke Latin, the people mainly continued to speak Punic. As to religion, Rome merely forbade human sacrifices and not even this restriction was observed in the peripheral sanctuaries. In all other respects the Punic cult continued for a long time to be practised by a well-organized priestly order and associations of believers formed near the temples.

The Numidian kingdom presents a further phenomenon. After the rival Carthage had been defeated it seems to have aspired to become her cultural heir. There are interesting accounts of Massinissa's sons collecting what was left of the libraries of Carthage, and one of their descendants, Hiempsal, wrote important works on the subject. Equally remarkable was the assertion of Punic religion in Numidian territory, particularly evident from the archaeological remains of the *topheth* of Cirta (Constantine), the capital of Numidia, and, above all, from the stelae. Of course, the Punic religion of this late period had its own development, assimilations, and convergences, as is proved by the stelae of the Ghorfa, found in a sanctuary in central Tunisia.

The fall of the Numidian kingdom marks the decline of Punic culture. When Caesar annexed Numidia and Carthage was rebuilt with Roman settlers the process of Romanization developed rapidly, not because of a concentrated effort of the empire, but because the independent centres of resistance vanished. In the second century AD the Punic inscriptions disappeared, while the spoken language – as witnessed by St Augustine[24] and confirmed by the so-called 'Latin-Libyan' inscriptions – survived for a few more centuries. Punic religion, too, was abandoned for Roman religion, or rather absorbed by Roman religion to the point of losing all characteristic traits. And so, slowly but surely, Carthaginian civilization ended.

7 Political organization

The system of the city-state, so characteristic of Phoenician political organization in the East, continued on the whole in the West, or at least left its mark there. As we have pointed out, even at the height of her power Carthage was never an imperial power in the accepted sense of the term. If the other Phoenician colonies in the West were tied to Carthage and virtually dependent on her, this was because of her strength rather than a policy of annexation and direct rule. The citizens of the various Mediterranean colonies were never regarded as Carthaginians; the colonies struck their own coins (Sicily, Ibiza, and Cadiz); their government, as far as we know, was autonomous (suffetes are mentioned in Malta, Tharros, and Cadiz, and a Maltese inscription cites a governmental system – suffetes, senate, people – in every way similar to that of the Carthaginians).[25] Carthage was, of course, the protector of the minor cities, which turned to her in times of need.

According to the system peculiar to the city-state in the East, every urban centre in the West gained control over a small surrounding territory. Carthage was no exception to the rule, even if, on account of the expansion of her power, the territory in question had spread some way into the interior by the fifth century. Within the territory amplified in this way, however, towns like Utica and Hadrumetum retained their independence.

If the spread of the surrounding territory was not such as to transform the basic urban character of the Carthaginian state, it did expand the economy in view of the great fertility of the soil. And while the urban population was prevalently of Phoenician origin the population of the country was prevalently indigenous, but interbred with slaves of various origins.

As far as the government is concerned, various indications suggest the presence of a king in the earliest phase of Carthaginian history, as there had been in East Phoenicia. Apart from the title of *basileus* given by the Greeks to the Carthaginian leaders with whom they came into contact in Sicily, the Malchus mentioned by Justin may be shown to be royal by his name. His story, on the other hand, shows that the government was not absolute: returning to his homeland, he had a quarrel with the senate and got the worst of it. Half-way through the sixth century, therefore, there appear to be two main elements in the Carthaginian political organization: the king and the senate.

The power of the Magonids who succeeded Malchus for three generations probably indicates the continuation of the monarchical system. The Magonids certainly commanded armies and are sometimes referred to by a royal title. On the other hand, the reaction against this family, around the middle of the fifth century, is of special importance for the evolution of the governmental system in Carthage, as we see in a celebrated passage from Justin:

At length, however, as so numerous a family of commanders was dangerous to the liberty of the state, since they themselves managed and decided everything, a hundred judges were chosen out of the senate, who were to demand of the generals, when they returned from war, an account of their proceedings, in order that, under this control, they might exercise their command in war with a regard to the judicature and laws at home.[26]

The exile of the Magonids was therefore accompanied by a readaptation of regal power. It was probably about this time that the title changed to suffete and the duties were temporarily reduced. Furthermore, the senate instituted a third governmental body, the Court of One Hundred, intended to supervise the royal power (maybe the senate itself was later deprived of authority by this oligarchy, as Picard points out).

Aristotle, who wrote in the fourth century, describes a well-established governmental system in Carthage,[27] consisting of two magistrates (kings or suffetes, maybe elected every year), a senate with three hundred members, a limited court of one hundred and four (probably corresponding to the one hundred already mentioned), and a general assembly of the people. This system remained substantially unaltered until the fall of Carthage: whether the Barcids renewed the supremacy of a family which, like the Magonids, owed its authority to the army, or acted independently from the suffetes and put the senate in the position of ratifying rather than taking decisions, the political structure of the state remained the same. Even in the second century, when Polybius was writing, there remained the fundamental tripartition of magistrates, senate, and general assembly.

Passing on to the intrinsic nature of the various bodies of government, the title 'king' covered an executive position over a period of time which stretched from the sixth or fifth century to the second century B C. The title 'suffete', which appears in various Latin authors, clearly corresponds to the Phoenician šōphĕtīm and is confirmed by the Punic inscriptions where it designates the highest citizens magistrates. The term means 'judge' and it was probably also used for normal judges; but in the sense of 'head of state' it is characterized by the duality of the functions and the comparison, made by the classical authors themselves, with the Roman consuls. The duration of office was certainly a year in the third–second century, and was probably not much longer at an earlier period. Investiture cannot have been due to birth, but, as Aristotle states,[28] to election on a basis of wealth and merit. The electoral body was presumably the general assembly, and it is likely that re-election was possible.

It was the king's duty to summon the senate, preside over it, and submit decisions; to summon the assembly of the people; maybe to exercise certain judiciary functions, about which we are not informed; and to command the armies, although this function was often delegated to military leaders. We do not know about any religious functions he may have had.

According to Aristotle,[29] the senate contained bodies of five members, pentarchies, probably put in charge of individual groups of questions, like permanent committees. But although this is hypothetical, since it is not mentioned in the sources, we do know that the pentarchies elected the One Hundred. How the senators were elected we cannot say: Aristotle tells that the pentarchies held a longer office, which seems to imply that power was not for life, even if re-election was possible, and it is quite likely that the senators were members of the richest and most influential families. In Carthage, as in Tyre, the power must have been in the hands of the commercial aristocracy, although we have no direct information on the subject. The senate, on the other hand, had to be consulted on all the main political and administrative matters. The sources are such that it seems to have been bound above all to decide about war and peace; it also received and dispatched messengers, organized the enlistment of mercenaries and slaves, and assessed the performance of military operations. With regard to internal questions, it was primarily the guarantor of the security of the state against personal ambition; it legislated and controlled the administration and the treasury. In conclusion, the duty of the senate was to control all state activity, and it undoubtedly constituted the main power of Carthage.

We do not know about the composition of the popular assembly. Slaves and foreigners could certainly not belong to it, and it may have consisted of elderly Carthaginian citizens with some private income. The assembly had to elect the generals and probably also the suffetes, and, according to Aristotle,[30] had to be consulted on matters about which the kings and senate did not agree, although it could also be consulted on other matters. It had, therefore, vast but primarily advisory prerogatives.

On the whole the political régime of Carthage was closely bound to the Phoenician tradition. We see that it was probably the class of rich merchants who held the power through the senate and the smaller body, the Court of One Hundred. It was mainly an aristocratic and oligarchic régime which survived all vicissitudes. The Carthaginian political system was, in fact, not very different from that of the Greeks (the tripartite government of Athens) or that of the Romans (consuls, senate, public assemblies). Their organization was, therefore, a convergence of the Phoenician heredity and the characteristics of the environment with which the Phoenicians entered into contact in the West. Although there is no proof of direct derivation, it is impossible not to notice cases like that of the function of the suffete: unquestionably of Phoenician origin (also in name), it presents the duality of person and the annual length of office of the Roman consulate.

An interesting development of the Carthaginian organization of the state which clearly shows Phoenician influence was the widespread use of mercenaries. The eminently commercial nature of Carthaginian policy was such that even military enterprises resulted from economic necessity and were ultimately more defensive than offensive. Since the Carthaginians had no intention of building a large empire, they did not wish to risk the diminution of the urban population by war. If war was part of business, it could have its contractors. Besides, the exemption of the proletariat from military service was a means of perpetuating the rule of the prosperous classes and of satisfying, or at least rendering inoffensive, the working classes. A mercenary militia also had considerable advantages from the point of view of military efficiency, so much so that the Greeks soon followed the Carthaginian example. But apart from the potential peril which a militia always presents for a state, the fact that the army could easily contract alliances with the Libyan subjects was a particularly serious disadvantage and one of the main causes for the fall of Carthage.

We now come to the government exercised by Carthage outside the city limits. Carthage gained control over the Phoenician colonies in the West when they were already in existence, founded and controlled new ones, but never made any annexations or aspired to direct rule. Local governments continued everywhere; independent coinage was struck; individual citizenships remained. There was probably a certain hierarchy amongst the colonies: Utica, and maybe Cadiz, remained official allies, but the same title was certainly not conferred on all the colonies. On the other hand, it seems certain that Carthage did impose restrictions on the autonomy: she cannot have authorized confederations between the colonies; she must have dealt with all foreign policy and forbidden local armies except for immediate requirements, otherwise supplying garrisons and organizing the defence of the colonies herself. She may – although this is not certain – have had inspectors of revenue in the various cities, and she controlled all trade. Only in certain cases did she go farther: she imported Africans to Sardinia, a well-known sign of direct colonization, probably aimed at the agricultural and mineral resources, and, between the First and Second Punic Wars, the Barcids turned Punic Spain into a province which provided soldiers in time of war and paid a tax.

What must have been a temporary situation in Spain, connected with historical circumstances and the Barcid policy, seems to have been permanent in North Africa, that is, in the territory flanking Carthage. The ties between the North African colonies and Carthage were therefore particularly close, even if there was no question of imperial unification. We know from Diodorus Siculus[31] that the Libyphoenicians, or the settlers in the maritime cities founded by the Phoenicians or Carthaginians in Africa, had the same connubial rights as the Carthaginians. In the preface to the treaty of Hannibal with Philip of Macedon, Polybius[32] mentions, after the Carthaginians, 'all under the dominion of Carthage who live under the same laws'. This seems to imply that the Libyphoenicians enjoyed the same private rights as the Carthaginians. It is also likely that a municipal autonomy persisted in the North African cities, although this did not prevent the forcible levy of military contingents and the imposition of taxes from causing outbreaks of dissatisfaction, as is proved by the Libyan revolts. On the whole, however, these revolts were rare, and we can say that the North African cities supported Carthage in the constitution of her dominion.

Finally there is no doubt that Carthage laid the foundations of a vast state and wisely applied the principle of local autonomies. However, her mercantile origins and the typical city tradition, inherited from the Phoenician homeland, did not allow her to develop these foundations into a solid empire. Carthage subjugated the colonies, exploited them despite their relative autonomy, but did not provide their population with prospects of a better life integrated in a large unitary community. So if the state remained substantially compact during the period of greatest prosperity, at a time of crisis it dissolved rapidly and completely.

CHAPTER 10

RELIGION

1 Introduction

Religion undoubtedly plays a dominant part in the civilization of Carthage. Sacrifice was the principal element, and is reflected in every sort of artistic production, in the temples, tombs, stelae, sarcophagi, figurines, and amulets. The literary documentation which we possess, with certain intrinsic limitations, is deeply concerned with religious life practised not only on an official level or by the educated classes. The thousands of votive stelae, and the minute and frequent objects peculiar to belief in magic, prove that widespread religious feeling existed on every level of the population.

However abundant a testimony we have of an intensive religious life in Carthage, the specific documentation of beliefs is considerably less abundant, and the mythology is almost completely unknown to us. This state of affairs is the result of the sources at our disposal. To begin with, the inscriptions give many divine names and repeat the main ones thousands of times, but they add little about the nature and functions of the deities, only occasionally providing, as in the 'tariffs', certain indications about the sacrifices offered. Besides, as in East Phoenicia, it is sometimes doubtful whether the name was proper or simply a title of the deity (for example, Baal and Milk).

The abundance of the theophorous names preserved both by the Punic inscriptions and by the Greek and Latin adaptations undoubtedly helps us to identify the divine names and get an idea of the general concept of the gods. So we have Abdeshmun 'servant of Eshmun', Eshmunyaton 'Eshmun has given', Shaphatbaal 'Baal has judged', etc. Certain names indicate familial and emotional ties: Himilk 'brother of Milk', Batbaal 'daughter of Baal', Arishatbaal 'beloved of Baal', etc. But above all the relationship indicated is one of subjection: Abdmelqart 'servant of Melqart', Amatbaal 'servant of Baal', Germelqart 'client of Melqart'. And there is the deep-rooted concept that the well-being of man depends on divine favour: Eshmunhanno 'Eshmun has favoured', Melqartazar 'Melqart has

136

helped', Baalshamar 'Baal has protected', Melqartshama 'Melqart has listened'.

A further source of knowledge of the Carthaginian deities is provided by their Greek and Latin interpretation, which, through assimilation to classical gods, clarifies certain characteristics. So we find Baal Hammon identified with Kronos/Saturn, Tanit with Hera/Juno, Melqart with Heracles (already identified as such in Phoenicia), etc.

Finally the illustrated monuments serve either to qualify the deities or to distinguish between them. But the deities rarely appear in anthropomorphic shape, and this limits the possibilities provided by the illustrations; besides, particularly in the amulets, the forms are typically and exclusively foreign – Egyptian in this case – so that they usually suggest importation.

The material for the reconstruction of Carthaginian and Punic religion, in North Africa, therefore, is apparently abundant but, in fact, very limited. We can gather indications about divine names, the current concept of the gods and certain forms of the cult, but not about the relationships between the gods, their functions or mythology. Carthage does not even have such a dubious and controversial source as Philo of Byblos in East Phoenicia.

2 The gods

It is evident that the pantheon of Carthage originally had Phoenician elements – the most natural result of historical conditions. But the Phoenician pantheon was not homogeneous: each city had its own version, although there were usually certain recurrent themes such as the convergence of the various divine figures in the triad of the supreme god, the goddess of fertility, and the young god who dies and is resurrected.

These beliefs also exist in Carthage, although their dislocation naturally determined developments and differentiations which were considerably influenced by Libyan and classical elements, in other words by the environments with which the West Phoenicians remained in lasting contact.

This consideration applies particularly to the two Carthaginian deities who largely predominate over all the others in the thousands of votive inscriptions which have been brought to light: Tanit Pene Baal and Baal Hammon, both mentioned in the majority of these inscriptions together in such a way as to form a veritable couple. The history of the two deities differs in that Tanit only appears after the fifth century and thereafter usually takes precedence, while the earlier inscriptions are dedicated to Baal alone, who is represented as a plain stone pillar. The primitive documentation corresponds wholly to what we know of the

Phoenician religion, while the couple constitutes a development and systemization to be placed in the fifth century, a period which witnessed evolution in every field. But the development does not lack Phoenician components, because Tanit has possible Oriental antecedents and is anyhow the equivalent of Astarte, therefore the mother-goddess. On the other hand, there are noticeable local components, such as the name, which might be the result of the Libyan environment.

Baal Hammon already exists in the East and is specifically mentioned in the inscription of Zincirli (ninth century). According to the most likely interpretation, the name means 'lord of the perfume altar', referring to the widespread practice of offering incense, indicated by the stelae where this altar (with the Greek name *thymiaterion*) frequently appears. On the other hand, the obvious etymology suggests here, as in Phoenicia, the prevalence of the function over the name, and therefore makes it possible to identify this god with the Phoenician El, rather than with Baal, although it is possible to identify him with both of them. The proposed identification with Amon, an Egyptian god whose cult had for some time been widespread in the Libyan area, seems unlikely as an original fact, but is possibly a secondary development obviously connected with the assonance of the names. The Greek and Latin identifications are evident: for the Greeks Baal Hammon corresponds to Kronos (like the Phoenician El), and for the Romans to Saturn.

The most convincing depiction of this deity is on a stele of Sousse: the god has a human form, a tall crown, beard, and long robe. He is seated on a throne flanked by winged sphinxes. In one hand he holds a spear, while he raises the other towards a believer in sign of blessing. On the whole this iconography can be considered typically Phoenician.

The name of Tanit does not appear, or appears very rarely, in East Phoenicia. The qualification 'Tanit of the Lebanon'[1] in an inscription might suggest Oriental origin, but it is insufficient and there could be various interpretations. Another indication is the component of certain toponyms (Aktanit, Aintanit, Kafr Tanit) attested by Ronzevalle in modern Lebanese toponymy. The vowelization of the name is hypothetical, particularly since certain stelae in Constantine have the consonantal form *Tynt*. We can add that some Punic inscriptions in Greek characters give the forms of Thinet and Thennit. Of course, since the inscriptions are late they may be no more than evolved provincial forms. But the doubt remains, as does the uncertainty, about the origin of the name which has sometimes been attributed to the Libyan environment.

The title 'face of Baal', which accompanies the name of Tanit, is noteworthy. It is clearly reminiscent of the title 'name of Baal' of Phoenician Astarte and is a clear indication of an original dependency from Baal. This dependency had actually disappeared in Carthage when Tanit started to appear at the head of the inscriptions. In other places, however, like Hadrumetum and Cirta, Baal Hammon is named before Tanit and sometimes stands on his own. This suggests that the phenomenon of Tanit's prevalence was not only late but was also restricted to the Carthaginian area.

In any case, Tanit definitely corresponds to Astarte of the East Phoenician pantheon. Rare in the inscriptions of Carthage, and yet contained in the theophorous names, Astarte evidently gave way to Tanit. The significant title of mother, accorded to the latter in certain inscriptions, indicates her nature, which is confirmed by the Greek identification with Hera and the Roman with Celestial Juno. The symbols which accompany her in the illustrations – dove, pomegranate, fish, palm tree – clearly suggest her functions as goddess of fertility.

Passing on to the depictions, we cannot be certain, but it seems likely that the female figures holding their breasts reproduced on the stelae and cippi are images of Tanit, as are probably the female protomai found in certain Carthaginian tombs, in addition to other female figures on coffins, like that of Ste Monique, with birds' wings folded on its body. On the whole all the female depictions which cannot, for various reasons, be identified as human seem to refer to the leading female deity.

From the depictions we come to the symbols. To begin with there is the famous 'sign of Tanit' about which a lengthy controversy has developed (which we shall mention in the chapter on art): either a decoration composed of a betyl and a solar disk divided by a horizontal arm or a development of the Egyptian *ankh* or something else. This sign is typical of the goddess and, in its development if not in its origins, represents a clear anthropomorphic interpretation. Another symbol used for Tanit is the 'bottle', which a stele recently discovered in Akziv proves to have its antecedent in the East. The symbol of the open hand is also probably connected with Tanit, as well as the crescent moon, sometimes pointing downwards and combined with the solar disk.

If Tanit and Baal Hammon are by far the most important deities in Carthage, they are not the only ones. Melqart, the leading god of Tyre, was also worshipped in Carthage, where a votive stele proves that a temple was dedicated to him.[2] Every year, as we know, a Carthaginian embassy went to Tyre to offer a tribute in his temple – a significant indication of the lasting connexions between the East and West Phoenicians. Finally, numerous monuments bear his image – that of the Greek Heracles to whom he had been assimilated both in the East and West. The particular veneration in which this deity was held by the Barcids has been taken to imply a spirit of conservation, or even return to antiquity, which both the religion and policy of the famous family enforced. This is possible, but not certain.

Eshmn, familiar to the East Phoenicians, was also worshipped in Carthage. His temple stood on the acropolis of Byrsa and was, it is said, the most beautiful in the city. The last stronghold in 146, it was entirely destroyed by the Romans. The Greek identification with Asklepios and the Latin with Aesculapius suggests that special healing qualities were attributed to this god. Besides, the fact that the cult of Asklepios/Aesculapius was so widespread indicated the importance of the deity. The possible identification with Iolaos, the nephew and companion of Hercules in numerous ventures, will be mentioned with reference to Hannibal's oath. There are no depictions which we can attribute with certainty or probability to this god.

Other deities are rarely mentioned. The proper names indicate a formerly Oriental god, Pumay or Pumayon, in other words Pygmalion. Reshef seems also to have existed and to be assimilated by Apollo. Saphon, a component of the Phoenician Baal Saphon, exists in various proper names. The other deities of Oriental origin, known from theophorous names, are Sakkon, Miskar, and Shed. Shadrapa, whom we know was adapted by the Greeks as Satrapes, appears in a bilingual inscription of the imperial era as corresponding to *Liber Pater*.[3]

At this point we can further our knowledge of the Carthaginian deities in the now Hellenizing period (third century) by examining Hannibal's celebrated oath in the treaty with Philip v of Macedon, recorded by Polybius. The treaty, of the year 215 bc, contains a series of clauses which Hannibal indicates by undertaking to observe them and calling the main Punic deities to witness the oath. Whether or not they belonged to the Greek pantheon, the adaptations are certain, and so is the Greek interpretation revealed by the treaty:

In the presence of Zeus, Hera, and Apollo; in the presence of the Genius (*daimon*) of Carthage, of Heracles, and Iolaus; in the presence of Ares, Triton, Poseidon; in the presence of the gods who battle for us and of the Sun, Moon, and Earth; in the presence of Rivers, Lakes, and Waters; in the presence of all the gods who possess Carthage; in the presence of all the gods who possess Macedonia and the rest of Greece; in the presence of all the gods of the army who preside over this oath . . .[4]

The document is of great interest. It must have been the Greek translation of a Punic text and might be a list of the pantheon made by somebody who knew it directly and venerated it. But there are some problems: Kronos and Asklepios, two of the main deities, corresponding to Punic originals (Baal Hammon and Eshmun), are missing from the oath. On the other hand, there are minor figures such as Iolaos (probably a secondary version of Eshmun), Ares, Triton, and Poseidon (figures for whom it is difficult to find an equivalent). It is likely that the difficulty results from a fluidity of the Greek adaptations: so, for example, Zeus would be Baal Hammon instead of the usual Kronos. Hera is undoubtedly Tanit. Apollo seems to correspond to Reshef. The 'Genius of the Carthaginians', according to an interpretation by Dussaud, would be Astarte. Heracles is Melqart.

Another peculiarity of Hannibal's oath is noteworthy: the mention of the deities in groups of three. This fact could suggest a tendency to family organization and a hierarchy of the pantheon such as we see in the Phoenician religion. The relevant data, however, are scarce: there is the connexion between Tanit and Baal Hammon (in this order or the other way round) which undoubtedly suggests a divine couple; and the title of Tanit Pene Ball which provides a further bond between the two elements of the couple. It is also possible that the votive cippi with triads of betyls represent a grouping of the pantheon.

The Greek deities were adopted in Carthage without necessarily accurate equivalents in the local pantheon: for example, Dionysus, Aphrodite, Demeter, and Kore. The cult of Demeter, who was to become Ceres in the Roman era, was especially widespread, and there is no doubt that this diffusion, as with the cult of Dionysus, was connected with the affirmation of the religious mysteries.

Special mention must be made of the Egyptian deities. Their cult does not, generally speaking, appear in the inscriptions or the onomatology. The amulets, however, show us their images in quantity: Ptah, Horus, Bes, Thot, Isis, Min, Khonsu, Shu, Amon-Re, Sekhmet, Anubis, Tueris are the most common. The solution of this apparent contradiction between literary sources and archaeological documentation is relatively simple: Egyptian magic enjoyed great success and development in Carthage, but remained on an essentially popular level, as opposed to that of the official and public beliefs.

3 The cult

In rightly saying that the essential act of Punic religion is sacrifice Picard bases himself on the fact that most of the texts and monuments handed down to us refer to sacrifices. This can obviously also appear to be coincidental, because there must have been in Carthage ordinary and extraordinary ceremonies in temples and religious feasts on established ·days. But for these we have no documentation, while we have a great deal for the sacrifices which must therefore have been a predominant part of religious life and conscience even if they were not the only manifestation.

Human sacrifice was as prevalent over the other forms of sacrifice as sacrifice in general was over other religious forms. In the precinct of

Tanit, a little west of the ports of Carthage, thousands of funerary urns have been brought to light together with votive stelae. Here there is archaeological proof of the existence of a *topheth*, or of a sanctuary where children were sacrificed. If the name is biblical, and if the Bible gives us a clear account of what these places of sacrifice were,[5] we must keep in mind that not one of them has been found in the East. It is the Punic West that testifies this typical Phoenician rite, primarily in Carthage, and also in Sicily (Motya) and Sardinia (Nora, Sulcis, Tharros, Monte Sirai).

The Phoenician and Punic word for sacrifice in the *topheth* is *molk*: it is connected to a root that implies possession, in the sense that the offering was given to the possession of the deity. At a later period, and in Latin adaptation, an amplification of the noun appears which specifies and diversifies its nature: it is *molchomor*, which means '*molk* of a lamb' and clearly indicates a substitute sacrifice which replaces the human being by an animal. Indeed, the excavation of certain *topheths* has brought to light the bones of small animals. The finds in the *topheth* at Sousse are particularly indicative of a temporal evolution, because it is only in the fourth century that animal bones start to appear instead of those of children. However, it is still difficult to be sure about the matter.

The *topheth* of Carthage was in use throughout the history of the city, as its successive strata prove clearly. The sacrifices were initially made only to Baal Hammon: in a celebrated passage Diodorus Siculus[6] says that the victims were placed in the hands of a bronze statue and then dropped into the flames, and the deity to whom the sacrifice was dedicated was Kronos. As we know, however, Tanit was soon to join Baal Hammon, and even precede him in the inscriptions.

Diodorus[7] also clarifies the purposes and the actual nature of the sacrifice. When Agathocles defeated the Carthaginians, in 310, and brought the war to Africa, the Carthaginians believed they had seriously offended the gods by replacing the children of the best families, formerly sacrificed to Kronos, by children acquired for the purpose. They decided to redeem themselves by sacrificing two hundred children picked from the best families, and, in their eagerness to contribute to the offering, the citizens assembled as many as three hundred children.

What was the intrinsic nature of this 'passage through fire'? Diodorus says that the relatives were forbidden to weep: this might simply have meant that they did not wish to diminish the value of the sacrifice with grief, but it is also possible that tears did not suit a sacrifice which led to the deification of the children. This theory of Dussaud may imply a connexion with the Elissa-Dido sacrifice from which this ritual would have originated. On the basis of interesting similarities with the Ugaritic texts Dussaud also suggested that the sacrifice of blood rejuvenated and strengthened the deity to whom it was dedicated, at the same time binding him to the offerer of the sacrifice. The concept of offering the first fruits to the deity, whether they were human, animal, or vegetable, was typical of the ancient Near East, as is clearly proved by the Bible.

If child sacrifices were the most characteristic and widespread, they were not the only ones. We also have clear indications of adult sacrifices, in this case foreigners and enemies. When Hannibal captured Himera in 409 he sacrificed three thousand prisoners to expiate the death of Hamilcar in the battle of 480. On another occasion, after a victory against Agathocles, the Carthaginians, according to Diodorus,[8] burnt the most handsome prisoners as a sign of gratitude to the deity. Finally, we are told that a human victim was sacrificed annually to Heracles.[9]

After the human sacrifices we must mention those of animals. The inscriptions list the animals sacrificed to the gods: bulls, lambs, rams, sheep, and birds. We also know of various categories of sacrifices which present immediate similarities to those mentioned in the Bible: the burnt offering, where the entire animal was burnt; the communion sacrifice, where part of the slaughtered animal went to the offerer and part to the sacrificer; and another type of offering, where the whole victim went to the priest. Furthermore, a percentage was due to the priests for the sacrifices which they performed. Details were provided by the 'tariffs', and of these the best known is that of Marseilles, which begins as follows:

Temple of Baal Saphon. Account of the dues which the thirty controllers of dues have fixed . . . For each ox whether the sacrifice be a sin offering or a peace offering or a burnt offering the priests shall have ten pieces of silver for each . . .

The tariff goes on to list the quotes established for every animal and every sort of sacrifice. In addition to animal offerings those of food and drink were also performed: flour, oil, milk, etc. Incense played an important and specific part in the cult of Baal Hammon.

The complex cult practised in Carthage required a large priesthood. The inscriptions mention priests and priestesses, either with no further specification or indicating the particular deity to which they were attached. There was also a hierarchy: a head of the priests, a priest, and a second priest. The head of the priests superintended the entire staff of a temple (for example, the head of the priests of Elat is mentioned), but the same title probably also designated the high priest in the town. The office could be hereditary: indeed, the inscriptions mention the succession of priestly functions for several generations in the same family. They were also connected with the city aristocracy, and certain episodes, like that of the son of Malchus and the suffetes during the wars against

143

Rome, remind us of the priestly functions assumed by some members of ruling families in Phoenicia. However, the phenomenon is limited and sporadic, and the priesthood never seems to surpass its functions in the cadre of city life. A secondary staff was also attached to the temples: servers, scribes, musicians, and barbers. It is not certain whether sacred prostitution, so characteristic of the East, continued in Carthage.

Belief in an after-life is clearly indicated by the votive gifts which accompanied the deceased to their tombs. What the specific elements of this belief were, we do not know. Magic certainly played a large part in the concept of the after-life, as we see from the pre-eminence of amulets among the funerary objects. The usual form of burial was inhumation, but cremation also existed, not only at a later age, as was at first thought, but also in an early period.

CHAPTER II

ART

1 Introduction

Phoenician-Punic art in North Africa is considerably better known than that of Phoenicia. A vast and prolonged excavation of Carthage has brought to light a series of monuments which provide an uneven documentation, but on the whole give a direct idea of Carthaginian artistic production. The case of the Phoenician cities, mainly buried under medieval and modern buildings, is not repeated, and Carthage, although the most productive, is not the only art centre. A series of North African towns have contributed to the integration and comparative evaluation of its documentation.

The documentation is uneven: the radical destruction of Carthage by the Romans was such that there are few architectural remains. On the other hand, large sculpture must have been virtually non-existent in the West as in the East, so we are left mainly with relief, together with the various forms of 'minor arts'. The majority of this material comes from the tombs, and can be termed largely funerary in its characteristics and origins.

There is a strong tie between Carthaginian and Phoenician art. Here, more than in any other aspect of the civilization, it is possible to assess the closeness of relations with the homeland. The Phoenician motifs are naturally accompanied by Egyptian ones: a large part of the material discovered in the tombs of Carthage is, as Vercoutter has pointed out, Egyptian or Egypticizing. But Carthage, far more than Phoenicia, was exposed to contact with Greece, so that material of Hellenic, and later Hellenistic influence or make, plays an important part in its art history. Finally, the historical contacts with the Etruscans also influenced the production and determined a new artistic component which was obviously unknown to the East Phoenicians.

As a result of this convergence of influences Carthaginian and North African art has few characteristics of its own. De Vögué's conclusion that the Phoenicians had no originality was the basis of decades of study devoted to the East Phoenicians, and is undoubtedly paralleled by the limited and partial studies on the art of the West Phoenicians. In this respect we can quote Gsell:

Carthaginian craftsmen displayed no originality either in their technique or their ornamentation. They invented no new processes and did not rejuvenate their repertory by contact with nature and life. They always copied. Carthage remained in close relationship with the metropolis and to begin with Carthaginian workshops, they were nothing but branches of those of the Phoenicians who had borrowed their technique and models from Egypt and introduced certain elements of Mesopotamian origin. In certain objects this Egypticizing style lasted for centuries and was even more tenacious in Africa than in Phoenicia proper. However, certain Greek influences made themselves felt in the seventh century, apparently coming through the East Phoenicians who lived close to the Greeks in the island of Cyprus. Then Greek art prevailed. It probably arrived mainly through Sicily where the Greeks fell subject to Carthage at the end of the fifth century, while, between the wars, other Greeks traded continuously with the Carthaginians.[1]

Gsell provides a basis for all successive studies, and a further passage is of interest in that it presents a criterion which will be developed later:

The technique degenerates after the fifth century. We can attribute the poor quality of the jewels found in the tombs to a wish to curb expenditure which was deemed useless. But does this apply to pottery? Well-made local crockery would not have been any more expensive than the imported vases which abound in the tombs. The truth was that the Punic craftsmen no longer took the trouble to work well: they left that to the Greeks. They performed their daily task without enjoying it. There was a great demand for cheap objects, while the commercial monopolies almost put the buyer at the mercy of the seller . . . The artistic talents of a nation appear in the commonest objects and these prove the hopeless incapacity of the Carthaginians who were not even able to imitate their Greek models.[2]

As we see, Gsell noticed a sudden decline of Greek influence as early as the fifth century. Picard makes a still more accurate assessment of Carthaginian art. It flourished in the seventh and sixth century with an astonishing abundance of Greek material, imported rather than imitated, and was accompanied by ample Egyptian material also mainly imported, probably by the Greeks. This is proved by the abundance of scarabs originating from the city of Naucratis, founded in 630 in the Delta, while Greek commercial mediation is significant as a threat to Phoenician control of trade along the Mediterranean coasts.

Either because of a reaction to this peril or a policy of isolation in the decades following the defeat at Himera, the Carthaginian tombs reveal a sudden reduction of imported Greek and Egyptian material and a consequent lack of objects of value in the fifth and part of the fourth century. Picard attributed this crisis to the fact that the government of

Carthage realized the damage caused by commerce with the Greeks who despoiled the country of its primary matters and only gave relatively useless luxury goods in return. Carthage then ceased striking coins and continued her trade on an exchange basis which must have been far more exhausting. Furthermore, Justin's account[3] of the senate's attempt to prohibit the teaching of Greek after a case of high treason at the beginning of the fourth century shows the results of this general policy in other than artistic fields.

So, just as Hellenic civilization was imposing itself on Phoenicia, Carthage reacted against it. But the phenomenon only lasted for a limited period of time: after Alexander the policy of alliance with the Hellenistic state of Egypt and the change in the balance of power in the Mediterranean determined a reconciliation between Carthage and the Greek, now Hellenistic world. In the third and second century Greek material reappeared in quantity in the Carthaginian necropolises, while a local art developed, although it was always of a commercial nature, and persisted until the fall of Carthage.

Passing on to a reconsideration of the characteristics of Carthaginian and Punic North African art, we can say that here, as in the Phoenician homeland, there was little aspiration to great art and a prevalence of crafts containing numerous foreign elements and lacking adequate coherence and stylistic tradition. Besides, here, as opposed to what happened in the East, external influence came mainly from importations – whether they were objects or craftsmen – rather than from imitations.

In spite of this the Carthaginians made repeated attempts, clearly perceptible, for example, in the stelae, to express a language of their own, however coarse and popular. And there was also the characteristic element of the graduation of the various influences – the most dominant and direct was the Egyptian influence which already prevailed in Phoenicia, while the decentralization in the West brought to the fore Greek influence, which continued from the earliest times, with the exception of the period already mentioned.

In the little architecture that remains Greek influence prevails. In the goldware and glyptic art the Egyptian influence is dominant. In the stelae Egyptian and Greek elements overcome an independent local basis which frequently re-emerges. The male masks contain truly autonomous elaborations. These are only a few examples, by way of introduction, of the results to which a detailed examination of the artistic production might lead.

Finally, the transfer of Phoenician production and its characteristics so far into the West is a unique and original factor. The distance from the source obviously caused assimilation of new and diverse elements, but also determined a continuity of ancient elements through the ages which corresponds to the characteristics of lateral areas of culture and avoids the natural evolution taking place in the homeland. So, from various and complex factors, emerges the phenomenon of Punic art.

2 Architecture

The plan of ancient Carthage could constitute an excellent means of reconstructing a typical Phoenician settlement and its development. However, in view of the radical destruction effected by the Romans in 146 BC little is left of the Punic phase. Apart from stelae and small objects we have a few remains of walls, the necropolises and the *topheth*. For everything else we must refer to later literary sources.

The town plan, however, is clear. The city was built on the triangular promontory between the lagoon of Sebkhet Er Riana to the north and Tunis to the south. The first Phoenician settlement must have been in the area of Salammbo, where a *topheth* and the earliest ports have been discovered. But expansion to the hill of Byrsa must have been immediate, since Byrsa already exists in the tradition of the foundation of the city. The necropolises north-east of Byrsa have also yielded early objects. So the city of the first centuries probably included the zone of the bay of Le Kram to the south and the acropolis of Byrsa to the north, also comprising the area of the necropolises of Douimes and Dermech to the east. Subsequently, after about the fifth century, the entire peninsula must have been occupied and inhabited.

The acropolis of Byrsa was therefore the centre of the city, together with the two hills of St Louis and Juno. On the acropolis stood the temple of Eshmun, the last refuge of the defenders of Carthage. Byrsa was surrounded by a line of fortifications, and all that remains of the entire complex are walls of late houses (third century BC) in the south-western area of the acropolis. Large blocks from this zone, which were long thought to be Punic defences, must instead be Byzantine.

At the foot of the acropolis, in the area between the acropolis and the port, were the living quarters with the main square or forum surrounded by porticoes and serving as the commercial and administrative centre of the city. The building of the senate and the building where the suffetes administered justice were probably in the vicinity. Appian writes that three streets led from the forum to the acropolis and that they were flanked by tall narrow houses of five or six stories built against one another.[4] A small gold plaque found on the islet in the middle of the circular dock shows a house with four stories. But while these houses constituted the more popular quarters, the residential area was, as we shall see, in the zone of Megara, to the west of the acropolis.

The earliest anchorages in the area of Carthage must have been the two lagoons to the north and south of the promontory. Appropriate docks were soon built on the southern area of the coast, however. This artificial harbour, specifically known as the *cothon*, and which we will find elsewhere in the West, consisted of a rectangular dock for mercantile vessels and a further circular harbour for warships. The access to the rectangular dock was guarded by a fortified quadrilateral, the foundations of which still exist. Small canals were built from the dock to the sea for the exchange and discharge of water. The circular harbour was surrounded by arsenals described by Appian, and the residence of the admiralty stood on the islet in the centre. Appian describes it as follows:

The harbours had communication with each other, and a common entrance from the sea seventy feet wide, which could be closed with iron chains. The first port was for merchant vessels, and here was collected all kinds of ships' tackle. Within the second port was an island which, together with the port itself, was enclosed by high embankments. These embankments were full of shipyards which had capacity for two hundred and twenty vessels. Above them were magazines for their tackle and furniture. Two Ionic columns stood in front of each dock, giving the appearance of a continuous portico to both the harbour and the island. On the island was built the admiral's house, from which the trumpeter gave signals, the herald delivered orders, and the admiral himself overlooked everything.[5]

If the zone to the south-east of the acropolis was occupied by the forum and the living quarters, and, on the sea, the harbour buildings, the zone to the north-east contained vast necropolises, of which the most noteworthy are those of Douimes-Dermech and Ste Monique. North-west of Byrsa, on the other hand, towards the base of the isthmus which joined the promontory to the mainland, was the elegant quarter of Megara with gardens, orchards, and scattered houses.

The whole city was surrounded by a wall with three lines of defence on the front. According to Appian,[6] the fortifications were of the same size, but Polybius[7] is probably correct in mentioning a ditch and a palisade, evidently the outer defence. The centre defence must have been a fairly low bastion where the armed soldiers could gather. It seems that the dimensions attained were seventeen metres in height and ten in breadth.[8] Every sixty metres was a four-storied tower protruding outside the walls.[9] Within the defences was a series of casemates which could hold vast quantities of animals (elephants and horses) as well as men (foot-soldiers and cavalry). On the sea front the defences consisted of a single curtain fortified at intervals. The huge blocks of stone still in existence between the bay of Le Kram and Bordj El Djedid are probably Roman, but stand on previous Punic constructions.

With regard to hydraulic supplies, the Fountain of a thousand amphorae at the foot of the northern cliff of Bordj El Djedid near the sea is certainly Punic in its origins. Otherwise, since the wells of Carthage did not supply drinking water, the cisterns gathered the rain and preserved the water for the city.

While the data provided by Carthage was virtually unique until a few centuries ago as far as Punic civil architecture was concerned, the recent excavations at Kerkouane have altered the situation considerably. Here houses have appeared with well-preserved mosaic pavements, walls with purple stucco, bathrooms and hygienic installations, toilet articles like flasks and perfume-burners, all going back to the fourth and third century BC.

Passing on to religious architecture, nothing remains of the great temples attested by literary tradition. The largest of all must have stood on the acropolis of Byrsa – the temple of Eshmun (Asklepios) – surrounded by a sacred wall to which a flight of sixty steps led. Tanit and Baal Hammon (identified respectively with Hera/Juno and Kronos/Saturn) must have had their temples between the hill of St Louis and the sea, where thousands of stelae dedicated to them have been discovered.

The most important religious building of Carthage to have remained is the *topheth*, situated in the area of Salammbo, hardly fifty metres east of the rectangular harbour. It is probable that Elissa landed and died here: at any rate, the cult must have been very ancient and connected with decisive events in the history of Carthage. The earliest phase of the *topheth* is represented by the *Cintas chapel*: a chamber of about a metre square, with a small 'holy of holies' dug into the rock which contained terracotta vases ascribable to the eighth century. Before the chamber is a courtyard, not much larger, with an altar. And before this are three curved concentric walls forming a sort of labyrinth through which the worshippers had to pass to reach the shrine.

After the eighth century, and on successive strata throughout the history of Punic Carthage, thousands of urns with ashes and bones of children (occasionally of birds and other small animals) have been found deposited in the *topheth*, clearly confirming the rite we know from the Bible and of which we find further evidence in the Phoenician-Punic world of the West. The urns are accompanied by cippi and votive stelae with incisions and inscriptions. Taking each stratum in turn, the first, lying on the virgin soil, is of the eighth and early seventh century: it contains urns with the bones of cremated children scattered on the earth and covered by heaps of small stones. The second stratum contains more urns, placed under large blocks of stones, or under altars or aedicules, or even under stelae representing betyls or the sign of Tanit. Also on this stratum (but according to some archaeologists on a different stratum) there appear new types of stelae shaped like pointed obelisks polished on one of the four sides, bearing inscriptions or decorations, during the fifth century. The stratum ends in the fourth century and is followed by a third stratum, from the third century to the destruction of Carthage, with small urns and few stelae, much disturbed by later buildings on the site. The whole site is covered by late Roman and Byzantine buildings, putting an end to a sanctuary which survived throughout the history of the city. No other sanctuary in North Africa has such a long history: the one in Sousse was founded later (sixth century), while those of Bir Bou Knissia, Constantine, and others begin in the Hellenistic-Roman phase.

Passing on to the tombs, we note close ties between the Phoenician homeland and the North African colonies. The Phoenician tombs, consisting of vast chambers dug several metres into the rock on the sides of a deep shaft, are paralleled in Carthage by the necropolises of Bordj El Djedid and Ste Monique: footholds cut in the sides of the shaft give access to the burial chambers. There are also tombs with *dromos*, always cut in the rock, but usually with a single chamber, as at Djebel Mlezza on Cape Bon.

The other North African colonies abound in necropolises, and we can even say that they are known mainly for their necropolises. The most typical of these is the necropolis of Mahdia, to the south of Sousse, with shafts cut in the rock leading to rectangular burial chambers accessible by steps. The chambers contain benches for the coffins and niches for lamps on the walls.

We also know that in Phoenicia certain tombs were built or semi-built on the surface of the rock, like the one of Eshmunazar at Sidon. Carthage also has tombs consisting of recesses built over shallow pits, as in the necropolis of Dermech. In the necropolis 'of the island' at Utica the tombs also consist of recesses dug in the earth covered by large slabs of stone. The monumental tombs, like those of Amrit in Phoenicia, are represented by the mausoleum of Dougga in Tunisia, going back to the third–second century BC.

The main system of burial throughout the history of Carthage was inhumation. Cremation also existed, however, and attained special development and significance in the rite of child sacrifice which characterizes the Punic religion.

3 Statues, cippi, and stelae

A marble head, discovered by Cintas in Carthage, is the earliest example of Punic sculpture yet brought to light: stylistically it resembles certain masks of terracotta of the seventh–sixth century B C. Cintas also ascribed a further piece of sculpture to a later period (third–second century) – this is a female figure seated on a throne enveloped in a veil and flanked by two sphinxes. More or less of the same epoch is a group of sculptures found at Leptis Magna: two male heads, one of which has a short beard; two male figures with a short tunic preserved from the neck to the knees; and two fragments of similar figures. Some torsos and fragments of statues in sandstone originating from Sabratha, in which Di Vita pointed out the traces of a more archaic Punic tradition, are also of Punic-Hellenistic epoch.

Although the remains of Punic statuary are scarce and doubtful, the cippi and stelae are very numerous, and appearn ot only in Carthage but in other cities, totalling several thousand, allowing us to undertake a large-scale study of this aspect of North African Punic art.

Beginning with the stelae of Carthage various strata, as we know, have been distinguished in the *topheth* of Carthage, and we can group the material found into two main categories: the first and earliest (seventh–sixth century B C), is characterized by cippi shaped like thrones, altars, and *naoi*; the second and most recent (fifth–second century) is characterized by stelae with triangular tips. This general typological subdivision incorporates a vast iconographical variety which we shall mention later.

The earlier cippi are blocks of limestone varying in height from thirty centimetres to one and a half metres. They are rough on three sides and worked on one side. The throne cippus consists of a parallelepiped base, usually surmounted by deep horizontal fluting forming Egyptian mouldings in which a solar disk may be inserted. Above the base rises the rear part of the back of the throne flanked by two arms; in the centre is a cavity intended to contain the divine image. The altar cippus is similar to the throne cippus, also usually having a back. It may have no arms, while the front part has two perfume-burners shaped like parallelepipeds contracting at the top; a central cavity is intended for the sacrificial urn or the betyl (fig 32). Finally, the *naos* cippus looks like a small chapel. The votive cella is dug in the base on which stands the idol. The cella is flanked by two pillars supporting a cornice with Egyptian mouldings (often with the solar disk in the centre), frequently surmounted by a frieze (figs 33, 34).

The Phoenician derivation of these cippi is evident. We have examined the votive shrine of Amrit (fig 2), but we must also recall the *naos* of Sidon, now in the Louvre (plate 2), which already contains the essential elements of the Carthaginian cippus, in other words the base surmounted by Egyptian mouldings, the cella, the pillars supporting the cornice (on which soars a winged solar disk), and the upper frieze with a series of uraei. The upper part of a second fragmentary *naos* of Sidon represents the characteristics of the former. Another important element of comparison is the stele from Burg Esh Shemali (plate 26). Of course, this entire production goes back to Egyptian models where the *naos* was widely used from an early date. So once more we note the Egyptian influence in Phoenician art and the subsequent spread of Egyptian elements and motifs in the Punic world.

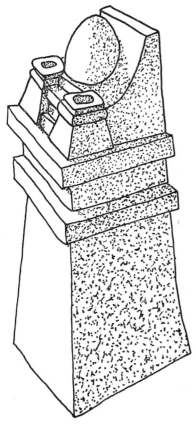

32   Scheme of altar-cippus

We now come to the iconography of the religious objects which are represented within the cellae of the *naos* cippi, and often within the mouldings that border the cellae themselves in one or more frames. To begin with we have the pillar-shaped betyls (plate 14), rectangular or slightly tapering at the top, single, double, or triple. The Phoenician stele from Burg Esh Shemali attests the Oriental prototype of this iconographical motif. Occasionally, but rarely, the pillars are surmounted by the solar disk and sometimes by the crescent moon pointing down. Other betyls are shaped like hexagons, lozenges (fig 33), and bottles (fig 34). We have already recorded the Phoenician prototype of this last motif discovered on a stele of Akziv (plate 22). From the B stratum of the *topheth* anthropomorphic motifs also appear, and in particular a naked figure with its arms to its sides and its legs stiffly joined standing between two pillar-shaped betyls or on an altar. In certain examples we see the *klaft*, or Egyptian wig, which immediately recalls the Oriental origin of the motif.

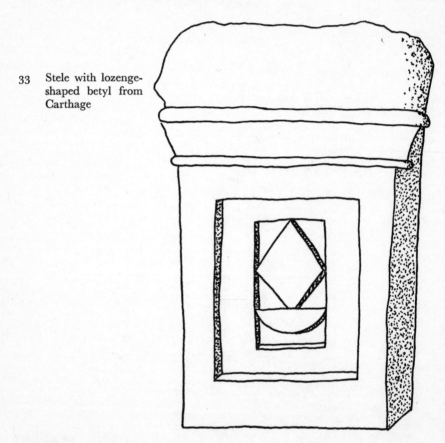

33   Stele with lozenge-shaped betyl from Carthage

The cippi diminish in the fifth century in correspondence to the beginning of the new period, while in this period the stelae with a triangular tip, sometimes flanked by two acroters, prevail. Besides eventual inscriptions, the stelae contain depictions partly familiar to us, like the solar disk (which frequently assumes a point in the centre) and the crescent moon (plate 19), or the bottle (often mounted on a base with Egyptian mouldings and integrated in the upper part with signs which tend to give it a human aspect (plate 30). In addition to these motifs, familiar even if elaborated, new ones appear, and amongst them the famous 'sign of Tanit' (plate 37), constituted by a triangle surmounted by a horizontal arm (rarely missing) and a disk. Long and complex studies have been devoted to this symbol, suggesting precedents in eastern monuments, but they are inconclusive (nor, for that matter, has Tanit any definite precedent in Phoenicia). It is also possible that the sign derives from the combination of formerly Oriental elements,

34 Stele with bottle-idol from Carthage

like the betyl and the solar disk. In any case, it assumes a definite aspect and undergoes considerable development in the Punic world, progressively turning into the anthropomorphic interpretation of a stylized female figure.

There are other iconographical motifs of the second phase of Oriental origin: the hand raised in prayer, which occurs in a celebrated stele from Hazor; the so-called Proto-Aeolic capital; and the palm tree. But the Greek world has now assumed an important part, with the Ionic

155

and Doric column, the caduceus, dolphin, birds, flower motifs, etc. Of the human elements, we have priests sacrificing (plate 38) and figures worshipping (plate 39); furthermore, as from the fourth century, we have numerous images of the dead on stelae on the tombs (plate 27).

In the third–second century BC the last and most active phase of stelae production took place in Carthage. These products are so clearly developed that we need not give a detailed account of them. On the whole, the decoration becomes far more complex. The geometrical motifs, used to compose dividing or border bands, fish spines, hoops, ovules, reticulae, and ivy leaves develop. In addition to the numerous vegetable motifs, animal motifs appear and spread (horses, panthers, rabbits (plate 55), swans, elephants, fishes, birds, frogs, cocks, ostriches, doves, rams, bulls). Certain liturgical objects are reproduced, such as offertory tables, jewel cases, vases, hatchets, knives, as well as chariots and ships. The human figures are infrequent but extremely interesting. There appear two types, mainly on the pediments: a standing figure, probably the offerer, holding a vase or a lotus leaf in one hand while he raises the other in prayer; and a naked boy seated on his left leg with his right leg folded under his body, evidently similar to the so-called *temple boy* of Cypriot origin. The main subjects of the stelae, on the other hand, are scenes of sacrifice, in addition to single figures, sometimes of Oriental aspect and sometimes Greek. In general this last phase of the *topheth* not only shows the appearance of new motifs but also a confusion and combination of pre-existing motifs in varied and unusual forms.

The North African locality to have supplied most stelae after Carthage is Sousse, the ancient Hadrumetum. The *topheth* of Sousse, excavated by Cintas, offers no material which can definitely be dated before the sixth century. So what we are left with corresponds to the second phase of Carthage. On the whole the iconographical motifs of Sousse are similar to those of Carthage (plate 28), although they do not lack particular elaborations (like the fluted columns enclosing betyls (plate 24), the sign of Tanit with hands raised, the distorted bottle, etc.), and certain lacunae (there is no lozenge idol, hand, or palm tree). But above all there are some isolated stelae typical of Sousse.

To begin with there is an interesting stele of the earlier period showing a worshipper confronting a god seated on a throne (fig 35). The god wears a tall conical crown and a long robe, and is on a larger scale than the worshipper. He raises one hand in blessing and holds a long spear in the other. The throne, with a high back, is flanked by winged sphinxes: despite the profile view the whole face of one sphinx is visible. The entire scene has typically Phoenician origins and the figure in the throne recalls numerous precedents, from the sarcophagus of Ahiram to the base of Fi.

Two other stelae from Sousse, both resembling each other, depict a female figure enveloped in a long robe and seated on a stool (fig 36). Her arms, supporting a sphere, are extended towards a brazier with a globe on top surmounted by the solar disk and crescent moon. Here, too, direct Phoenician models can be recalled, and the same can probably be said for a stele showing a betyl confronted by an altar and flanked, together with the altar, by two tall palm trees at the foot of which are two animals. This would seem to represent a typically Phoenician cult in the open air. Finally a frontal bust of Isis testifies Egyptian influence through Phoenician.

35 Stele with worshipper before a god from Susa

A third productive centre of Punic stelae was Cirta (Constantine). Here, however, the material is late, going no farther back than the third century, and is therefore of secondary interest. The stelae of Constantine, which display classical influence, are probably the earliest and are derived from Carthaginian models. This production has a local development in which the sign of Tanit is considerably humanized, holding in its hand the caduceus (plate 18) or a branch; there are also various types of arms, like helmets, shields, spears, swords, trumpets; leaves, rosettes, and palm trees, also abstracted; geometrical or astral symbols, including stars, a plain disk or a disk emitting rays, the crescent moon pointing up; animal figures like dolphins, rams, bulls and horses; and infrequent human representations including a frontal view of a seated deity (fig 37).

36   Stele depicting a
      woman from Susa

Here we should point out that the fall of Carthage did not in any way interrupt the production of the stelae. On the contrary, they flourished in the Neo-Punic period, at times showing the tenacious persistence of Punic motifs and at others the strong development caused by the Hellenistic-Roman environment. Maybe the most typical examples of this evolution are to be found in the celebrated stele from the Ghorfa (plate 25) in the second century AD characterized by the humanization of the pantheon: the dedicator is bordered at the base of the stele by the precinct of a temple, while the upper field of the stele shows various divine figures placed in an ascending position and converging towards the summit. Another large and significant group of Neo-Punic stelae comes from Dougga. While a part of them, going back to the second–first century BC, still show a series of Phoenician motifs in the upper field, others, going back to the first–second century AD, show clear developments particularly evident in the sign of Tanit: the disk is sometimes separated from the cross-arm, sometimes substituted by the crescent moon pointing up, and the arms become sometimes filiformed and

37   Stele depicting a deity from Constantine

159

produced beyond the curve, and the disk assumes the aspect of a human face (fig 38).

Having completed the study of the North African Punic cippi and stelae, we can pass on to certain conclusive considerations. In the first place the influence of the homeland is unquestionable: the typology clearly goes back to Phoenician models, and Phoenician are some iconographical motifs which persist throughout the ages, such as the

38   Stele with the humanized
     sign of Tanit from Dougga

aniconic betyls and the astral emblems. In the second place, the Egyptian influence is as predominant in Punic art as it is in Phoenician: the architectural frames are the most obvious example of this, as are some specific motifs like the uraeus, the winged solar disk, etc. In the third place, independent iconographical motifs emerge in Carthage, as is evident from the vastness and variety of the production, particularly in the animal and human motifs. In the fourth place, just as Phoenician art is the vehicle of multiple components, including non-Egyptian ones, we find some of these components in the Punic world, such as the palm tree and the hand; and most evident of all is the Cypriot influence which we get, for example, in the Proto-Aeolic capitals, the palmettes, and the *temple boy*. In the fifth place, the Greek influence, particularly in the final phase of the production, intervenes with decisive force and gives us the Ionic and Doric columns, the complex floral friezes, as well as certain divine figures.

In conclusion, the North African production of the cippi and stelae emerges as a development of the Phoenician production and absorbs its multiple components. Then, because of independent circumstances, it undergoes a notable development and lives a separate life consisting of new elements and influences, and a series of internal developments in which the conservatism typical of a peripheral area plays a certain part.

4 Sarcophagi

The typical Phoenician art of carving sarcophagi in relief, showing the image of the deceased on the upper part, was obviously imported from Egypt and submitted to Greek influence: in Carthage it finds its counterpart in a group of coffins in the necropolis of Ste Monique datable between the end of the fourth century and the beginning of the third century B C.

Of these sarcophagi the most Oriental in inspiration bears the flat-fronted image of a Carthaginian *rab*, Baalshillek (plate 12): the figure, with a long beard and flowing pleated robe going down to his feet, raises his right hand, while in his left he holds a bowl on a level with his chest. The coffin is on a very small scale, and must therefore really be considered a cinerary urn.

Two other sarcophagi, strongly resembling each other, show two priests, both bearded and clad in long tunics, holding bowls; one of the two has his head covered and wears a sort of stole. On the whole, Greek influence predominates in these figures.

A fourth sarcophagi is of special interest (plate 9). It represents a female figure wearing a tunic and enveloped from her hips down by two large wings which fold over each other – a motif taken from the Egyptian figures of Isis-Nephthys. Her head is clad in a scarf surmounted by a hawk's head – another typically Egyptian motif. Of the two arms the right lies by her side and the hand holds a dove-shaped incense-brazier, while her left arm is folded forward with a bowl in the hand. On the whole, in spite of the motifs of Egyptian origin which we have mentioned, the figure is typically Hellenistic.

Nine more sarcophagi complete the group of Ste Monique. They all show predominant Greek influence, indicated, besides the depictions, by the shape of the coffins – Greek temples with acroteria.

5 Terracotta figurines

While we will deal later with the typology of the pottery and its significance for Punic chronology, we will here mention the numerous animal
and human-shaped figurines made in terracotta which reveal artistic
or at least religious concepts (note the absence of the metal figurines so
widespread in Phoenicia and other parts of the Punic world). Of course,
in this sort of production, common to the whole of the Mediterranean,
it is not always easy to tell what was produced in North Africa from
what was imported.

It is certain that this production appears at Carthage from the earliest
times. On the lowest stratum of the precinct of Tanit a duck-shaped vase
was found which repeats a characteristically Oriental typology (plate
53). From the same level comes a crudely made figurine of great interest
because it anticipates a typology which we shall find in other regions of
the Punic West, and particularly in Bythia in Sardinia (plate 69).

There is an interesting vase from Douimes of the sixth century. It has
seven small receptacles shaped like tulips, with a cow's head surmounted
by a head of Hathor in the central front part: the inspiration is clearly
Egyptian, although it probably passed through Phoenicia. Similar
receptacles, but without the head of Hathor, come from Sardinia and
Ibiza.

After the sixth century a vast production of female figurines, partly
of Egyptian and partly of Greek origin, starts to spread. If the problem
of possible importations still exists (moulds could easily have been
imported to Carthage to imitate a local production), we can say that
the Egyptian figurines (plate 64) have the stiff aspect of mummies,
while the Greek ones (plate 65) are partly erect (distinguishable by their
head-dress, robe, and the dove or disk which they frequently hold
against their chest) and partly seated on a throne (characterized by the
tall crown or veil, and holding their hands on their knees).

This Greek type of production continues into the following centuries
with the usual phenomenon of provincial retardedness, while in Greece
new forms prevailed. But these new forms were, of course, also known
in North Africa: draped female figures with a fan, bearing a child or a
vase on their shoulder; dancers; players; figures at a banquet; deities
of Greek mythology; head-shaped perfume-burners (plate 104). Local
manufactories certainly existed, as is proved by the moulds and the
cast-offs found at Dermech.

In this period we also have Punic subjects: men with a cap and long
tunic; women in priestly garb in the act of prayer; and divine figures of
various imitation – a coarse and incoherent production, which does,
however, have its parallels in the rest of the Punic world.

6 Masks

Masks are another typical Carthaginian production in terracotta. They have Oriental antecedents, as can now be proved by the discovery of a mask of this kind in Hazor, going back to the late Bronze Age. They also have equivalents in other parts of the Punic world, in Ibiza, in Sardinia, and, according to the recent discoveries of the archaeological mission of the University of Rome, in Sicily.

The category of masks includes works which differ from each other considerably: on one side there are the female protomai with impassive or smiling faces, on the other male faces usually grimacing (grotesque masks). Both categories are slightly under life-size, while the masks of the second category are accompanied by smaller ones, like necklace pendants, of glazed terracotta, glass paste, ivory, and bone. So, if the categories and dimensions of the pieces generically described as masks are different, they do, however, have certain traits in common.

As to the function of these pieces, they cannot have been used as masks are now used, since they were too small to be worn. They may have been hung on the walls by the suspension holes, and were certainly placed in the tombs, where they had a protective function, either conciliating the evil spirits with the smile, or, more probably, frightening them away from the deceased with the grimace.

The female protomai recur in the earliest tombs of the seventh and sixth century. They are made mainly from moulds and subsequently daubed with pink and black. There are two main types, one under Egyptian and the other under Greek influence. In the first the head usually has a *klaft*; the face is impassive; the eyebrows are in relief and at right-angles to the line of the nose (plate 62). In the second type the head has a veil which leaves the ears free and hangs down the neck; the face is smiling, with large slanting eyes, a pointed nose, and arched eyebrows continuing the lines of the nose and jutting-out chin (plate 61).

Passing on to the grotesque masks, they also come from the earliest tombs of the seventh and sixth century. Cintas's accurate study has enabled us to distinguish various groups of which we shall enumerate the main characteristics. A first group presents a youthful beardless face, a squashed nose, holes for the eyes, and the mouth which is drawn up on one side (plate 72). A second large group presents an old but beardless face, heavy lines on the forehead and cheeks, crescent-shaped eye sockets, and large hole for the mouth turned high up on both sides (plate 73). A third group, similar to the second and perhaps a mere variant, is characterized by an oval crease surrounding the mouth, which is often smaller (plate 74). A fourth group hitherto consists of two isolated but very characteristic pieces: they are the only male faces which are not grimacing; a suspension ring is on the top of the head and the eyes are sculpted and not perforated (plate 75). Finally a fifth group consists of bearded Silenus faces, with pointed animal-like ears and small almost round eye-holes (fig 39). These examples are probably later than the preceding ones.

39   Silenus mask from Carthage

The earliest examples of the smaller necklace-pendant grotesque masks (seventh–sixth century) come from Dermech and faithfully repeat the motifs of the masks. Those of ivory, bone, and polychrome glass paste (the latter rare) are connected to the masks of the first group. Those of soft glazed siliceous paste, instead, resemble the fifth group, presenting the figures of running satyrs, devils, and Bes, as well as Silenus figures. At a later period the pendants differ still more from the models and can no longer be easily divided into groups (plate 91).

We now come to the subjects of these masks. The female protomai are probably divine images, so the apotropaic function would be non-existent or secondary, while the protective and votive function would be fundamental. The grotesque masks, on the other hand, probably represent demonic figures, in which the apotropaic function is always essential.

The grotesque masks have been compared to African masks, and this is undoubtedly justifiable, particularly when we think of the tattoos which accompany both types, but of which it is hard to judge the historical implications. Comparison with Greek masks, on the other hand, and especially with those of the sanctuary of Artemis Orthia in Sparta of the same epoch (seventh–sixth century), furnishes better results. Opinions differ, and the connexion between Punic and Greek masks is considered plausible by some and equally improbable by others. If there is a connexion, however, it is generally thought (particularly after the discoveries at Hazor) that the influence was exerted by the Phoenician-Punic production on the Greek and not vice versa.

7 Amulets

From the earliest times the Carthaginian tombs have been found to contain numerous amulets depicting on a small scale gods, animals, objects, and divine symbols. The amulets are made of porous, crumbly siliceous paste protected by enamel. They were cast in moulds, while the enamel was superimposed later. This material is of undoubtedly Egyptian inspiration and even, according to Vercoutter, of Egyptian origin, or imported to North Africa. Cintas, instead, accepts Egyptian origin for part of the material, but claims that the other part could have been produced in Carthage.

The most common figurative themes are the eye, *ujat* (plate 97), the uraeus, and the Ptah-Patechus (plate 98). We also have the hawk, Horus, Bes, and Thot. Less frequent, but repeatedly attested, are certain divine beings like Isis, Horus, Min, Khonsu, Shu, Khnum or Amon-Re, Sehkmet, Anubis, Tueris; certain animals (always connected with divine beings) like the monkey, the dog, the boar, the hare, the cat, the crocodile, the ibex, the lion, and the bull; and certain symbols like the *waj*, the crown of Upper Egypt, the heart, the hand, and the lotus flower.

The amulets of the seventh and sixth century are very frequent; they suddenly decrease in quantity in the fifth century, evidently in relation to the reforms of the period; they resume in the fourth and third century with less intensity and gradually disappear. The necropolises vary considerably in the amount of material yielded, probably because the amulets were widespread in the wealthier tombs (like those of the *rabs*), and rarer, because of their value, in the others.

Passing on to the origin of the amulets, Vercoutter has made certain interesting observations comparing the spread of types in Egypt and

Carthage. A significant parallel emerged both in the abundance and scarcity of documentation according to various periods, so it seems definite that most, but not necessarily all the material (as Vercoutter suggests) was imported. The siliceous paste was certainly worked at Carthage, as we saw with regard to the masks, and there is no reason to suppose that the working was limited exclusively to masks. The very fact that part of the production should be inferior seems to suggest local imitations of better-quality Egyptian models.

Before drawing general conclusions about this nature of the artistic production we must take into consideration a distinct category of amulets – the small cylindrical and octagonal metal tubes (plate 100), containing rolls of very fine metal engraved with depictions and sometimes brief inscriptions. The earlier tubes are mainly of gold and silver, the later ones of bronze or lead. On the tip of the tubes is reproduced the head of a divine Egyptian animal: those of gold and silver usually represent Sekhmet, and, less frequently, a hawk and a ram; while those of bronze or lead nearly always represent a ram.

Only metal rolls contained in the tubes have been found, because only metal is preservable. There are, in fact, three in gold, but we must assume that they existed both in other more perishable metals and in cloth and papyrus. Of the three rolls which have come down to us, the largest is twenty-seven centimetres long and 2·3 centimetres wide. It is divided into four registers, seven to four millimetres wide. In the registers, in close-spaced and minute relief, is a series of representations of Egyptian origin, inspired by magic texts; the frequency of serpents, lions, crocodiles, scorpions, and antelopes recalls the Egyptian texts against serpent bites. So the artist was well acquainted with Egyptian models; it is, however, dubious whether he was an Egyptian, and still more dubious whether the roll was imported from Egypt, since it has some inaccurate detail and a Punic inscription begging for protection which is closely connected to the engravings and seems contemporary. The other two golden rolls, which are smaller, present a partial but accurate repetition of scenes from the larger roll, thereby confirming the existence of a single text which served as a model for the engravings.

As to the general nature of the amulets, there is no doubt that the tubes had a magic purpose and were directly inspired by Egyptian magic. The same can be said of the other amulets which show certain significant signs. We note the pre-eminence of the *ujat* eye, the specific magic functions of which are well known, as well as the uraeus. In other words, the two types of amulets were not imported *en masse* by chance, but because of their magic qualities. This also applies to other types of amulet found at Carthage: Ptah is a particularly powerful god in magic, and the Pathecus shape gives him a special quality against the stings of scorpions and serpents. The other gods and animals reproduced on the amulets also have magic gifts, particularly against the bites of poisonous animals and the evil eye. Furthermore, the absence of typically funerary amulets, like scarabs of the heart, the four sons of Horus, etc, among the other amulets of Carthage, is equally significant.

So the amulets show a considerable development of superstition and magic in Carthage, as well as the extent of Carthaginian dependency from Egyptian beliefs from which a large number of the amulets originate.

8 Razors

Metal objects have obviously been found at Carthage and in Punic Africa, but they are usually vases, weapons, musical instruments, utensils of everyday life, and not works of art in the accepted sense of the term. Until now none of the bronze figurines which characterize Phoenician art in the East have been found.

On the other hand, one type of metal production appears in Carthage which is new, at least as far as Phoenician documentation is concerned: the so-called hatchet razors. Here again, however, the precedents are to be found in Egypt, where, as Vercoutter proved, the blades were moulded in the same way. The Carthaginian razor, however, lacks the metal handle of the Egyptian razor, and is characterized by a narrow stem in the shape of a bird's head. It must also be noted that the Egyptian razor never bears engravings, while the Punic one, especially at a later phase, has them in plenty. Finally, while the Egyptian influence in this type of artistic product seems evident, it does assume independent developments, the first of which is the use of the razor for religious purposes.

Gauckler accurately noted that the first razors appear in tomb 57 of Dermech and are ascribable to the second half of the seventh century BC. Although they do not appear previously, they appear from then on with remarkable frequency. The earliest razors have special characteristics: the largest represent a duck's bill, while the others are forked. The blades are mainly without decoration and those with decorations have *pointillé* as opposed to outlined engravings. Of fifty-one razors, Vercoutter observed, only ten are engraved, and of these four have fish on only one side of the blade, while the others have zigzags, dots, and palmettes.

With the fifth century we have a sudden decline of documentation, as it happens in other forms of artistic production. There are no decorations on the very few examples which have survived. In the fourth–third century, instead, the production resumes and increases rapidly, also assuming new characteristics. The forked form disappears and all the

167

razors assume a duck-billed stem, at the base of which is nearly always a large bird's wing. The blade is elegantly decorated with motifs which are rarely Greek, and frequently Egyptian or Phoenician-Punic.

As an example of Greek decoration we can cite the razors bearing figures of Heracles and Asklepios. The motifs which dominate the repertory of Egyptian origin are the Isis/Horus couple and the hawk on the lotus. Even the seemingly Punic motifs contain details of Egyptian origin, like the crown of Lower Egypt, the *ankh* sign, and the lotus flower. The main Punic motifs are the divine figures with conical head-dress and long robe, but even the gods not of this type show traces of Egyptian influence (plate 112).

We now come to the problem of the actual functions of these Punic razors. The lack of proper handles and the decorations exclude their usual practical use, so we are left with the possibility of ritual functions in general, or magical in particular. The suspension hole in the stem suggests a votive purpose, while the predominantly divine images point to a religious function. As Vercoutter observed, however, there is a way of formulating more precise observations. Not all the razors bear divine images, but there is, for instance, a razor from Byrsa which represents a bird catching a serpent on a squatting lion. This sort of example evidently suggests magical functions, so the divine images may also have some connexion with magic: hence the reappearance of the *ujat* eye already known from the amulets.

Although we have still to come to a conclusion about the purpose of the razors, we can say that they constitute the typically Punic develop-ment of objects which existed in Egypt, but which have assumed new functions, and that this development, with several iconographical aspects of its own, has a ritual and probably magical character.

9 Ivories

The working of ivory, so important in East Phoenicia, has sporadic parallels in Carthage, and it is hard to tell whether the pieces were produced locally or imported. In fact, it was not difficult for the Car-thaginians to procure ivory: the African elephant reserves rendered this easy in the West as well as in the East. But there is nothing in Carthage or North Africa comparable to the abundant productions of the Phoeni-cian homeland; and, of the Punic colonies in the West, it is undoubtedly Spain, with the celebrated series of the ivories of Carmona, which pre-vails in this type of production.

But there is no dearth of ivories in Carthage. Two mirror handles of the seventh century, coming respectively from a tomb on the hill of Juno (fig 40) and another tomb in the necropolis of Douimes, present a standing female figure with Egypticizing hair style, holding her breasts in her hands and clad in a long girdled robe ending in a fringe. We cannot tell whether these two pieces, which have precise parallels in Phoenician art, are local products or importations.

40   Ivory female figure
      from Carthage

Another typical ivory object is the comb. One, again from the hill of Juno in Carthage, ascribed to the sixth century, bears a dove perched on a squatting sphinx before lotus plants engraved on one side, and a bull with lotus plants on the other (fig 41). The semicircular nicks on the edge reappear on the combs of Carmona and provide an interesting typological parallel. It is, of course, impossible to know whether the production of combs is local or imported.

41   Ivory with sphinx and bull from Carthage

10 Jewellery

Goldwork played an important part in Carthage, as literary sources prove. We learn of the offering of crowns, of golden fittings for the shrines, and silverwork. The gold came from the African interior, the silver from southern Spain, and some ready-made objects may have been imported.

At this point we must observe that numerous objects already mentioned or about to be mentioned could be classed as jewels, such as the masks of small format, the amulets, and scarabs frequently pierced or strung like necklace beads. But there are certain objects which can only be classified as jewels, and we shall deal with these now. From the seventh to sixth century the tombs of Carthage provide silver rings with scarabs set in gold; plain gold bracelets with one or two spirals, or engraved with decorations like palmettes and scarabs; small round golden plaques decorated with the winged solar disk or flanked by uraei; a vase flanked by uraei; the crescent moon with or without solar disk, or inscriptions; ear-rings and trinkets shaped like half-moons, often with pendants; gold or silver diadems; nose- and ankle-rings, mostly of silver; and pearls of various types and shapes, pierced to be strung on necklaces (plate 93). On the whole, this production denotes prevalently Egyptian influence, probably transmitted by Phoenicia, where a similar production was already widely established.

After this early phase of production, there was, as always, a later one in which Greek influence appeared and affirmed itself. Here there are some doubts as to the origin of certain objects, although there are indications that the art persisted locally, such as the appearance and spread of the sign of Tanit.

11 Scarabs

Several hundred scarabs and scaraboids, found in the Carthaginian tombs, prove the particular importance of these objects among the funerary offerings: they were sometimes the only objects, apart from the ritual vases, to accompany the deceased.

We can distinguish scarabs of glazed paste, jasper, and cornelian, while lapis lazuli, agate, rock crystal, and basalt are less frequent. If we consider the distribution of these elements through the various phases, we see that scarabs of glazed paste are predominant in the first phase (seventh–sixth century), while those of jasper and cornelian prevail in the second (fourth century); here, as elsewhere, the fifth century is badly documented.

This clear distinction in time and frequency corresponds to another intrinsic differentiation. All the characteristics of the scarabs of glazed paste suggest Egyptian make (plate 90): subject-matter, form, technique of engravure, hieroglyphic inscriptions ultimately accompanied by a divine figuration. Furthermore, they appear and disappear independently from the development and decadence of the corresponding types in Egypt. In particular, most of the examples from Carthage are similar to those found by Petrie at Naucratis, while in other examples the prevalence of figurations with Ptah and Sekhmet seems to suggest origin from Memphis. Finally, according to Vercoutter's analysis, the scarabs of glazed paste of the earliest period (seventh–sixth century) were imported directly from Egypt.

The situation is different for the jasper and cornelian scarabs which predominate in the later period (fourth century). Starting with the jasper scarabs, the shape is no longer quite the same as the Egyptian. And the figurative motif can be both Graecizing and Egypticizing. The Egypticizing themes are the god Bes in various shapes and attitudes (frequently fighting with a lion); the hawk Horus preceded by a uraeus; Isis both in human shape with Horus and in the shape of a cow giving milk; and the sphinx, generally winged and squatting. The Graecizing motifs are human heads in profile, warriors in action, deities, animals attacking their prey; and various animals. These Graecizing motifs prevail, as is natural, in the later period of the production. On the whole, there is no question here of an Egyptian make, but rather of an imitation of Egyptian models. The excavations in Sardinia have recently brought to light a vast quantity of green jasper scarabs, corresponding typologically and iconographically to those described above. It is to Sardinia, therefore, that the origin of this production has been traced, and both Phoenician-Punic and Greek craftsmen probably contributed.

The scarabs of cornelian and other materials parallel the diffusion of the jasper scarabs. They are earlier, however, and apart from establishing themselves in the fourth century, they are to be found in a limited quantity in the seventh and sixth century. Here, too, we can distinguish Egypticizing and Graecizing motifs, but there are more of the former. Of these we have Bes, Isis and Horus, Horus (or Ra) in the shape of a god with a hawk's head, and the sphinx with and without wings. The Graecizing motifs are human heads in profile, warriors, the lion chasing an antelope, the scorpion, together with a few other subjects less easy to interpret. According to Vercoutter the examples of the seventh–sixth century were probably imported from Phoenicia, while those of the fourth were produced in Sardinia together with the jasper scarabs.

We must remember that, with the end of the fifth century, the scarab was no longer made in Egypt. A large quantity of scarabs were probably directly imported from Egypt in the seventh and sixth centuries, although some (like those of cornelian) suggest Phoenician origin. After the crisis of the fifth century, when Egyptian production ceased, the Carthaginians continued to use scarabs, to which they evidently attributed great value. Since they could no longer import them from Egypt, they now imported them from Sardinia, where a notable local production had developed with its own characteristics (in particular the use of jasper and cornelian instead of glazed paste). It is probable that the scarabs owed their importance to predominantly magical attributions.

12 Further 'minor' products

A typical and widespread Carthaginian product, for which we know no Phoenician antecedents (maybe because the objects were perishable), is that of decorated ostrich eggs. They were made into bowls and vases, painted in red or black or engraved with geometric designs, palmettes, lotus flowers, animal images, or even human faces, probably serving an apotropaic purpose. In Carthage ostrich eggs appear, however infrequently, in the seventh century, abound in the sixth, then diminish, and recur frequently in the third and disappear in the second. Apart from the vases, there are many fragments adapted as small masks, with the essential features of a painted face (plate 75). Other examples of this singular production are found again in North African localities (Djidjelli, Gouraya), in Spain (Sexi, Villaricos), in Ibiza, Sardinia, and Sicily.

A few words must also be said about glass production. Although many objects already mentioned are made of this material, such as the masks, amulets, jewels, and scarabs, the small and elegant flasks shaped like amphorae, made of dark blue glass with added trails in a lighter colour, are peculiar to Carthage. The process of manufacture, studied by Gauckler, indicates designs on the inside of the paste with successive trails of colour (yellow, lemon, white, turquoise) applied to the warm and sticky shell. Other small vases are shaped like the ox Apis or a squatting monkey. It is probable that this production originated at least partially from Phoenicia.

The first Punic coins were struck in Sicily at the end of the fifth century to pay the mercenaries of Carthage on the island. They are gold coins on the Phoenician standard or silver tetradrachms on the Attic. The inscriptions bear the names of Motya, Panormus, and other Sicilian towns, as well as Carthage and 'the camp', or the headquarters. On the obverse was a head of Tanit in the guise of Persephone, on the reverse a horse, a lion, or a palm tree. Coins were not struck directly in Carthage before the fourth century – they were on the Phoenician standard, in gold, electrum, and bronze, and bore the motifs of the horse and the palm tree (plates 101, 102). When, at the end of the third century, Hamilcar gained possession of the mines in Spain, silver coins were also struck in Carthage. Finally, in the last years of Carthage, there was a prevalence of bronze coins, which have been found in places as far apart as Britain and the Canary Islands, and provide significant evidence of Carthaginian diffusion.

In conclusion we can mention the remains of painting that have come to light in the tombs of Djebel Mlezza: the subjects of these simple and dissociated exercises in elementary compositions are a building or a mausoleum, an altar, a cock, a city, and certain geometric motifs. The artists used a solution of ochre, outlining the figures directly on to the rock.

13 Pottery

A great quantity of pottery has come from the Carthaginian shrines and tombs. It was undoubtedly exported, because it has exact parallels in other parts of the Punic world (Spain, Sicily, Sardinia), and potters' workshops have been brought to light near the port of Dermech, so we can consider the means of manufacture directly.

The main clay pits were north of the necropolises and provided a reddish material of excellent quality. The Punic potters worked with crude wheels on which the large loaves of clay were modelled. They were then baked in a coarse brick oven consisting of a central pillar and a high cylindrical chimney. In general we can say that the production was strictly utilitarian, contrasting with the elegant foreign pottery of which there is no dearth in Carthage and which constitutes a valuable element for chronological purposes.

The earliest pottery of Carthage (plate 103) presents familiar Phoenician forms, like the mushroom-lipped and trefoil-lipped jugs which appear towards the end of the eighth century and continue until the beginning of the sixth. This pottery has the familiar burnished red colour which has already been mentioned in the East and which also characterizes the earlier Punic crockery in other parts of North Africa and Spain. Another early form of possible Oriental origin is the *chardon* vase with a long broadened lip. There are further types from Carthage of the same period with a more or less globular body and small horizontal or vertical handles; they often have a ring half-way up the neck. This category of vase usually has a painted linear design of horizontal bands on the body and 'triglyphs and metopes' on the shoulders. The jugs with a single handle between the lip and the bulge, on the other hand, have no design. The lamps are of a fairly large type with two open beaks (plate 107) and a band lip. A lamp with seven beaks found in Utica in an eighth-century tomb is interesting because it is archaic and the only one of its sort. There are also certain examples with an umbilicated saucer. The large amphorae are more or less biconical, with square shoulders and no neck.

The mushroom-lipped and trefoil-lipped jugs do not seem to go as far as the fifth century in Carthage, during which the *oinochai* with a cylindrical neck of maybe Corinthian origin came into fashion. The vases with painted designs continue with later variations, together with a two-handled urn with a lengthened swollen body narrowed in the centre or at the top. The lamps continue with the same forms but gradually reduced dimensions.

After the fourth century the crockery of Carthage changes considerably in shape and decoration and appears very influenced by Hellenistic culture. The typical lamps and trefoiled *oinochai* continue with later forms. Large groups of pots and jugs, with spouts and beaks on which painted designs develop, appear, probably under the influence of Egyptian Hellenism. The amphorae become shorter with a thick stem lengthened at the base.

Towards the final phase of the Hellenistic period these types are joined by others current throughout the Mediterranean, like the tapering ointment jars and the cups the shapes of which are connected with the black-glazed products of southern Italy. Certain typical Punic forms, such as the lamps, still exist.

CHAPTER 12

ECONOMY AND TRADE

1 Economy

The economic life of Carthage constitutes an excellent guide to the continuity and development of Phoenician civilization in the West. This even applies to the territorial premisses, because the Carthaginians, like the Phoenicians in the East, worked on a restricted territory and developed similar forms of economy within it. It is not always easy to prove whether the Phoenicians imported their own methods of cultivation directly or whether they developed local forms already in existence, as they had done in their homeland. But on the whole the analogy between East and West remains and is one of the most characteristic connexions between the two sides of the Phoenician world.

In the territory of Carthage we must make a distinction. The zone lying closest to the capital was directly cultivated by the Punic settlers. During the expeditions of Agathocles and Atilius Regulus the sources describe this very fertile region where the wealthy Carthaginians had vines, olive groves, orchards, and pastures.[1] Beyond this region, farther inland, was an area cultivated by the Libyans, who remained in possession of their land at the price of heavy tributes. The zone produced mainly grain, of which a percentage went to Carthage.

The importance attached by the Carthaginians to the cultivation of their fields is attested by the accounts of treatises which they wrote on the subject. The best-known authors are Hamilcar and Mago. Through Latin tradition we are acquainted with a series of passages from the latter, and thereby get a glimpse of otherwise unknown Carthaginian literature. From the technical point of view, of course, Mago was not exempt from criticisms from the earliest times. In the first century AD Columella writes: 'Other precepts of husbandry are not to be concealed from the tiller of the soil; and while Punic writers from Africa have handed them down in large numbers, yet many of them are assailed as erroneous by our farmers.'[2]

Anyhow, it is probable that Mago, who lived around the time of the Punic Wars, helped himself to Greek sources. But these reservations do not diminish the interest of the quotations with which we are left.

Starting with the cultivation of cereals, we know that grain and barley were largely cultivated in North Africa by the natives. And, as long as they were partially in the possession of Carthage, Sicily and Sardinia also provided grain in abundance. We have few details about the methods of cultivation, but the stelae depict the type of plough used, which was made of wood, had no wheels and was drawn by oxen. It is interesting that this plough should be similar both to the one used in ancient Israel and in modern North Africa. A harvesting machine mentioned by Varro,[3] called *plostellum punicum*, must also have been of Carthaginian origin. It was a sort of wooden sled with dented rollers which may have had remote Eastern antecedents, to judge from certain modern analogies as well as a passage from St Jerome about Palestine.[4] The grain was gathered in store-houses and silos, which were frequently subterranean, and must have been introduced to North Africa and the West by the Carthaginians.

We now pass on to the vine and the olive, the most characteristic crops of the Phoenician-Punic world, on which the Carthaginians concentrated in the countryside surrounding the capital. It was a point of honour to cultivate one's own property personally, and Mago even made a precept of it in his treatise:

'One who has bought land should sell his town house, so that he will have no desire to worship the household gods of the city rather than those of the country; the man who takes greater delight in his city residence will have no need of a country estate.'[5]

The manual labour was mainly performed by slaves. Mago recommends interesting them in their work and according them privileges, by allowing them to save up enough money to purchase their liberty and form a family. He explicitly states that this should be done not for reasons of humanity but to get more out of the human tools.[6]

The vine and the olive were cultivated by the Phoenician settlers with special care; and it is probable, even though it is not certain, that they imported the cultivation to North Africa. Some quotations from Mago[7] indicate the Punic method of cultivating the vine: to have the vineyards facing north in order to avoid the heat as much as possible; to plant the vines in trenches scattered with stones to protect the roots from water in the winter and from the heat in the summer; not to fill the whole trench at once, but to do it gradually, from year to year, in order to push the roots deeper into the ground; to manure the plants with sediment of grapes and dung. Mago also gives us precepts on grape harvesting, which he thinks should be done in the spring rather than in the autumn,[8] and recipes for making good wine. That lime should be added to the must, as Pliny says,[9] might simply have been a device to sweeten the wine and not a system in general use (Pliny writes at a much later period). Although it is certain that the Carthaginians traded in wine, it is not sure whether they exported their own. According to Diodorus, they actually received it from Agrigentum in the fifth century.[10]

It is related that Hannibal filled a large part of Africa with olive groves, putting his soldiers to work on them in order to prevent them from idling. Whether or not this is true, it does indicate the spread of the olive at the time of the Punic Wars. But the cultivation was earlier: the Carthaginians probably took grafts from the wild olives and planted new ones together with them.[11] Plantation must have taken place in the autumn, and the trees placed about twenty-two metres apart (a similar spacing has recently been observed in certain Tunisian regions). Pliny's claim[12] that certain olives were taken as landmarks because they produced a thousand pounds of oil a year is evidently exaggerated, but it does indicate the fertility of the North African olive groves. Oil, like wine, was also imported from Agrigentum,[13] and this again seems to indicate that the local production was of high quality rather than quantity.

An abundant production of fruit accompanied that of wine and oil. It was probably the Phoenicians who imported figs to North Africa, or at any rate those good qualities which they assumed. To prove how close they were to Carthage and urge his fellow citizens to the attack Cato allegedly showed them fruits which were still fresh. In any case, Cato and other authors praise the qualities of the 'African figs' in their treatises.

Equally appreciated in Rome was the North-African pomegranate, called the *mala punica*. Columella quotes a series of recipes from Mago for the conservation of this fruit, such as storing it in clay or sawdust.[14] It is probable that this cultivation was also imported from Phoenicia, and, unlike other products, it was exported and certainly reached Italy.

The date-palm was widespread, as is proved by the frequent depictions on the stelae and coins. The best fruit, however, did not come from the coastal regions, where the palm flourished (particularly between the two Syrtes), but from the hinterland and the oases, although we are still uncertain whether Carthaginian control extended this far.

Certain precepts of Mago[15] concern the planting of the almond tree, its season and the best way to improve its quality. The walnut and the pear tree may also have been cultivated, but the diffusion of these plants was considerably smaller. There were, of course, vegetables like cabbages, thistles, garlic, peas, and lentils, and Dioscorides[16] mentions medicinal African plants frequently bearing a Semitic name. The main industrial plant was flax.

Stock-raising was widespread. Polybius writes:

For the number of horses, oxen, sheep, and goats in the country is so large that I doubt if so many could be found in the rest of the world, because many of the African tribes make no use of cereals but live on the flesh of their cattle and among their cattle.[17]

In fact, stock-raising was most widespread among the nomads living on the borders of the cultivated land, and Carthage undoubtedly had dealings with them, allowing them access to Carthaginian territory in the dry seasons and using their livestock in exchange. To start with, the horses, which occasionally appear on Punic coins, were probably a local breed ultimately improved by cross-breeding. Then there were the particularly strong Barbary mules, about which Mago gives us further information.[18]

But above all Mago writes at length about the oxen, and his famous description is quoted by many authors:

The bullocks which should be purchased are those which are young, squarely built, with large limbs and horns which are long and blackish and strong; the forehead should be wide and covered with curly hair, the ears shaggy, the eyes and lips dark in colour, the nostrils bent back and wide spreading, the neck long and muscular, the dewlap ample and falling almost to the knees, the chest broad, the shoulders huge; the belly should be capacious and have the appearance of pregnancy, the flanks extended, the loins wide, the back straight and flat or even sinking slightly, the buttocks round, the legs compact and straight but short rather than long and the knees not ill-shaped, the hoofs large, the tail very long and bristly, the hair all over the body thick and short and of a red or brindle colour and the body very soft to the touch.[19]

Rams are reproduced on the votive stelae and resemble the type with long thick tail now so common in Tunisia. The fowl were cocks, hens, doves, pigeons, all frequently depicted on the stelae. The bees were particularly important, and famed for their honey and wax, called *cera punica* by the Latin authors and used for medical purposes. The Carthaginians also used elephants, but only in war, and camels were unknown.

A typical industry of the Punic West was that of salting fish. The production of the *garum* earned Cadiz fame throughout the classical world, and the entire zone round Cadiz has yielded remains of factories. The same applies to North Africa, as has been proved by the recent finds on the north-western coast of Morocco. The saltworks which developed in the area of Punic dispersion were closely connected with the industry of salting fish.

The wide development of craftsmanship in Carthage is shown by the votive stelae. Mentioning the various trades of the dedicators, they indicate that they were not slaves but free citizens. There were specialized metalworkers who primarily served the armed forces, but also produced domestic articles, as is proved by the objects found in the tombs – knives, forks, scissors, strigils, and mirrors. And there were plenty of vases, particularly of bronze and sometimes decorated, bowls, plates, and lamps. The razors and the objects made of precious stones have already been mentioned in the chapters on art.

The textile industry was of great importance, and here again there is an essential link with the Phoenician homeland. To start with there was a private family industry, but the inscriptions also speak of professional weavers, and we can assume that factories existed. Cushions, carpets, and Carthaginian embroidery are said by the ancient authors to have been of particular quality, while the industry of purple dye was imported from Phoenicia and expanded: heaps of murex shells have been found in various North African localities, and the island of Djerba was famed for its dye.

In Africa the Phoenicians again found the cedars which had rendered their homeland famous. Their skill as carpenters, in building and repairing ships, was acclaimed by all; and Latin terms like *fenestrae punicanae* and *lectuli punicani* show the particular talent which the Carthaginians must also have had for the manufacture of furniture and fittings. The tombs have provided numerous lids of coffins, and the depictions on the stelae show us that the instruments used included hammers, pliers, hatchets, and squares.

The potters, glassmakers, goldsmiths, and other types of craftsmen have already been mentioned in the chapter on art; so finally we can say that the production was intensive, mostly dependent on commercial demands, but on the whole lacking particular originality.

2 Trade

Carthaginian trade continued, developed and established the policy inaugurated by the Phoenician cities on a Mediterranean level. There is a collection of anecdotes about the type of the Carthaginian merchant: resourceful, wily, and unscrupulous, he seems to be the natural predecessor of the more recent 'Levantine'. Of the various portraits, Plautus's merchant in *Poenulus* is possibly the most characteristic, but apart from these anecdotes one fact distinguishes this merchant of antiquity from his successors: he was supported by a powerful state and therefore combined personal initiative with the reflection of a general policy which was one of the most potent forces in the ancient Mediterranean basin.

Carthage's trade was deliberate policy, and Gsell's definition of it is still the most valid:

(The aim of the Carthaginians was) . . . to open markets by force or by treaties or by the foundation of colonies; to reserve exploitation in countries where it was possible to avoid all competition; to regulate the transactions through agreement stipulating reciprocal advantages in countries where this monopoly could not be established; and to ensure navigation, the cities and the maritime trading-posts against piracy.[20]

The basic principle of Carthage, and even her origin, can be seen in her capacity to trace and exploit the metal routes. According to Diodorus Siculus,[21] the Phoenicians discovered the silver mines in Spain and realized that the natives did not fully appreciate their value. So they founded a series of trading-posts, the last of which was Cadiz, to control the traffic of the precious metals which they acquired in exchange for goods of little value and resold in the East on very different terms. This situation has been rightly compared to that of the Spanish and Portuguese *conquistadores* in America: they both made a fortune by connecting two worlds where precious metals had totally different values.

But if the silver of Spain was an important element of Phoenician and Punic commercial policy, it was not the only one. Another metal which the Phoenicians discovered in the West, and of which they assumed control, was tin, extracted from mines in places as distant as northwestern Spain and Great Britain.

With the gold from the African interior we complete the picture of Phoenician metal traffic, a necessary premiss for understanding the historical development of Carthage. Starting as a trading centre in the West, she ended by assuming increasing independence and finally becoming in her turn the centre of the complex widespread commercial activity which we have described. This activity was not limited to metals, but covered all Phoenician-Punic crafts as well as crafts of other nations which the Phoenicians could propagate. But the metal routes between the East and West were the basic cause of the prodigious development of Phoenician and later Punic trade in the Mediterranean.

The history of Carthage illustrates the events which accompanied this commercial policy. The conquests in Sardinia, Sicily, Africa, and Spain, as well as the creation of colonies up to the shores of the Atlantic ocean were the political instruments. The Carthaginians wished to install trading-posts everywhere – some isolated in unconquered lands and others to conquer the surrounding area with the basic purpose of ensuring protection. War was continually necessary to protect the trading-posts and the communications, so a strong naval force was built which brought Carthage to the zenith of her power in the fourth century.

But colonization and war were constantly being checked by a diplomacy intended to define the rights and conditions of commerce. As far as the Etruscans were concerned, Aristotle[22] informs us that they not only had political alliances with the Carthaginians but also commercial treaties concerning importations. And thanks to Polybius we are particularly well informed about the treaties with Rome, in which the conditions concerning the control of the trade routes and trading-posts are pre-eminent. Piracy was also controlled by the treaties, so that what was legally forbidden by the agreements could not be illegally performed.

The only surprising fact in so circumspect an organization as that of Carthaginian trade is the lateness of striking coins. As we know, this did not take place before the fifth century in Sicily and the fourth century in Carthage. Admittedly, many of the lands to which the Punic settlers sailed would not have accepted coins in view of the retarded and primitive conditions of their commercial activity; but there is no doubt that the late introduction of money played an important part in the decline of Carthaginian trade.

The main Punic imports were metal, one of the main sources of Carthaginian commerce, and slaves, sometimes captured by piracy. Foodstuff was also obtained from the colonies, and we have seen how Sardinia provided grain, and Sicily grain, wine, and oil. In exchange Carthage followed the Phoenician tradition by exporting cloth dyed purple, carpets, jewels and small ornamental objects, amulets, decorated ostrich eggs, glass, arms and metal utensils, crockery, and perfumes. Of course, Carthage often acted as intermediary for the merchandise of other nations. So Greek objects found their way to the West through the Carthaginian merchants, and the abundance of foreign material in Carthage, like the Egyptian and Egypticizing material found among the funerary objects, implies intensive importation from Greece and, still more, from Egypt.

To increase her commercial expansion Carthage promoted a series of long voyages, which constitute a major chapter in the history of exploration. These voyages were also the result of a policy initiated by the Phoenicians with the circumnavigation of Africa c. 600 B C on the orders of the Pharaoh Necho.

The first major voyage was undertaken by Himilco, who sailed up the Atlantic coast of Spain and France as far as the British Isles c. 450 B C. We have incomplete and scanty information about this journey from the quotations from earlier Greek sources given by Avienus in the fourth century in his geographical poem *Ora maritima*. It is certain that Himilco wanted to follow the tin route to its remotest sources and that he visited Ireland after coasting the whole of western Europe.

Hanno's voyage along the Atlantic coast of Africa c. 425 B C is better known. Hanno himself had an account of it engraved on a stele in the temple of Baal Hammon, and our knowledge is based on a Greek version of this account (with certain alterations). In other words, we have a Punic text, even if it is adapted, and here is its translation:

This is the story of the long voyage of Hanno king of the Carthaginians into Libyan lands beyond the Pillars of Heracles, which he dedicated on a tablet in the temple of Kronos:

I The Carthaginians decided that Hanno should sail beyond the Pillars of Heracles and found cities of Libyphoenicians. He set sail with sixty pente-conters and about thirty thousand men and women, and provisions and other necessaries.

II After sailing beyond the Pillars for two days we founded the first city which we called Thymiaterion. Below it was a large plain.

III Sailing thence westward we came to Soloeis, a Libyan promontory covered with trees. There we founded a temple to Poseidon.

IV Journeying eastward for half a day we reached a lake not far from the sea, covered with a great growth of tall reeds, where elephants and many other wild animals fed.

V A day's journey beyond this lake we founded cities on the coast called Karikon Teichos, Gytte, Akra, Melitta, and Arambys.

VI Passing on from there we came to the large river Lixos, flowing from Libya, beside which nomads called Lixitae pastured their flocks. We stayed some time with them and became friends.

VII Inland from there dwelt inhospitable Ethiopians in a land ridden with wild beasts and hemmed in by great mountains. They say that the Lixos flows down from there and that among these mountains Troglodytes of strange appearance dwell, who according to the Lixitae can run more swiftly than horses.

VIII Taking interpreters from the Lixitae we sailed south along the desert shore for two days and then for one day eastward and found a small island five stades (about one km.) in circumference at the farther end of a gulf. We made a settlement there and called it Cerne. We judged from our journey that it was directly opposite Carthage, for the voyage from Carthage to the Pillars and from there to Cerne seemed alike.

IX From here sailing up a big river called Chretes we reached a lake, in which were three islands bigger than Cerne. Completing a day's sail from here we came to the end of the lake, overhung by some very high mountains crowded with savages clad in skins of wild beasts, who stoned us and beat us off and prevented us from disembarking.

X Sailing from there we came to another big wide river, teeming with croco-diles and hippopotamuses. We turned again from there and came back to Cerne.

XI We sailed south for twelve days from there, clinging to the coast, which was all along occupied by Ethiopians who did not stay their ground, but fled from us. Their speech was unintelligible, even to our Lixitae.

XII On the last day we came to anchor by some high mountains clad with trees whose wood was sweet-smelling and mottled.

XIII Sailing round these for two days we reached an immense gulf, on either shore of which was a plain where by night we saw big and little fires flaming up at intervals everywhere.

XIV Taking on water here, we sailed on for five days along the coast until we came to a great bay which our interpreters called the Horn of the West. In it was a large island and in the island a salt-water lake, within which was another island where we disembarked. By day we could see nothing but a forest, but by night we saw many fires burning and we heard the sound of flutes and of beating of cymbals and drums and a great din of voices. Fear came upon us and the soothsayers bade us leave the island.

XV We sailed thence in haste and skirted a fiery coast replete with burning incense. Great streams of fire and lava poured down into the sea and the land was unapproachable because of the heat.

XVI We left there hurriedly in fear and sailing for four days we saw the land by night full of flames. In the middle was a high flame taller than the rest, reaching, as it seemed, the stars. By day it was seen to be a very high mountain called the Chariot of the Gods.

XVII Thence sailing for three days past fiery lava flows we reached a gulf called the Horn of the South.

XVIII At the farther end of this bay was an island, like the first, with a lake, within which was another island full of savages. By far the greater number were women with shaggy bodies, whom our interpreters called Gorillas. Chasing them we were unable to catch any of the men, all of whom, being used to climbing precipices, got away, defending themselves by throwing stones. But we caught three women, who bit and mangled those who carried them off, being unwilling to follow them. We killed them, however, and flayed them and brought their skins back to Carthage. For we did not sail farther as our supplies gave out.[23]

So ends this account, unique of its sort, of the process of colonization and exploration characteristic of the Punic people. It has long been observed that the Greek translation contains inaccuracies, which may even have been intentional, in order not to reveal the routes and landing-stages of Punic diffusion in North Africa. It has also been suggested that the account is largely a literary exercise based on dubious authenticity. There are, however, certain possible identifications: the river Lixos with the Draa and the Lixitae with the Berbers; the Ethiopians with the negroes; Cerne with an island near the mouth of the Senegal (Chretes in the account). Here the colonies end and the more questionable part of the journey begins: according to some it ended in

Sierra Leone, and according to others (which is more likely) it ended in the Cameroons or Gabon.

The reason for Hanno's voyage, and for Punic colonization in general along the African coast beyond the Pillars of Hercules, is once again the search for precious metal, this time gold. And it was gold that induced the Carthaginians to cross the caravan routes of the Sahara. Athenaeus[24] writes with evident exaggeration that a certain Mago crossed the desert three times without drinking. The desert must really have been crossed by the Carthaginians, who had good intermediaries for their trade with the African interior, like the Garamantes, who lived in what is now Tripolitania, and the Gaetulians, who lived farther west.

Finally the Phoenicians probably got as far as Madeira, the Canary Islands, and the Azores in the Atlantic. Diodorus[25] tells that a ship from Cadiz, lost in the ocean, landed on a large island with an excellent climate, possibly Madeira? The Etruscans, adds Diodorus, wished to found a colony there, but the Carthaginians prevented them. The position of the Canary Islands suggests that they were known to the Phoenicians, but we have no direct proof. Eight Punic coins of the third century BC were found in 1749 on Corvo Island in the Azores.

CHAPTER 13

SCRIPT AND LANGUAGE

1 Script

The script and language of the Punic world provide an interesting indication of the continuity and development of Phoenician culture in its transplantation from the East to the West. We can observe the strong conservative force of both the script and the language, and the establishment of the developments, which obviously exist, on essentially internal lines resulting from the detachment from the homeland and contact with a new environment.

Starting with the script, we note the survival of a clearly Phoenician type of archaic aspect, with broad, massive signs, throughout the early period, and especially on the islands. It has been attested in Sardinia, and Malta, and in various Carthaginian texts of the sixth century, although in a slightly less archaic form.

If the script hitherto described can be called Phoenician, it is paralleled by the development of the actual Punic script with elongated, slightly curved characters, which appears to be the official script in Carthage and the Punic empire until 146 BC. After this date it continues for a brief period in the monumental inscriptions of the African princes, and appears sporadically on the coins, but is generally substituted by so-called Neo-Punic script.

That Neo-Punic script was in current use long before 146 is proved by certain inscriptions, and above all by the fact that some votive stelae bear the ritual dedicatory formula in Punic, but add information about the dedicator in Neo-Punic, evidently because the engraver was only familiar with the current system.

We are not going to examine the characteristics of Neo-Punic, which vary according to time and place. We can simply say that it is a cursive derivation of Punic, characterized by a notable evolution in the form of many letters and a strong schematization often leading to confusion. For example, it is often hard to distinguish between the letters *b*, *d*, and *r*, represented in the later period by simple vertical strokes.

2 Language

Like the script, the Punic language is a continuation of Phoenician. The differences between both languages are minimal, although the official language is accompanied by a vulgar form in which the differences increase, and the later official texts present further autonomous traits differing from the ancient texts. In each case the language seems to have developed on essentially internal lines.

Starting with the consonantal system, Punic shows a progressive weakening, followed by a crisis, in the pharyngeal and laryngeal series. While official documents tend to follow the historic spelling, the vulgar inscriptions indicate a tendency to reduce all the consonants of the two series, and a subsequent free graphical exchange or a dropping, indicating a realization which is no longer perceptible.

Other less evident uncertainties are also peculiar to the Punic consonantal system: the articulation of *d* and *l* is sometimes weak, and causes droppings, like *Bomilkar* for *Bodmilkar* and *mochomor* for *molchomor*; in late Punic we also note oscillations within the sibilant and liquid-nasal series, as well as emphatics and non-emphatics.

Vulgar Punic has important developments of the initial double and doubled consonants, and vocalic registration; and here we have clear divergences from the basic Semitic norms. The initial double consonants, which Semitic avoids through prostheses or anaptictic means because they are contrary to its syllabic system, are widely registered in vulgar Punic with no difficulty. The doubled consonants, on the other hand, are registered twice, in Graeco-Latin fashion, instead of once, in Semitic fashion. Finally the vowels are registered by laryngeal-pharyngeals and semi-vowels, not only like *matres lectionis* in the way of some Semitic languages, but also to replace short vowels.

In the morphological sphere the same differences between Punic and Phoenician must be noted, evidently resulting from secondary developments: so the possessive suffix of the third person singular, masculine and feminine, is –' instead of –*y*.

The only sphere in which the developments of Punic are visibly conditioned by the other languages with which it came into contact is the syntax. But here again the phenomena are rare and always peculiar to the late or vulgar language. So we have an infinitive with *l* after the verb which evidently adapts the Latin predicative gerund.

In conclusion the script and language appear to us as important aspects of a culture in which Phoenician tradition survives its dispersion and the passage of time. They are an essential guiding line of Phoenician-Punic unity and continuity.

III

THE COLONIES IN THE WEST

CHAPTER 14

MALTA, GOZO, PANTELLERIA

1 History

This island is a colony planted by the Phoenicians, who, as they extended their trade to the western Ocean, found in it a place of safe retreat, since it was well supplied with harbours and lay out in the open sea.[1]

This is how Diodorus describes the settlement of the Phoenicians in Malta: he obviously realized the importance of its position on the Mediterranean trade routes. We do not know exactly when the first Phoenician settlement was founded, but it was certainly before the eighth century, to which some Phoenician tombs in the region of Rabat can be ascribed.

Furthermore, there is no doubt that the settlers did not limit themselves to the coast, but spread inland, founding at least one large city, which must have stood on the site of the present Rabat-Medina. So far no remains of this city, which would correspond to the *Melite* mentioned by Ptolemy,[2] have been discovered because they are probably covered by the modern town, but numerous tombs have come to light in the vicinity which are evidently connected with the ancient settlement.

Another fact indicates the importance of the Phoenician colony in Malta. Stephen of Byzantium[3] informs us that the North African city of Acholla, opposite Malta on the eastern coast of Tunisia, was founded by Maltese people, in other words Phoenicians from the island. So if Malta was in a position to found her own colonies she must have been of considerable importance. We have no precise information about the period when Acholla was founded, but it seems reasonable to assume that this happened before the power of Carthage absorbed the surrounding region, which would presumably be before the seventh century.

In the account about Malta, Diodorus adds that the Phoenicians also colonized Gaulos or Gozo. The name of the island is of Phoenician origin and denotes a type of round mercantile vessel. Pantelleria must have been occupied at about the same time, but we do not know whether by the Phoenicians directly or by the settlers from Malta. The steep coastline of this islet opens on to a good port to the north-west, which was probably the first landing-stage. Here again the earlier name, Iranim, is of Phoenician type, and even the classical name, Kossyra, is of possible Phoenician etymology.

The supremacy of Carthage undoubtedly marked the incorporation of the islets in her sphere of influence. The Periplus of Pseudo-Skylax,[4] written half-way through the fourth century, suggests that the Carthaginians occupied Malta, Gozo, and Lampedusa, without specifying the date. We cannot tell, therefore, whether this account refers to occupation or reoccupation. In any case the Carthaginians probably occupied the islets at least from the sixth century. Pantelleria may have been an exception, and in the third century the Roman annals of the First Punic War mention a victory 'over the Cossyrians and Carthaginians' which could be taken to imply a relative independence of the islet.

Once under Carthaginian rule Malta shared Carthage's misfortunes. During the First Punic War, according to Naevius,[5] Malta was laid waste by the army of Atilius Regulus, who disembarked there before sailing for Africa. The possible dates for this expedition are 256 or 253, the latter being more likely.

That this expedition was a raid rather than a conquest is confirmed by the fact that Rome had to occupy Malta again during the Second Punic War. According to Livy,[6] the consul, Tiberius Sempronius Longus, was appointed commander in 218 of the expedition which Rome sent against Carthage in Africa. He went to Messina and thence to Lilybaeum, and while preparations were being made for proceeding to Carthage he sailed to Malta, where the small Carthaginian garrison under Hamilcar, son of Gisgo, surrendered. There is no reason to suppose that the local population rebelled, but simply that the Punic force was too small and lacked a fleet to protect itself.

In 218 Malta entered the Roman dominion, as did the other neighbouring islands. Although the Roman epoch is outside our period, one event is connected with this earlier era: the shrine of Juno was plundered by Verres, who was then denounced by Cicero in his famous speech.[7]

Certain accounts of the late period indicate institutions in Malta which were similar to those of the Phoenician homeland and Carthage. To the second century BC we can probably ascribe a Greek inscription[8] which mentions two *archontes*, or two suffetes, and speaks of a decision of the senate and the people of Malta. To the third or second century belongs a Punic inscription of Malta[9] which refers to the annual magistrature of an official ('In the year of Hannibal, son of Bodmilk'), while a more or less contemporary Punic inscription from Gozo[10] concerns the 'people of Gozo' and certain magistrates and officials.

On the whole, we can say that Phoenician-Punic culture established itself in Malta and the neighbouring islands. The ample information about the celebrated textile industry (women's clothes, remarkably fine and soft hats and cushions are mentioned)[11] confirms Malta's role in Mediterranean trade. Furthermore, Phoenician and Punic culture was slow to disappear, despite the Roman conquest, as we see from the coins with Punic legends struck in Malta and Pantelleria as late as the second and first century B C.

2 Archaeology

Information about Phoenician-Punic culture in Malta is still scarce, because of the rarity of excavations of this phase of Maltese history. Only recently, since 1963, has an Italian archaeological mission seriously tackled the problem of Phoenician and Punic antiquities, immediately obtaining important results. However scarce information had been until then, it was nevertheless extremely indicative: the tombs, pottery, inscriptions, and coins constituted an incontestable proof of the Phoenician-Punic phase of Malta.

Furthermore, there is no doubt about the Phoenician origin of this culture as far as the finds are concerned, and the distinction from the Punic phase is perfectly clear, not because the date of Carthaginian occupation is known, but because there is so far a certain interval between the earliest finds, which are definitely Phoenician, and the later ones, which are definitely Punic.

The Phoenician-Punic settlements of Malta, apart from those of Gozo, can be reconstructed from the indications given by the geographer Ptolemy.[12] He mentions four centres on the island: the city of Melite (now Rabat-Medina); that of Chersonesus (now perhaps Valetta); the shrine of Hera, and that of Heracles. Of the settlements the only archaeological remains to come to light until recently were the tombs in the neighbourhood of Rabat-Medina, near Paula and in Ghain Qajjet. The two shrines, on the other hand, were theoretically located near Valletta (that of Hera) and near Marsaxlocc (that of Heracles). In fact, as the Italian excavators proved, the shrine of Hera must be located in the area of Marsaxlocc. In November 1963 inscriptions to the goddess appeared in the locality of Tas Silg, together with numerous fragments of plates with Punic dedications to Astarte and Tanit, the Phoenician and Punic equivalents of Greek Hera and Roman Juno. The sanctuary identified is therefore the one rendered famous by Cicero's oration against Verres.

The sacred area of Tas Silg presents a complex series of constructive phases: a first pre-historic phase, a second Punic phase, a third Roman phase, and a fourth Byzantine phase. The Punic phase can be placed between the sixth and second century B C and consists of a proper acropolis surrounded by a thick wall of parallelepiped blocks of limestone. Access to the acropolis was gained by a paved ramp which has been excavated. Within the precinct there must have been various buildings, as was usual in a *fanum*. So far a small zone has been excavated which, judging from the animal ashes and the remains of various offerings, seems to be a sacrificial area. There are certain interesting architectural remains with close affinities to types which have so far only been discovered in the East. In particular we have a newel of a similar type to the ones seen in the balustrade reproduced on the Phoenician ivories showing the 'woman at the window'.

To the south of the wall of the precinct a particularly interesting area has been identified, characterized by a stratum of organic ashes mostly lying just above prehistoric remains. In this area several hundred fragments of plates have been found, engraved before baking with a dedication to the deities Astarte and Tanit. Together with the fragments bones belonging to small animals, sheep or birds have appeared. It was evidently a refuse area of the shrine.

The necropolises of Malta present tombs of Phoenician type – inhumation-tombs, and access shafts with one or two chambers at their sides. The ascription of these tombs to the eighth or seventh century is confirmed by the pottery: mushroom-lipped jugs, trefoil-lipped jugs, umbilicated plates, two beaked lamps, various types of cups, all found together with Greek material which confirms the date. After the seventh century numerous autonomous developments can be noted in Maltese production, and there is a unique fragment of a jug from Tas Silg, originally painted like a human face, in which can be seen one eye and the nose adapted to a symbol of Tanit (plate 107).

Casual discovery of objects sometimes subsequently lost confirms the Phoenician-Punic *facies* of Malta. Certain clay and stone statuettes recall the Phoenician homeland on account of their Egypticizing appearance. A fifth-century clay coffin of anthropoid shape also provides similar indications. A stone bust discovered at Tas Silg in 1964 is particularly noteworthy: the stylistic traits suggest an example of the type of standing worshipper which immediately recalls Cypriot models of the fifth century (plate 33). There are also some interesting terracotta protomai studied by Mayr, who noticed certain autonomous characteristics with respect to the Carthaginian models. The amulets, which are nearly all of enamelled glass paste and under prevalently Egyptian influence, are also fairly numerous in Maltese collections. They represent deities, *ushabti*, Bes uraei, *ujat* eyes, and *jed* pillars, and sometimes bear hieroglyphic signs. They were mainly parts of necklaces found together with scarabs and pearls of the same enamelled glass paste or of stone. A gold amulet-bearing tube with the head of a bearded man, containing a rolled golden lamina on which are engraved two rows of superimposed figures, mainly Egyptian demons in animal shape, is of particular interest. As for the ivories, a few fine fragments were found in Tas Silg by the Italian Mission in 1964. The jewellery is of silver and gold, and includes the fragment of a golden bracelet with repoussé figures of gryphons on either side of a sacred tree composed of Phoenician palmettes and flowers, surmounted by the winged solar disk between two uraei.

The coins which Malta started to strike shortly before the Roman occupation are also of considerable interest. The earliest present the word '*nn*, probably the Phoenician name of the island, and depict a bearded male head with caduceus and a pillar and urn, the Egyptian deity Osiris between Isis and Nephthys, and a veiled female head similar to that on the Cyrenaican coins. Egypticizing figures appear still later, towards the middle of the second century BC. In Gozo the coins show a female head, bare or with a helmet, surmounted by the crescent moon – this may be a type of Astarte, who appears to have had a shrine on the island.[13] On the reverse the coins of Gozo represent a warrior accompanied by a star.

Our knowledge of the Phoenician-Punic phase of Pantelleria is so far limited to casual finds, and the research undertaken by P. Orsi in the winter of 1894–5 and the University of Rome in the spring of 1965. The acropolis stood on the two hills of St Teresa and St Marco, rising above the present town. Parts of a walled precinct several times restored have come to light. The remains of terracotta heads and protomai of the Punic type with *klaft* or head-band originate, according to Orsi, from the locality of Bagno dell'Acqua. Typically Punic jewels, ear-rings and necklaces were found in a tomb in the Ghirlanda quarter. Various coins with Latin-Punic legends depict figures of Isis, confirming the Egyptian elements of this culture in the late Punic phase. In the necropolises which stretched in an arc round the acropolis numerous oblong clay amphorae with a peg-bottom have been found. On the whole, the research of the University of Rome has shown a marked prevalence of Roman remains: Punic pottery is scarce, and this would lead us to imagine a settlement of limited dimensions. We have no decisive archaeological proofs of the preceding Phoenician settlement.

3 Religion

The cult of Heracles-Melqart and Hera-Tanit-Astarte is attested in Malta by the two temples already mentioned, while two bilingual Graeco-Punic stelae of the second century BC are dedicated to 'our lord Melqart, lord of Tyre'. And besides the dedications on fragments of vases in the area of the *fanum Iunonis* a newel of the *fanum* is dedicated to Astarte. But the most interesting problem is the alternation of dedications to Astarte and Tanit: one answer to the problem could be a variation of certain characteristics in the development of the two deities in the Maltese world.

Passing on to other deities, Baal Hammon is attested in Malta by an inscription coming from the outskirts of Rabat-Medina. As for Tanit Pene Baal, her name appeared on inscriptions privately owned several decades ago. But the origin of these inscriptions has not been established, and they could equally well have been North African. In any case, the symbol of Tanit appears on a fragment of pottery distorted to resemble a nose. The origin of a Neo-Punic inscription, which has been lost, is also doubtful: it was dedicated to Baal Addir (this is probably how the inscription should be read, instead of Mayr's Baal *ndr*). Finally the figures of Isis, Osiris, and Nephthys on the coins of Malta, like the figures of Isis on those of Pantelleria, recall Egyptian cults, but are probably reduced to plain iconographical symbols.

CHAPTER 15

SICILY

1 History

The Phoenician origins in Sicily are the object of considerable chronological controversy, and the question arises whether it is possible to distinguish a Phoenician phase from a Punic phase on the island.

The main reason for this problem is a passage from Thucydides to which we have alluded previously:

Phoenicians, too, had settlements all round Sicily, on promontories along the sea coast, which they walled off, and on the adjacent islets, for the sake of trade with the Siculi. But when the Greeks also began to come in by sea in large numbers, the Phoenicians left most of these places and settling together lived in Motya, Soloeis, and Panormus near the Elymi, partly because they trusted in their alliance with the Elymi and partly because from there the voyage from Sicily to Carthage is shortest.[1]

Pareti, the most radical critic of the antiquity of Phoenician settlements in Sicily, submits this passage to rigorous criticism, denying the possibility of pre-Punic Phoenician colonization on the island. Motya, Panormus, and Solunto, in his opinion, were not inherited from the Phoenicians, but simply founded by the Carthaginians in the first phase of their expansion (seventh century) at the same time as other foundations, like those of Ibiza, Malta, Gozo, and Pantelleria. In this case the historical situation would be altered: the Sicilian colonies would not be the result of Phoenician commercial colonization on the routes of the West, but of Carthaginian policy intended to curb Greek diffusion in the Mediterranean.

There does not, in fact, seem to be any good reason for contradicting all that Thucydides says. It is hardly possible to talk of a Carthaginian commitment to Sicily before the seventh-sixth century, while the archaeological excavations in Motya reveal a Phoenician settlement from the eighth century. The co-existence of Phoenician and Elymian elements, also indicated by the excavations, confirms the affirmation of Thucydides. The find of a bronze statuette of a walking god in the sea near Selinunte suggests Phoenician presence on the southern coasts a few centuries earlier. Finally, the examination of prehistoric cultural phases in southern Sicily, recently undertaken by Bernabò Brea, indicates alterations and fractions around the tenth century, which can be attributed to the Phoenicians.

In conclusion, most studies and criticisms tend to reassess Thucydides's passage. It is likely that Phoenician origins in Sicily preceded the intervention of Carthage by some centuries; that they were connected with commercial expansion and were localized in an area far larger, even if restricted to the coast, than the one which was later to develop; that the withdrawal and concentration of the Phoenicians in the West was due to the arrival of the Greeks; and that the Phoenicians were supported primarily by the Elymi, and only later by the Carthaginians. So in Sicily, as later in Sardinia, there does seem to have been a Phoenician phase before a Punic one, although documentation is scarce.

Very little is known about the earliest Phoenician and Punic history in Sicily. In Gela commercial relations between the Punic and Greek settlers are mentioned around the middle of the seventh century.[2] The archaeological remains of Motya show that Carthaginian presence was active in the sixth century and definitely established itself in the fifth. Tradition confirms these indications and records, as the first military venture of the Carthaginians in Sicily, the general Malchus's victory over the Greeks, and, according to Justin, his subsequent subjugation of a part of the island.[3] He then proceeded to Sardinia, where, as we know, he was heavily defeated. It seems evident that Malchus acted in agreement with the Phoenician colonies, and we must not forget that the walls of Motya were reinforced in this period. The other cities, too, Panormus and Solunto, were probably fortified and Punicized together, and present no documentation of an earlier period.

The Spartan Doriaeus renewed the struggle in Sicily c. 510. Doriaeus founded Heracleia on the slopes of Mount Eryx and formed an anti-Punic alliance with the Selinuntines, the Himerans, and the Sicanians. The struggle lasted for a long time and fortunes were varied, but the Elymi and the Carthaginians finally got the better of their adversaries and destroyed Heracleia.

The next episode of the war between the Carthaginians and the Greeks in Sicily was in 480, at the same time as the encounter between the Persians and the Greeks in the East. The alliance between Gelon, tyrant of Syracuse, and Theron, tyrant of Agrigentum, created a grave danger for the Carthaginians, which came to a head when Theron occupied Himera and drove out Terillus, the ally of Carthage. We have already mentioned the phases of the expedition sent by Carthage to Sicily under the command of Hamilcar: the Carthaginians were defeated at the battle of Himera in 480 and were not to have any offensive force in the area for a long time. Thanks to the policy of Gelon, however, who did not want his Agrigentine ally to become too powerful, they retained their possessions on the island.

The struggle between the Carthaginians and the Greeks resumed in 409, when Hannibal, a descendant of the Hamilcar fallen at Himera, destroyed Selinunte and Himera. Three years later, in 406, a new Carthaginian expedition commanded by Hannibal (who was to die soon after) and Himilco, attacked and conquered Agrigentum and Gela. Dionysius of Syracuse, who had assumed command, concluded an unfavourable peace in 405 which gave him time to recover his strength. Besides the colonies (Motya, Panormus, Solunto) and the allied territory of the Elymi, Carthage was left with the tributary region of the Sicanians and the cities of Selinunte, Agrigentum, Himera, Gela, and Camarina. When Himilco returned to Carthage about half of Sicily could be said to be under Carthaginian control.

The peace of 405 gave Dionysius enough time to make the necessary preparations for a new encounter with Carthage. When this took place, in 398, Dionysius exhorted his people to war against the eternal enemies and allowed them to plunder Carthaginian property in Syracuse and elsewhere. A true 'Sicilian Vesper' followed, resulting in the injunction of war in Carthage and the beginning of a swift march along the southern coast of the island, during which all the cities and local populations rallied to Dionysius. By the spring of 397 Dionysius was confronting Motya with an army of about eighty thousand foot soldiers, three thousand horse, and two hundred ships. They had laid waste the neighbouring territories and were blockading the island when Himilco arrived from Carthage with a fleet of a hundred ships which dropped anchor in the mouth of the port. Dionysius had his fleet transported over the peninsula on narrow wooden rails, and managed to reach the open sea. Threatened by encirclement, the Carthaginian fleet decided to withdraw. Motya was finally conquered and sacked, while its remaining inhabitants were sold as slaves.

But the reverse of fortunes soon proved that the destruction of Motya, although a serious matter in itself, was no more than another episode in the struggle between the Carthaginians and Greeks in Sicily. In 396 the Carthaginians, having fitted out a powerful army, intervened once more in Sicily, under the command of Himilco, and, after landing at Panormus, advanced inland. While Dionysius retreated to Syracuse, Himilco made for the straits and conquered Messina. Finally, when a Punic unit under Mago advanced to Catania, the fleet of Dionysius attacked but was defeated. Then, hardly two years after the destruction of Motya, the military situation was reversed and Dionysius was blockaded by the Carthaginians in Syracuse. He managed to escape because of a plague which broke out in the enemy camp and to regain control over the eastern part of the island.

After Himilco's return to Carthage and suicide as a result of opposition to his work, Mago remained in Sicily and had further encounters with Dionysius in 393 and 392. A treaty followed by which the Siceliots and the Siculi remained with Syracuse, and the Sicanians and Elymi with Carthage. According to Diodorus,[4] the situation of 405 was repeated.

Further years of truce followed, together with more preparation for the war. On the one hand Dionysius tried to lure over to his side the Sicanian towns under Punic control, while on the other Mago sought alliances with the Siceliote towns in order to be able to attack Dionysius on both fronts. This was a bold policy of considerable significance, which further broadened the horizons of Carthage and is explicitly testified to by Diodorus.[5] War broke out in 382 and probably lasted until 374. The first major event was the battle of Kabala, where the Carthaginians were defeated and Mago killed, but a truce allowed them to recover their strength. The second was the battle of Kronion, near Thermae Imeresi, where the Syracusans were defeated, but the Carthaginians, having suffered heavy losses, signed a treaty placing the frontier at the river Halycus. It was to remain here for about a century, establishing the dominion of Carthage over a third of Sicily.

Some years later, in 367, Dionysius tried once more to drive the Carthaginians from the island. He attacked the territory under the control of Carthage, occupied Selinunte, Entella, and Eryx, and besieged Lilybaeum (whither the remainder of the population of Motya had moved). But after he had sent part of his fleet back to Syracuse, and remained with a hundred and thirty ships at Drepanum, two hundred Carthaginian ships suddenly appeared. In order to avoid an encounter which would not have benefited either side, a peace was signed which restored the *status quo*. Dionysius died shortly after, without having been able to fulfil his plan of destroying Carthaginian power in Sicily.

A fairly long period of peace elapsed, and then war resumed once more. Between 342 and 341 Timoleon the Corinthian advanced to the territory under Punic control and occupied Entella, while, according to Diodorus,[6] many cities still subject to Carthage joined him. The Carthaginians then intervened in force and the encounter took place east of Segesta, on the river Crimissus: the Carthaginians were heavily defeated and had to retreat to Lilybaeum (340). But Timoleon did not manage to obtain the expected results from the victory because many allies rebelled against him. Hicetas of Leontini, Mamercus of Catania, and Hippo of Messina gave aid to the Carthaginians, and although they were defeated Timoleon found himself forced to sign a peace treaty confirming the frontier on the river Halycus (339).

Further years of peace followed this treaty. Carthage had no reason to fight and skilfully prevented the reinforcement of a unitary power in eastern Sicily which would have caused another war. She did not succeed for long, and, however paradoxical it might seem, it was she who paved the way for the new tyrant of Syracuse, Agathocles. In 318 the Carthaginian Hamilcar negotiated the treaty which enabled him to return to Syracuse, whence he had been banished. In 314 Hamilcar himself intervened in order to pacify Agathocles with Messina, but the subsequent treaty specified that the Greek cities in eastern Sicily should retain their independence, but recognize the hegemony of Syracuse. Hamilcar clearly intended to act as arbiter and so maintain a certain supremacy, but this position was obviously insecure: Carthage, growing suspicious, recalled and tried him, but he died before the verdict was given.

Agathocles now advanced into Punic territory with ever more obvious provocations. Carthage, suddenly altering her policy, put Hamilcar, son of Gisgo, in command, and he landed in Sicily with a powerful army and struck camp on the right bank of the river Himera. He routed Agathocles in a decisive battle (310), driving him back first to Gela and then to Syracuse, where he besieged Agathocles by land and sea. Except for the city the whole of Sicily was now in the hands of the Carthaginians.

At this point Agathocles took the celebrated initiative of invading Africa. In Sicily, Hamilcar made several unsuccessful attempts to conquer Syracuse, but he died in battle in 308 without having accomplished his task. In 307 Agathocles temporarily returned to Sicily and managed to relieve Syracuse and recover part of the territory which he had formerly controlled. After returning to Africa, where he was defeated in 306, he fled for the last time to Sicily, where a treaty with the Carthaginians enabled him to make peace on honourable terms. Sicilian territory was divided as before (by the Halycus) and Agathocles obtained a sum of money and a dispatch of grain (305).

After the death of Agathocles in 289 internal strife broke out among the Greeks in Sicily with new vigour and the Carthaginians took advantage of it. In 287 and 280 they defeated Hicetas, the new tyrant of Syracuse. At the same time they extended their control towards Agrigentum and Messina, and occupied Lipari. Finally, in 278, they besieged Syracuse, which had no alternative but to request the aid of Pyrrhus, then in Italy.

Carthage had already signed a treaty against Pyrrhus with Rome in 279. As well as the mutual spheres of influence (Sicily to Carthage and Italy to Rome) the two powers agreed to mutual aid, and in particular to Carthaginian aid at sea:

No matter which require help, the Carthaginians are to provide the ships for transport and hostilities, but each country shall provide the pay for its own men. The Carthaginians, if necessary, shall come to the help of the Romans by sea too, but no one shall compel the crews to land against their will.[7]

At the same time a Carthaginian fleet arrived at Ostia and the admiral, Mago, was received by the senate. Carthaginian ships also transported Roman soldiers to Rhegium, and remained to blockade the straits. In spite of this, however, the Carthaginians had to bear the brunt of Pyrrhus's attack virtually on their own. He landed in Sicily, was welcomed as liberator by the population of the island, and soon occupied the entire territory except for Lilybaeum. At this point Pyrrhus could have obtained peace on favourable terms, but he wanted at all costs to occupy the last Carthaginian stronghold. Defeated and abandoned by his local allies he was forced to leave Sicily in 276, thereby ending his venture.

This brings us to the Punic Wars. In 265 or 264 the Carthaginians installed a garrison in Messina, and soon afterwards the Romans declared war. In 241 the First Punic War ended and the whole of Sicily fell under Roman dominion.

2 Archaeology

The direct remains of Phoenician and Punic culture in Sicily are very limited. By far the most abundant source of material is Motya, the only city to have retained its independent physiognomy and to permit excavation on a large scale. Of the other two traditional Phoenician-Punic settlements, Panormus and Solunto, Panormus lies under the later town and has only yielded short stretches of wall, some tombs, and a few inscriptions and coins; Solunto was probably not on the site where the classical city later arose and is therefore an open problem, although Tusa's recent studies tend to place it on the site of the present Cannita, where two remarkable anthropoid coffins have been found. There is also Lilybaeum, whither the inhabitants of Motya who survived the destruction of their city escaped, and which the Carthaginians subsequently fortified, using it as the bridge-head of their advance into Sicily. Lilybaeum has already provided interesting material, including votive aedicules with painted figurations. We must keep in mind, however, that this material is late, since the city of Lilybaeum developed after the fall of Motya in 397 B C. The only archaeological evidence we possess of the Phoenicians and Carthaginians who lived farther east of these cities is the bronze male statuette found in the sea near Selinunte (plate 48).

Documentation being so scarce, we must return to the indications of Phoenician-Punic culture contained in the eminently Greek evidence in ancient Sicily. A study of this kind, being undertaken at present by Tusa, provides elements of considerable interest. At Segesta, for instance, an architectural fragment has been found with Egyptian mouldings, which seem attributable to Phoenician-Punic influence. This is all the more interesting since the Mango quarter of Segesta is yielding a probably Elymian shrine and inscriptions in Greek characters, but not in the Greek language: the Elymi, closely allied to the Carthaginians, were in a better position than the Greeks for preserving the elements of Carthaginian culture, since they knew them better. Equally interesting is the discovery of an *oscillum*, a disk-shaped terracotta object supposed to be suspended, which bears one word in Punic characters and one in Greek. While the Greek characters are incomprehensible and suggest a non-Greek language, *l* ('to') can be read in the Punic dedicatory prefix, followed by a name. From Solunto, another wholly classical town in structure and buildings, we have indications of Punic influence probably originating from the substratum of the population: a temple with open altar and a basin containing the burnt bones of small animals which recall the sacrifices in the *topheths*; two small altars with religious symbols like the sign of Tanit and the caduceus; the heads of female deities ornamented with the sign of the crescent moon; and two beaked lamps. In Selinunte the so-called Hellenistic buildings actually present indications of Punic influence, such as the 'loom-like' walls which are to be found also in Motya, and the typically Punic pottery (fourth/third century B C) found in a cistern. Finally the Punic and Neo-Punic inscriptions and the onomatology suggest Carthaginian origins.

If the Punic background occasionally emerges in Greek culture in Sicily, the Greek environment also influenced the Punic production. We can even say that the permeation of Greek elements, sometimes becoming almost indistinguishable, is a characteristic of Phoenician-Punic culture in Sicily, from which only Motya is partially exempt. So, the first Punic coins struck in Sicily present a head of Astarte clearly derived from the female head of Athenian origin which appears on the coins of Syracuse. Furthermore, there is the directly Greek material which seems associated to the Punic material and facilitates dating; the pottery of Motya is the best example of this, and Motya has an equally significant stuccoed Doric capital ascribable to the sixth century.

It is, of course, also difficult to distinguish between the Phoenician and Punic phase. All we can say is that the statuette from the sea near Selinunte and the earliest pottery from Motya suggest Phoenician models, while, after the sixth century, the documentation is of Carthaginian type.

Considering the architecture, Motya is an excellent example of town planning. The site is typically Phoenician-Punic: an islet lying close to the coast and well protected from the winds. After the sixth century

Motya was surrounded by walls which follow the line of the shore closely for a perimeter of about 2,500 metres. The walls, remade various times, present the 'loom-like' system: a series of monoliths at short distances apart, with intermediate spaces filled with smaller stones. The remains of towers are fitted into the walls, which have two main gateways, one to the north and the other to the south. Close to the southern port is a small *cothon*, another typically Punic construction. Its dimensions are considerably reduced (fifty-one by thirty-seven centimetres) and the access canal is only about seven metres wide, too small, evidently, to constitute the main port, which must instead have been in the lagoon between the island and the mainland. In the interior of the island there are two main buildings which have so far come to light: the Cappiddazzu, a public building or temple, possibly standing on an ancient open-air Phoenician shrine, and the 'house of the mosaics', so-called because of a floor of white and black pebbles with Orientalizing depictions.

The most recent finds in Motya include the *topheth*. Both Whitaker and Cintas had already brought to light stelae and urns, a sure proof of the typical Phoenician and Punic sacrifices; but it was only in 1964 that the archaeological mission of the University of Rome and the Department of Antiquities of Palermo identified the wall structure of what must have been the *topheth*, also finding some female protomai, a splendid male terracotta mask, and a large quantity of other stelae.

From the island of Motya an ancient sheep-track, barely visible under the water-level, led to the opposite shore of Birgi, where the necropolis of the city was situated. But, in fact, this necropolis is the later one (sixth century): an archaic necropolis exists on the island near the northern gate, partially covered by the walls built across it in the sixth century, and here there is a characteristic predominance of cremation over inhumation, although inhumation also existed and prevailed in the later necropolis. The corpses were inhumed in graves by means of usually monolithic coffins.

In the later Lilybaeum the necropolis called *dei Cappuccini* yields subterranean shaft-tombs at the bottom of which are funerary chambers of about two metres square. The chambers contain coffins, the remains of wooden chests, urns, and amphorae for ashes. The other necropolis of St Francesco has subterranean tombs accessible by steps surmounted on the outside by the familiar aedicules. There are further Punic necropolises in Panormus, of the sixth century and later, with an underground chamber and access steps; and in the locality of Cannita, where the two celebrated anthropoid coffins were found.

As far as sculpture is concerned, the categories best represented are the cippi and stelae on the one side, and the protomai and masks on the other. Further examples are as follows: from Motya, a large headless adolescent (plate 35), some terracotta heads and a relief from a gate with scenes of lions devouring a bull; from Panormus, a small altar with fighting animals; from Cannita the two anthropoid coffins with Graecizing female figures, one with a draped dress (plate 10), the other without; from Solunto a female deity on a throne flanked by sphinxes (plate 31); from Alesa, a fragment of a group with a lion biting a calf (plate 54). This list, composed by Pareti, is also questionable, because, as Pareti himself admits, 'all these statues reveal Siceliot influence, but some could have been made by Siceliot craftsmen trying to adapt themselves to Phoenician tastes, and others by Punic or native Sicanian craftsmen who had absorbed the Greek systems'.

Motya provides a wide documentation of cippi and stelae, completed in recent years by new finds. Before the fall of the city, in other words between the seventh and fifth century, cippi emerge with a quadrangular betyl heavily engraved (plate 15), occasionally flanked by flattened columns and surmounted by a pediment with Egyptian mouldings. There are sometimes two betyls, but never more. There is also the bottle-idol in its more stylized form. From the most recent excavations various stelae with long narrow betyls on high pedestals have emerged, but the most significant discovery was of a series of stelae with varied human depictions which often have no precedents. An example of these is a stele with a male figure under a reversed crescent moon with a solar disk (plate 16), in which the treatment of the nude suggests Greek influence.

Some interesting stelae of the fourth century come from Lilybaeum. A particularly important one ends in a low triangle and acroteria in which a priest is shown before a *thymiaterion*, a symbol of Tanit and a caduceus, surmounted by three betyls on Egyptian mouldings. The cornice encloses the human and solar symbols and an inscription below. We also have another stele ending in a triangle in which a female figure stands before a caduceus surmounted by a symbol of Tanit.

A few centuries later the typical *heroon*-shaped aedicules (plate 4) spread in Lilybaeum. Two columns with a smooth shaft support a large pediment containing the usual astral symbols. The aedicule represents a male figure reclining on a *kline*, offering an amphora to a female figure seated on a chair opposite him; in the middle stands a small table bearing food. Numerous objects and symbols accompany the depiction. Of these, especially on the columns, we note the symbol of Tanit, the disk with the crescent moon and the caduceus. It is a hybrid art, marking the final encounter between Phoenician and Greek motifs in Sicily.

The excavations of 1964 in Motya have brought to light, in the *topheth*, a series of female protomai of the type already mentioned in

Carthage. Here, too, the protomai are made from moulds and bear the remains of pink colouring. The head is covered by an Egyptian wig and the hair is supported by a ribbon and falls behind the ears. The features are soft and regular, the eyebrows are at a right-angle to the lines of the nose (plate 60). In the same excavations a male mask in excellent condition came to light – the first to appear in Sicily. It is from the second group identified at Carthage by Cintas: face furrowed by heavy lines on the forehead and the cheeks, eyes formed by crescent-shaped sockets pointing downwards, and a very wide mouth-slit turning up on either side (plate 76): this is undoubtedly one of the best examples of grimacing Punic masks yet known.

Minor artistic products from the ruins of Motya are of great interest with regard to the continuity of certain artistic types in the Punic world. There are red terracotta figurines closely connected to the typology most amply manifested in Bythia (Sardinia); small amulets of cream-coloured paste with the Egyptian figurations usual in Carthage; brace-lets, ear-rings, rings, and necklaces of glass pearls, amber or black stone, sometimes with small masks; scarabs of lapis lazuli, cornelian, and other hard stones; fragments of ivory; ostrich eggs painted red. The necropolis of Panormus, too, has yielded objects of quality, the most interesting of which are an enamel pendant with Egyptian figures and a malachite scarab, also with Egyptian figures.

As we know, the first Punic coins were struck in Sicily towards the end of the fifth century to pay the Carthaginian mercenaries on the island. They are of gold and silver, and have the name of Panormus (*Ziz*, may be 'resplendent') engraved in Punic characters; the depictions are female heads and various animals (especially the bull and the dog) or chariots. After the fourth century the names of Motya, Karthadasht, and *mahanat* appear on the coins. Karthadasht corresponds to Carthage, but since this name means 'new city' it has been suggested that it refers to Panormus rebuilt (Cavallaro). *Mahanat* means 'camp'; in other words the Carthaginian headquarters. On these coins we have on one side a female head (probably Tanit, on the model of the Persephone of Syra-cuse), and on the other an animal (the lion and the horse prevail) or a palm tree.

Punic pottery in Sicily is widely documented at Motya, and generally appears to be closely connected to that of Carthage. In the earlier period (eighth–seventh century) jugs with mushroom lips and trefoil lips were very frequent. To these we can add the single-handled pots, and vases with painted design of 'triglyphs and metopes'. The lamps are of the usual two-beaked type and there are umbilicated plates. The fifth century presents new types, such as the jugs with cylindrical neck and a ring. In the fourth century there were numerous importations from southern Italy which clearly influenced the local production, and the majority of the large amphorae seem to be of this period.

3 Religion

The Punic religion in Sicily is testified to in Motya by the *topheth* and the sacrifices, first human, then animal, performed there, while the female protomai probably represent the image of Tanit-Astarte in wholly similar form to that which appears in Carthage. In Lilybaeum, too, the votive dedications to Tanit and Baal Hammon repeat the Carthaginian formulae and the one dedicated to Baal Hammon alone seems to be no more than episodic.[8] Finally, all we know about Punic religion in Sicily is necessarily connected with Carthage by the period of the finds. Of pre-Punic Phoenician examples we can only cite the Baal of the statuette found in the sea near Selinunte; but this is too tenuous an indication, because nothing proves that the statuette reflects local cults.

A significant encounter between the Punic and local cults is to be found in the worship of Erycine Astarte in the open air in Eryx. This is mentioned by Diodorus[9] to emphasize the contact between Elymi, Carthaginians, and then Romans. The sacred prostitution practised in the temple seems of clearly Oriental origin. Besides, from the sanctuary we had a Punic inscription, subsequently lost, which confirmed the presence of Carthaginians there.

CHAPTER 16

SARDINIA

1 History

The Phoenician-Punic origins in Sardinia are notoriously ancient, and what is problematic elsewhere can be taken as certain here, that is the existence of an appreciable Phoenician phase before the Punic one. On the other hand, the historical sources are scarce as far as the Carthaginians are concerned, and not even remotely comparable to what we possess on Sicily. While in Sicily the historical sources prevail over the archaeological data, in Sardinia the archaeological data prevail.

The considerations hitherto taken into account apply to the problem of the first Phoenician settlements. Certain classical authors tell of the earliest populations of the island, but the accounts are definitely legendary and bear no more than a faint resemblance to historical events. Here is what Pausanias writes:

The first sailors to cross to the island are said to have been Libyans. Their leader was Sardus, son of Maceris, the Maceris surnamed Heracles by the Egyptians and Libyans. Maceris himself was celebrated chiefly for his journey to Delphi, but Sardus it was who led the Libyans to Ichnussa, and after him the island was renamed. However, the Libyan army did not expel the aboriginals, who received the invaders as settlers through compulsion rather than in good-will. Neither the Libyans nor the native population knew how to build cities. They dwelt in scattered groups, where chance found them a home in cabins or caves. Years after the Libyans there came to the island from Greece Aristaeus and his followers. Aristaeus is said to have been a son of Apollo and Cyrene, and they say that, deeply grieved by the fate of Actaeon, and vexed alike with Boeotia and the whole of Greece, he migrated to Sardinia . . . At any rate, these colonists too founded no city, the reason being, I think, that neither in numbers nor in strength were they capable of the task. After Aristaeus, the Iberians crossed to Sardinia, under Norax as leader of their expedition, and they founded the city of Nora. The tradition is that this was the first city in the island, and they say that Norax was a son of Erytheia, the daughter of Geryones, with Hermes for his father. A fourth component part of the population was the army of Iolaus, consisting of Thespians and men from Attica, which put in at Sardinia and founded Olbia. However, many years afterwards the Libyans crossed again to the island with a stronger army, and began a war against the Greeks. The Greeks were utterly destroyed, or only few of them survived . . .[1]

Certain points of the account are repeated in brief by Solinus:

We do not therefore need to relate how Sardus born of Heracles, Norax of Mercury, the first from Africa and the second from Tartessus in Spain, came to this island, nor how the country was named after Sardus and the city of Nora after Norax . . .[2]

The legendary nature of the accounts is obvious: they are aetiological attempts at explaining the origin of the island and the oldest cities by persons of the same name. However, beyond the legend there appears a basis of historical facts: the ties between Sardinia and the African, Iberian, and Mycenaean world are obvious, and the concept of pre-urban life of the local populations is significant. It seems clear that the first Africans actually correspond to the Phoenicians, while the later ones are the Carthaginians; and the legend of Norax leads us to wonder whether the Phoenicians already settled in Spain did not play some part in the foundation of the earlier cities in general and Nora in particular.

The most important elements, of far more decisive value for the reconstruction of the Phoenician phase in Sardinia, are provided by epigraphy and archaeology. The inscription of Nora, which can probably be dated in the ninth century, is of special significance. In it history, as opposed to legend, provides the name of Sardinia for the first time; we find Tyre, the mother of the colonies in the West, and Pumay is possibly mentioned, a divine name which already appears both in the East and the West.[3] The archaeological evidence is only a little later: both Nora and S. Antioco yield finds of the eighth century, and therefore of the pre-Punic Phoenician phase.

Besides this direct evidence of the earliest phase of the Phoenicians in Sardinia there are certain indications deducible from the development of the pre-existing local civilization. As Lilliu has stressed, the development of the celebrated bronzes of this very early period was influenced by Phoenician bronzes which must certainly have been known on the island, while the very efflorescence of the Bronze civilization in Sardinia, curiously retarded in the middle of the Iron Age, can only be accounted for by the exploitation of the copper mines on the island introduced by the Phoenicians and taught to the local populations. Even the emergence of urban settlements on the foundation of proto-Sardinian villages seems conditioned by the arrival of the Phoenicians, and the development of navigation, which put an end to the isolation of proto-Sardinian society, may certainly have had precedents in the Mycenaean age, but owes its decisive impulse to the Phoenicians.

The Carthaginians were settled in Sardinia by the sixth century. Justin[4] tells us that Malchus led an expedition to the island in this period, probably in order to establish Carthaginian rule over the natives and protect the coastal colonies. Malchus was defeated and lost a large part of his army in the battle. But other expeditions soon followed. Justin[5] also mentions wars conducted in Sardinia by the sons of Mago, Hasdrubal and Hamilcar, towards the end of the same century. Hasdrubal died of a wound and command was assumed by Hamilcar. Other references have no date, but they confirm Punic establishment on the island: Strabo[6] says that the Carthaginians gained possession of it; Diodorus[7] says that with the growth of their power they fought for mastery of Sardinia.

We get a significant confirmation of the extent of the dominion of Carthage in Sardinia at the end of the sixth century from the first treaty concluded with Rome (508 BC). From this it appears that the Carthaginians controlled the commerce on the island, allowing nobody else to trade there except in the presence of a Carthaginian official. Repeating the text of the treaty, Polybius writes:

'Men coming to trade may conclude no business except in the presence of a herald or town-clerk, and the price of whatever is sold in the presence of such shall be secured to the vendor by the state, if the sale take place in Libya or Sardinia.'[8]

So Carthaginian presence was established on the island, and it is evident that its influence spread from the Phoenician colonies on the south-western coast, Nora and Sulcis. There were probably others, too, such as Inosim (Carloforte), Karalis (Cagliari), and Tharros, whose foundation can be hypothetically placed in the eighth century; the necropolises of these last two cities are certainly of the seventh century. The settlements in the area of Bythia must also be of the seventh century, and in particular the one recently discovered on the islet of Su Cardulinu. Cornus, Olbia, and other minor cities appear to be slightly later, and therefore probably of Punic foundation. The occupied area must have skirted the whole western coast of the island, from the area of Cape Carbonara in the south to the islands of Tavolara and Molara in the north. It is quite possible that future excavations will reveal Phoenician-Punic settlements on the remainder of the eastern strip (at Sulcis, for example), thereby closing the circle of the coastal occupation.

Punic settlers or traders certainly penetrated into the interior of the island as far as Othoca, Uselis (Usellus), Macopsisa (Macomer), Macomadas, Gurulis (Padria), and Nura. An important Punic stronghold has recently been discovered at Monte Sirai, and it seems that the regions to have escaped Punic penetration correspond approximately to the present province of Nuoro, and to the hinterland of Olbia, the Gallura.

If the coastal cities started as landing-stages on the maritime trade routes, the inland cities were founded to keep the Greeks away from this vital area of transit in Mediterranean commerce, to protect the coastal cities (as in the case of the settlement of Monte Sirai) and to exploit Sardinian agricultural and mineral resources. The mineral resources are indicated by the widespread use of bronze and the settlements of Sulcis and Monte Sirai in a zone particularly rich in lead and silver. As far as agriculture is concerned, numerous historical accounts confirm the fact that the Carthaginians attached special importance to it. They apparently imported African peoples to the island for agricultural purposes, thereby causing a process of direct penetration and ethnic superimposition which was not repeated elsewhere, and is the main difference between Punic occupation in Sardinia and in Sicily. We must also keep in mind the following incidents: in 480 Hamilcar, in command of the expedition in Sicily, sent part of his fleet to Sardinia to obtain grain; in 396 dispatches of grain were sent from Sardinia to the Carthaginian army blockading Syracuse, and soon after further dispatches were sent to Carthage. At the time of Agathocles, Carthage again had recourse to Sardinian grain.

That the populations of the hinterland were never completely subjugated by the Carthaginians seems clear from every available indication. Furthermore, we also have the evidence of classical authors, like Diodorus, who writes:

Thus the Carthaginians, though their power extended far and they subdued the island, were not able to enslave its former possessors, but the Iolaes fled for safety to the mountainous part of the island and built underground dwellings, and here they raised many flocks and herds . . . And although the Carthaginians made war upon them many times with considerable armies, yet because of the rugged nature of the country and the difficulty of dealing with their dug-out dwellings the people remained unenslaved.[9]

The political organization of the Punic cities in Sardinia must have been based on Carthaginian politics. The existence of two suffetes at the head of the city administration is proved by the trilingual Latino-Graeco-Punic inscription of Pauli Gerrei. The Punic text says: 'To the Lord Eshmun Merreh the altar of copper weighing one hundred pounds vowed by Cleon. (The Lord) has heard his voice and healed him. In the year of the suffetes Himilkat and Abdeshmun, sons of Himilk.'[10]

As in Carthage, the suffetes were joined by a city senate. A bilingual Latin-Punic inscription of the first century BC, incised on the base of a statue found at S. Antioco, says in the Neo-Punic text: 'To Himilkat, son of Idnibaal, son of Himilkat, who, by decree of the Sulcitanian senate, had this temple built for the Lady Elat, Himilkat his son erected this statue.'[11]

We only have sporadic information about the history of Punic Sardinia. According to Diodorus,[12] a terrible plague broke out in Carthage during the war of the Carthaginians against Dionysius of Syracuse in 379; taking advantage of this, the Libyans and Sardinians rebelled. It is not easy to judge the nature and the exact implications of this event, about which we have no further information. It seems that the rebellion involved both the local people and the Africans imported to the island. The same can be said of another account by Diodorus,[13] according to which the Romans sent a colony of five hundred men to Sardinia in 378. If Rome tried to establish a colony on the island at this time, the attempt must have failed.

In 348 the second treaty between Rome and Carthage forbade the Romans to trade and found cities in Sardinia. This clause, so peremptory as to indicate the firm control of the Carthaginians over the island, is reported by Polybius:

'No Roman shall trade or found a city in Sardinia and Libya nor remain in a Sardinian or Libyan post longer than is required for taking in provisions or repairing his ship. If he be driven there by stress of weather, he shall depart within five days.'[14]

The situation changed drastically with the Punic Wars. In 259-258, during the first of these wars, Rome occupied Olbia, in the defence of which the general Hanno was killed, and raided the coasts of the island. But the Punic counter-offensive soon forced her to abandon her aspirations of conquest. In 240, however, the Carthaginian garrison in Sardinia, composed almost exclusively of mercenaries, revolted against the homeland, killed the generals Bostar and Hanno and spread terror among the Carthaginians. In the meantime Carthage was deep in her war with the mercenaries and therefore at one of the most critical periods of her history. The Sards reacted against the rebellious garrisons of Sardinia and forced the mercenaries to flee to Italy. The mercenaries then turned to Rome, who took the opportunity to occupy Sardinia and Corsica in 238. The Carthaginians tried to organize an expedition, but, threatened with war by Rome, they finally withdrew. And so ended Carthaginian rule on the island, which, together with Corsica, became the first Roman province overseas.

Carthaginian influence in Sardinia, however, did not end immediately; on the contrary, it aroused considerable hostility against the Romans, who were considered far greater enemies than the Carthaginians. So, in 215, after the battle of Cannae, the Sards rebelled against

Rome under the command of Hampsichoras and secretly asked Carthage
to reconquer the island. An army commanded by Hasdrubal the Bald
set sail, but as a result of the defeat of the Sards and the suicide of
Hampsichoras in the battle of Cornus (215) the attempt failed. The
Carthaginian army was defeated and the general taken prisoner.

2 Archaeology

Apart from the homeland and Carthage, Sardinia is undoubtedly the
region where the marks of the Phoenician-Punic civilization lay deepest.
The first settlements are ancient and certainly pre-Punic-Phoenician,
and the penetration from the coast towards the interior of the island was
considerable and performed with the intent of lasting conquest.

We are therefore faced with complex phenomena of ethnic and
cultural symbioses which give Phoenician-Punic culture in Sardinia
characteristics of its own. On one side the Phoenician and Punic components are joined by the Libyan ones, originating from North Africa
as a result either of the transfer of populations attested by history or of
prehistoric contacts; on the other side there is a close contiguity between
Phoenician-Punic and Sard culture, and subsequent original reactions.
Finally, Phoenician-Punic culture in Sardinia is considerably freer from
Greek influences than in Sicily and perhaps in Carthage, and therefore
constitutes a source of primary importance for an authentic view of the
characteristics of the Phoenician-Punic world.

With regard to the actual Phoenician influence which certainly
existed and preceded Punic influence, it is interesting to note indications
of origin from Spain: the traditional founders of Nora come from Spain
and the earliest colonies seem orientated for commerce with the West.
Moreover, this commerce must already have been active when the first
Sardinian colonies were founded, if it is true that Nora was founded in
the ninth century (or shortly before) while Cadiz existed by the end of
the twelfth century. Other interesting indications, such as the possible
mention of the god Pumay in the inscription of Nora, and certain elements
of Cypriot appearance (in particular clay statuettes) seem to connect the
Phoenicians of Sardinia with the island of Cyprus.

The Punic components, on the other hand, establish themselves in
the sixth century, and while they prevail over the preceding components
in the coastal cities, they are unique in the inland cities, since there
does not appear to have been a pre-Punic-Phoenician penetration into
the hinterland. Besides, the Punic components have linguistic reflections
which must not be overlooked; so place-names, like Macomer and Mago-
madas, and common names like *mizza*, 'spring', are certainly Punic.

The problem of the Libyan cultural component is complex. Two phases can obviously be suggested for it: the prehistoric phase (second millennium BC) in the cadre of general Mediterranean contacts; and the historic phase, in the cadre of the displacements of populations already mentioned. The Libyan influence is testified mainly by lexical facts, which sometimes also extend to the Iberian world.

We have seen how the encounter with Phoenician-Punic culture promoted certain typical developments of proto-Sardinian culture, such as the production of bronzes. We can add that the recent discoveries of Monte Sirai provide exceptionally valuable material for studying the relations between these two cultures. In Monte Sirai the encounter between Sardinian and Punic elements is evident; and, from numerous other indications, of which the most typical is the reversed symbol of Tanit in a tomb which must have been the work of a craftsman who did not understand its meaning, it seems equally evident that Sardinian artists worked on commissions from Carthaginians, adapting extrinsic themes but clearly showing their particular origins and traditions.

Barreca has written a detailed and perceptive study of Phoenician-Punic town planning in Sardinia. According to traditional Phoenician principles the cities were founded on the promontories or islets lying just off the coast. They usually had two ports, on opposite sides of the promontory, so that each could be in use, whichever direction the wind was blowing. In Nora and Tharros the isthmus joining the peninsula to the mainland served as a double mole. The same happened at Sulcis, on the narrow tongue of land which stretched towards the island and was prolonged to form an isthmus along which ran a canal joining the two ports. Karalis, on the other hand, can only have had one port, on the eastern shore of the lagoon of S. Gilla, but this was because the lagoon was constantly protected.

The Phoenician and Carthaginian method of constructing harbour wharfs can be gathered from certain stretches of the coast at Nora and Tharros: these stretches, now under the surface of the water, appear to have been levelled artificially, and we can therefore assume that the natural rock was smoothed out to form the wharfs, while the change of base level of the Sardinian coast has now brought what previously emerged for at least a couple of metres under the surface of the water.

According to the current system in harbour towns, the market square, where the merchandise was displayed and sold, must have been beside the port. The excavations of Nora have brought to light a similar square, the remains of which are actually of Imperial Roman epoch, but do not correspond topographically to the Roman construction principles and can therefore be considered of Phoenician or Punic origin.

To the west of the square of Nora, Pesce excavated a living quarter which has retained its Punic character despite the Roman alterations.

There are small squares or rectangular areas, with floors of clay and holes at the foot of the walls for the amphorae, and some walls of the characteristic 'loom' type. The houses are sometimes composed of two adjoining chambers and sometimes of several chambers round a central area which probably served as courtyard. Certain houses have a cistern of the typical 'bath-tub' shape – long and narrow with the shorter sides rounded; while others have been identified on the hill of Bythia with courtyards in front. In Cagliari the floors of Punic houses found in the quarter of S. Avendrace are of red beaten earth with white limestone tesserae forming geometrical figures and the typical sign of Tanit. Finally, we have a quarter of houses in Tharros which has been so altered that it is no longer possible to distinguish what is Punic from what is Roman. There is, however, an interesting type of water system composed of terracotta tubes built in the wall, which has hitherto not been found anywhere else.

The cities were undoubtedly surrounded by walls. Barreca has brought to light the remains of fortifications in Nora, Sulcis, Monte Sirai, and Tharros, and managed to identify the pre-Roman remains incorporated in the Pisan walls of Cagliari. From what we can judge, and as far as the terrain permitted, the system of defences must have been the same as that of Carthage: an outer wall surrounding the entire inhabited area and an inner wall enclosing the acropolis. The walls of Sulcis are a good example of outer defences, built in such a way as to exploit the natural conditions, resting on the hills which open in a semi-circle behind the harbour quarter, stretching beyond the inhabited area. As an example of inner defences we have those of Nora and Tharros, where the acropolis was built on the extreme tip of the mainland; those of Caralis, where it must have stood on the inner hill of the castle; and above all that of Monte Sirai, which, in 1964, yielded the most impressive Punic fortress yet known in Sardinia.

The acropolis of Monte Sirai stood on the southern ridge of the hill and was defended on the outer sides by large steep crags on which the walls were built with megalithic technique. On the inner side, instead, it was defended by a double line of fortifications to which access was gained through a narrow gate defended by two embattled towers. On the highest point of the acropolis stood a powerful keep flanked by chambers in which numerous objects pertaining to cults have been found.

In Sulcis the old road round the city has been excavated. Starting behind the outer walls, it permitted the troops to move rapidly from one place to another. We know little about other roads in the Punic cities: in Nora and Tharros, however, there seems to have been a main road leading from the harbour and the square to the acropolis, and it is possible that other cities were also built round a main street.

In the countryside surrounding the urban centres – and here again Sulcis is a good example – abundant traces of buildings and tombs of the Punic period have come to light. As at Carthage, houses and farms were probably scattered in the outskirts with rich agricultural cultivations. Minor towns, like Mazzacara near Sulcis and S. Salvatore di Cabras near Tharros, may have developed in this way.

There are numerous remains of Punic temples in Sardinia, but most of them are late and have complex elaborations. To start with the characteristic Phoenician 'high place' – a sacred area consisting of an open precinct with the object of the cult (betyl, aedicule) in the centre – an example is provided by S. Antioco on the Collina del Fortino. It is a rectangular precinct formed by large blocks of stone built over a demolished *nuraghe* (proto-Sardinian round tower). The temple of Tanit at Nora has also been qualified as a 'high place'. Patroni found a pyramidal stone cippus retaining an aniconic image of Tanit, and Mingazzini thought that the rest of the walls indicated an open precinct; it is possible, however, that there were further partitions inside. Another religious building in Nora, developed as a result of successive transformations, has revealed an aedicule of great interest, because it is the only one discovered hitherto in Sardinia and recalls a celebrated Phoenician model (Amrit): the base and the pediment remain, on which can be seen, as in the Oriental and African models, a winged solar disk surmounted by a row of uraei (fig 42).

The temple of Bes in Bythia is perhaps the only reminder of the traditional Phoenician temple with three successive chambers. As regards the rest, the type that prevails in Sardinia, at a relatively late period, is the shrine consisting of a cella preceded by a flight of steps and surrounded by a *temenos* (a clear development of the 'high place'); such is the monumental temple of Tharros, with a cella reproducing the familiar type of stelae, open in front with two semi-columns with volutes on either side supporting an architrave with Egyptian mouldings; the whole is on a high pedestal led to by a monumental ramp (fig 43). The temple found in Via Malta in Cagliari must have been similar; this was also preceded by an auditorium of Greek type which could be used for theatrical performances, or, better still, for gatherings.

Finally, a different type of temple has been found by Barreca at Tharros (Cape San Marco) in 1958 and at Monte Sirai in 1963 (fig 44). It is a sacellum of rectangular type accessible along a flight of steps built against a long side; the inside consists of compartments irregularly divided, the most sacred of which is destined for sacrifices. Parallels of this type of temple can be identified in certain sacred buildings in Cyprus at the beginning of the first millennium BC.

Another type of religious building preserved in Sardinia is the

topheth. Topheths once existed at Caralis and Nora, but their significance
was not understood, and today they are almost destroyed. There is a
particularly interesting one in Tharros, the excavations of which are
still at an early phase. The best *topheths* to study at the moment are
those of Sulcis and Monte Sirai. In Sulcis, on the northern outskirts of
the town, the *topheth* stands on a craggy hill, and on its slopes is a locality
which, because of the urns, is called *Sa guardia de is pingiadas* ('the sentry

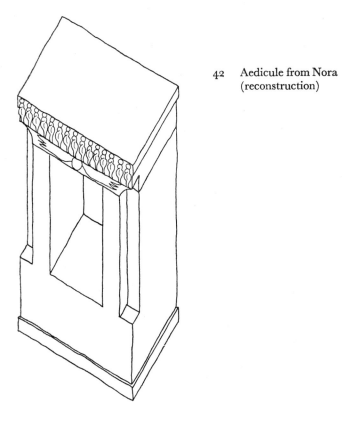

42   Aedicule from Nora
(reconstruction)

of the pots'). It consists of certain quadrangular courtyards of various
dimensions (fig 45): one large courtyard encloses three smaller ones,
two (one inside the other) near the top of the hill, and a third standing
free near the foot. The entrance is always on the southern side. One
stretch of large squared and embossed parallelepiped blocks remains of
the wall. The presence of single-beaked lamps suggests that the earliest
stratum goes back to the ninth century, and various successive strata
follow, which span the entire history of the city. In the *topheth* hundreds
of urns have been found containing children's bones and teeth together

with plates, lamps, terracotta figurines, betyls, and votive cippi bearing the image of Tanit in an architectural frame. The inscriptions attest that sacrifices to Tanit and to a male deity probably called Baal Addir were made here.

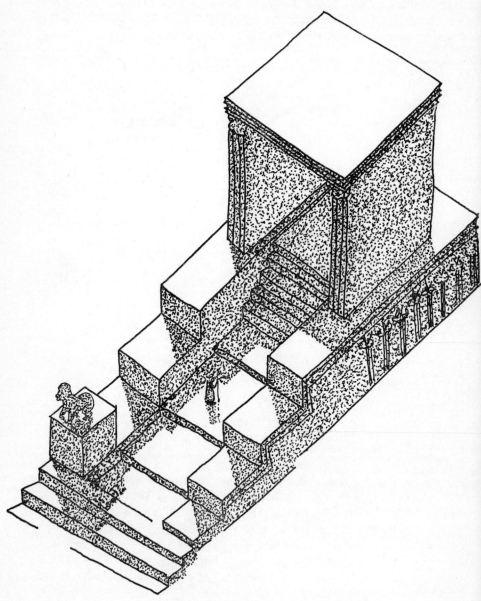

43   Temple of Tharros (reconstruction)

At Monte Sirai, as at Sulcis, the *topheth* is on the edge of the inhabited area. It consists of urns and stelae scattered among the rocks or on the earth amongst the stones, and probably has two strata, one of which can be ascribed to the fifth and fourth centuries at least, and the other to

0   1   2   3 m.

44   Temple of Monte Sirai

the third–first centuries. From the *topheth* a monumental flight of steps led to the temple we have described; and since a crematory oven with the remains of bones has been found, it is evident that the sacrifices were performed inside and not outside the temple.

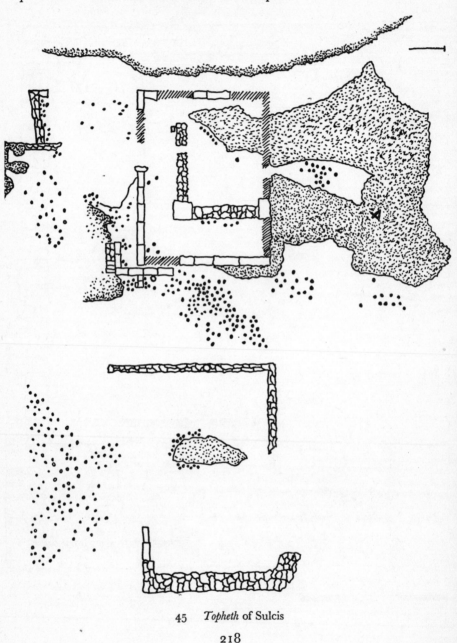

45   *Topheth* of Sulcis

Like the *topheth* the Punic necropolises were on the outskirts of the inhabited area. The situation varies, however, and, in addition to the tombs outside the walls, there are others within. The burials were mainly performed by inhumation and the tombs are of various types: they could be dug in the earth like plain graves, or made like 'chests' with blocks of stone, or cut in the rock with shafts or *dromos*. In this case the Phoenician prototypes are evident. The shaft-tombs (fig 46) consist of subterranean chambers accessible by shafts with footholds cut in the sides. The Carthaginian necropolis of Tuvixeddu at Cagliari is of this

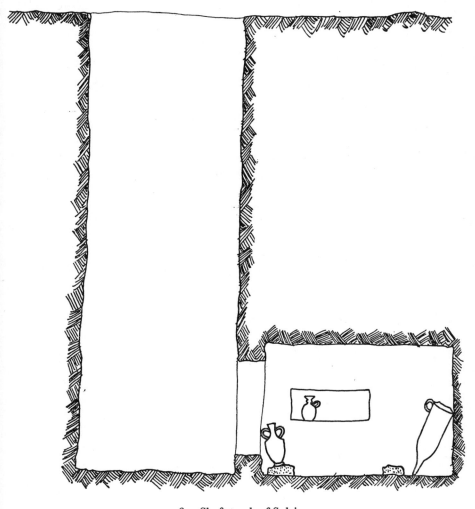

46   Shaft-tomb of Sulcis

type. The *dromos*-tombs (fig 47) are accessible along corridors with steps and consist of square or rectangular chambers, high enough for a man to stand in. The walls are covered by the tombs cut into the rock itself, or by small niches for vases and lamps. In the tombs the remains of wooden coffins varnished in red have been found. The funerary chamber can be divided into two parts, or into an antechamber and two chambers. The most important examples of necropolises with *dromos*-tombs are those of Sulcis and Monte Sirai. In this last locality there is an interesting tomb of which the central rock pillar remains, with the reversed sign of Tanit carved on it. Again at Monte Sirai, another tomb had a male head, perhaps of a demon, carved in the ceiling. It must have exercised an apotropaic function, and this recalls a similar custom in the later Punic tombs of Malta, as well as a tomb of Cyprus carved with a Gorgon's head. Finally we must note the absence in Sardinia, so far, of the stone anthropoid coffins so widespread in Phoenicia and the other parts of the Phoenician-Punic world.

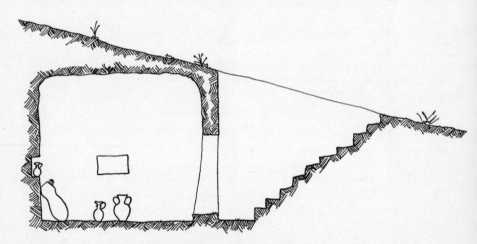

47   *Dromos*-tomb of Sulcis

Human statuary is scarce in Sardinia, although there are certain interesting examples. A divine image of great interest came from Monte Sirai in 1964 (plate 34). The head, accurately worked with clear volumetric masses, contrasts with the rest of the body of distinctly inferior porportions and hardly outlined. There are also other singular simplifications and stylizations: the arms barely outlined, curls on either side of the face, the ears reduced to two concentric circles.

A series of statues, conventionally defined as being of Bes, originates from Sardinia. The volumetric sensitivity suggests that most of them are of the Hellenistic era: this applies, for instance, to two statues from Maracalagonis, near Cagliari (plate 32) which also show (especially on the stomach) an accentuated feeling for the nude. Of the series of Bes, the best known is the colossal sandstone statue found by Taramelli in Bythia.

Another life-size statue in red granite, coming from the botanical garden of Cagliari and now in the local museum, also corresponds to the Punic tradition, even though it is late. It is a sphinx whose soft or almost inert features suggest models of the end of the fourth century or the beginning of the third (plate 52).

In the recent excavations of the monumental temple of Tharros a life-size sandstone lion has been found, squatting on its hind legs, one of its fore-paws pointed to the ground and the other stretched forward (plate 56). The extreme erosion of the statue suggests that it was long in the open air and it is probable that, like its remote Oriental archetypes, it was put in guard of the shrine. Pesce, the author of the excavations in Tharros, suggests a date in the fourth–third century B C. Not far away the thigh and tail of a similar lion, which probably formed a protective pair with the other on either side of the entrance to the sanctuary, was found.

A few words must be said about the betyls, large pillars in which the deity was thought to exist. While the rest of the Punic world has yielded a great quantity of betyls in relief on the stelae, Sardinia has yielded many completely round ones: one is from Monte Sirai and has a square pedestal and a base into which it fitted; others come from the Punta 'e su Sensu, where they suggest the presence of an early shrine in the open air.

Passing on to the smaller statuary, there are hardly any remains of the typical Phoenician production of bronzes. A statuette from the Nurra, twenty kilometres north-east of Alghero, represents a narrow head and bust of a bearded male figure with characteristic pointed cap; the left arm is folded forwards and the right raised in sign of blessing; the figurine is naked (plate 46). Pesce suggests an eighth–seventh century date. Another bronze statuette comes from Genoni (province of Nuoro) and represents a bearded male figure with a crown of feathers and a long close-fitting tunic, arms in the same position as the preceding example: however, this figure, assumed to be an image of the *Sardus Pater*, dated from the end of the fifth to the beginning of the fourth century, cannot definitely be considered a product of Punic craftsmanship. In the Hellenistic age statuettes of Isis suckling Horus, Osiris, and Harpocrates were imported from Egypt.

The small wood carvings remain the only examples of a production that certainly existed, but which perished owing to the nature of the material. One of them represents Osiris and originates from Olbia, and the other, in worse condition, may represent Bes and comes from Nora. We must note that, according to recent studies, the moulds of the proto-Sardinian bronzes must have been of wood and not of wax or clay.

Passing on to small sculpture in terracotta, Punic Sardinia presents a rich and varied production, extremely interesting because of the relationship with the other parts of the Phoenician-Punic world. Certain female figurines recall a Palestinian and Cypriot typology: a nude goddess standing and holding her breasts (cf. the example from Nora of the sixth century BC) (plate 67); a standing goddess in a draped robe and Egyptian headdress, holding her arms close to her body (cf. the example from Tharros, also of the sixth century); a standing goddess clad in a Doric peplos with a wide hem, her hands on her chest, one of which holds a crown and the other a lotus flower (cf. the example from Tharros dated towards the end of the sixth century); a standing goddess of Hellenic type, but with a Phoenician-Punic tambourine (cf. the example from Tharros dated in the sixth century); a seated goddess of Hellenic type, but also known in Punic tombs (cf. the example from Predio Ibba in Cagliari, dated in the middle of the sixth century); Bes of a type similar to that of the larger sculpture, and interesting on account of the high feathered head-dress and the remains of polychrome colouring which suggest characteristics similar to the larger statues (cf. the example from the burial ground of Via Ismalias in Cagliari, dated at the beginning of the Hellenistic age). Two fragmentary statuettes have a place to themselves of particular importance – one from Sulcis and the other from Monte Sirai, representing a male head with pointed beard jutting out: this detail suggests specific Cypriot influences. In other cases the typology is clearly Graecizing, so, despite the fact that it is sometimes found in the Punic world, it cannot be considered a part of the production which we define as Phoenician-Punic in Sardinia.

The major discovery of Sardinian sculpture is that of the votive *stipe* of Bythia by Pesce. Near the temple of Bes, in a large trench, about two hundred statuettes were found on two strata: the lower stratum, composed of sand mixed with black soil, contained complete figurines in more or less good condition; the upper stratum, composed of sand mixed with grey soil, contained fragments of figurines, like bodies lacking heads, arms, and legs. The statuettes had evidently once been removed from the temple and buried, and the complete examples were separated from the fragmentary ones. Other objects were found together with the statuettes: perfume-burners, lamps, vases, bronze rings, necklace beads, gold beads, amulets, shells. Although no other locality in Sardinia has yielded finds comparable to those of Bythia, we must mention the discovery of two similar statuettes in Nora and Tharros. This suggests the vast spread of this type of production which has important parallels outside Sardinia, in Carthage, Motya, and Ibiza.

The typology of the statuettes is as follows (plate 70): the body consists of a reversed bell-shaped vase modelled on a potter's wheel; the head, arms, and sexual organs seem to have been put on later. While the vases are evidently prefabricated, the characterization is individual so that no two figurines are identical. The arms in particular are always articulated in a different way, so that the hands, formed with pieces of dung, are placed on different parts of the body. Because of these characteristics Pesce supposed that the statuettes were *ex-votos* offered by the faithful to recover from diseases indicated by the position of the hands. The same author grouped the statuettes into typological and stylistic categories. In this respect the hands are of particular interest, and there can be distinguished a round type, a pear-shaped type, and a flattened type. The body also presents different typologies: chalice-shaped, bowl-shaped, bell-shaped, tube-shaped, glass-shaped. On the whole, it was a humble and popular art, but none the less expressive and skilful.

Passing on to relief, a small monument from Tharros has a position to itself. Forty-one centimetres tall and carved in sandstone, it has the aspect of a cippus around which are four dancing figures: the back view of three nude female figures, and the frontal view of one male figure wearing a skirt. Above the head of the male figure an ox-head emerges from the cippus. The cippus itself ends in a sort of pyramid with steps. According to Pesce, it can be ascribed to the third–second century BC. Also from Tharros we have a small cippus in sandstone on which the figure of a hero slaying a winged monster is carved in relief (plate 5). A date has been suggested at the end of the sixth century.

The stelae constitute a category of abundant and varied reliefs in which Sardinia again assumes a pre-eminent position in the Punic world. To start with, Punic production came into contact with the proto-Sardinian environment, where the production of betyls and stelae is notable. Indeed, Lilliu has emphasized the specific resemblance between a proto-Sardinian example from Biristeddi and a Punic one from Nora. In any case, the environment seems to have favoured the development of Punic production. Another singular fact is that there are no throne cippi or pointed stelae, so characteristic of the second phase of Carthaginian production. And usually the Semitic elements prevail over the Greek ones, although the latter ultimately appear in the lateral supports of Doric or Ionic small columns, or in the infrequent pediments with triangular tympanum and acroteria, but not in the main elements of the figurative field (and this in Sulcis, not in Nora).

Passing on to the examination of the various groups of stelae, the main centres from which they originate are Nora, Sulcis, and Monte Sirai. As far as Nora is concerned, the aniconic idols are widespread: so we have the pillar-shaped betyl, either on its own or composed in the betylic couple and triad, this last very frequent and sometimes surmounted by the symbols of the crescent moon and the sun; the lozenge on an altar flanked by other symbols on a smaller scale; and the bottle-idol, with a wide variety of frames and sometimes on a high base (plate 20). An interesting characteristic of the stelae of Nora is that the aniconic symbol tends to become iconic and a barely outlined human image emerges from the lozenge. The bottle-idol develops more clearly, both with the shaping of the form of the body and the juxtapositioning of short arms. Passing on to the iconic idols, the naked goddess holding her breasts and the goddess with a long robe holding a tambourine are widespread. Peculiar to the stelae of Nora are certain walking figures seen in profile facing right or left, which directly recall Oriental precedents. The symbol of Tanit appears from the fifth century and is the only indication of chronological development in a production which starts in the seventh–sixth century and whose characteristics undergo little alteration in the course of time. Patroni, who published the stelae of Nora, has observed that the only trace of Greek influence in this production is provided by the Doric column which appears once (as an architectural frame). Otherwise it is significant that the production of Nora should be connected to Carthaginian and directly Oriental models without following the Graecizing developments typical of Carthage.

The production of Sulcis differs from that of Nora in the prevalence of iconic depictions over aniconic ones. The latter only exist in a limited quantity in the earlier phase of the production (seventh–sixth century) and here again we have the betylic pillars, sometimes large and lightly incised at Motya, but always on their own or in couples, never in triads, and we also have the bottle-idols. Of the iconic figurations there are certain noteworthy rude male figurines, and in particular one male figure in profile facing right, with a long robe and left arm stretched out to hold a spear, which appears on a stele recently published by Pesce and believed to be the earliest in Sardinia, a pre-Punic-Phoenician product (plate 29). After this by far the most prevalent iconography in Sulcis is that of the female figure holding a tambourine to her breast; in other cases the figure either holds her right arm close to her body and her left folded on her breast, or holds a lotus flower on her breast with both hands, or has the *ankh* in her right hand and holds her dress in her left. The figure initially appears naked, but then assumes a long robe of Greek type, and the treatment of the figure and dress becomes Hellenized. A similar process of Hellenization can be noted in the aedicule, at first with Egyptian mouldings, uraei, and solar disk, and Aeolic-Cypriot capitals, but soon supported by Doric and Ionic columns. Independent currents, however, do not disappear at a later period: of the Hellenistic period we have a group of stelae with curved tips, astral symbols and a figure of a walking ram which suggests ancient Asiatic models (plate 49). There are also figures of Tanit coarsely treated in the local manner (stelae of Nora). Finally, we must note the appearance in Sulcis, among the most recent discoveries, of marble aedicules fitted in large sandstone cubes.

The settlement of Monte Sirai, recently brought to light, has so far yielded several dozen stelae dated between the fifth and first century BC. The settlement shares many characteristics with Sulcis, but the standard of production is inferior and Sardinian craftsmanship emerges with special traits. A first group of stelae presents an Egypticizing aedicule enclosing a female figure clad in a long tunic, usually holding a tambourine to her breast, more rarely holding a vase-shaped receptacle, or with one hand on her breast and the other by her side, holding the symbol of Tanit (plate 41). This iconography is connected to that of Sulcis and Nora, but the significant appearance of Sardinian peculiarities in the garb of some examples prepares the way for independent characteristics. A second and third group are more autonomous: the cornice is engraved on stone or is simply constituted by the edge of the stele, and a coarse human figure appears in the centre. The fourth group, typologically new, no longer has a cornice and the figure is simply engraved in its essential characteristics: a female image with a child (plate 21) indicates a figurative language more Sardinian than Punic. Finally, only one example has come to light of a fifth group, consisting of a very worn triangular stele with the coarse figure of a quadruped. Certain general observations can be applied to this material to compare it with that of other localities. There is no aniconism, so the stelae of Monte Sirai differ more from the African prototypes than the other Sardinian ones.

To Nora, Sulcis, and Monte Sirai we can add Tharros, whose stelae are so far unpublished. We can assume that they present an accentuated aniconism and that there is widespread use of the symbol of the bottle in an Egypticizing aedicule. Further stelae come from various parts of the island. The major production presented hitherto, however, suffices to illustrate the importance of this sort of art which had a flourishing development in Sardinia and was characterized by the long survival of archaic elements even at a late period, relatively advanced elsewhere. This applies above all to Nora and Monte Sirai, where there were also clear and singular emergences of the local Sardinian substratum.

While stone relief is completed with the head from the ceiling of a tomb on Monte Sirai (plate 40), another type of relief peculiar to the Punic world and which finds parallels in Sardinia are the protomai and terracotta masks. The typology of female protomai already brought to light in Carthage is repeated, and there is the same differentiation between protomai of Egyptian influence, with a *klaft*, impassive expression, and eyebrows forming a right-angle with the nose, and protomai of Greek influence, with a veil, smiling expression, slanting eyes, eyebrows continuing the lines of the nose in an arch, pointed nose, and jutting-out chin (plate 59). The best examples, belonging to the second type, come from Tharros and Sulcis. There is furthermore one male protome with long beard and curls found on Monte Sirai in 1964 (plate 63) which is worth noting.

The grimacing masks also find parallels in Sardinia. One of the best examples of the second type identified by Cintas at Carthage is a beardless face, heavy lines on the forehead and cheeks, crescent-shaped eye sockets pointing down, and a large mouth hole turning up on the sides, coming from a Punic tomb in S. Sperate near Cagliari. The fifth Cintas group – bearded face of Silenus, painted animal-like ears, and small almost round eye sockets – is represented in an example from a tomb in Tharros. Other masks, instead, are completely Graecizing, and do not really belong to this category (there is one of a bearded god from the Stagno di S. Gilla in Cagliari).

The tombs of Sardinia have yielded a series of small amulets which show close connexions with those found in Carthage. They are of soapstone, glass paste, bone, and hardstone. The most frequent divine figures are Horus, Bes, Thueris, Anubis, and Shu. The animals include sows, cats, lions, doves, chariots, and crocodiles. We note the eye, the hands, the sexual organs, and the figure of Tanit.

In Sardinia, too, there are the characteristic amulet-bearing tubes. They have been found in Tharros and Olbia, are about four centimetres tall and have a lion- or sparrow-headed lid. They are both in bronze and gold, and a fine example from Tharros with a lion's head contains a golden lamina engraved with scenes from the Egyptian last judgement.

The characteristic Punic razors, already found in Carthage, also reappear in Sardinia. Altogether about fifty have been found, with handles in the shape of heads of ibises (frequently forked), ducks, waders, and swordfish. The suspension hole does not protrude, but, as in the majority of Carthaginian examples, is on the blade. Only six of the Sardinian razors hitherto known are decorated, by means of incisions either engraved or chiselled. The earliest is an example nineteen centimetres long and three and a half centimetres wide, with a handle in the shape of an ibis head with a very long forked beak bearing, engraved on one side of the blade, an Aeolic capital, a Phoenician palmette, and a rose with ten petals. A sixth-century date has been suggested. Of Hellenistic age we get a razor bearing on one side a nude female figure and on the other a strange Gorgonian mask with a bust formed by a solar disk and crescent moon; another bears on one side a male figure sitting under a vine-branch, maybe in the act of shaving, and on the other a swan in profile; another bears on one side the figure of Isis poised over the coffin of Osiris and on the other a procession of magic Egypticizing figurines. As Pesce, who published the razors, says, the production is similar but not identical to that of Carthage. Both in the form and ornamentation we have new and distinctive aspects which suggest local craftsmanship with a repertory of its own.

Coming to the objects in ivory and bone, we note, besides the amulets, the reliefs in bone of a casket from a tomb in Nora: they show hares and calves squatting. Other bone objects are a flute from a tomb in Tharros and an engraved bird, formerly part of a casket or the handle of a mirror, from a tomb in Sulcis. Excavations in Monte Sirai have brought to light various fragments of worked gold, one of which represents the bust of a male deity with arms folded on his breast (plate 88). There are also smaller objects, like hairpins, spoons, spatulae, and pen-holders.

Gold and silver jewels were widespread in Sardinia, perpetuating characteristic motifs. The best examples are from Tharros, where pendant ear-rings abound: so we get a gold ear-ring consisting of an upper part shaped like a half-moon, followed by two rings, a hawk, two more rings and finally an acorn-shaped pendant-box. The granulation technique suggests a seventh–sixth century date. The bracelets in which the Phoenician motifs of the palmettes and scarab are particularly evident are also widespread: so we get another example from Tharros (plate 92) composed of five laminae joined by clasps of which the centre bears a four-winged scarab and the head of a hawk, the two intermediary ones palmettes with volutes, and the last two Proto-Aeolic capitals; here again the granulation technique points to the seventh–sixth century, although a later date was suggested.

A large series of scarabs comes from the Punic tombs of Sardinia, and in particular from Tharros and Cornus. The classification already made in Carthage is repeated: some are of glazed pottery, others of hardstone like green jasper. In the first group, as at Carthage, the iconography is typically Egyptian. In the second group it is partly Egypticizing and partly Graecizing. On the whole the production of green jasper prevails in Sardinia, and probably originated there.

Ostrich eggs, cut in the shape of disks or crescent moons and sometimes engraved or painted to resemble human faces, eyes, flowers or geometrical figures, come from certain Sardinian tombs, mainly from Cagliari and Tharros. The glass, as at Carthage, has given polychrome perfume flasks, enamelled and iridescent cinerary urns, and necklace pendants shaped like small masks. There are numerous amulets in glass paste; in the necropolises of Olbia, Levi found some of very varied typology (naked Astarte, Bes, the hawk, the serpent, the uraeus, the cock, the monkey, the pig, lion protomai, the breast, the heart, and the hand). Coins were struck in Sardinia from the fourth century: on the obverse they bear the head of Tanit, on the reverse, the horse, the bull, ears of corn (and as complementary elements the palm tree and the sun emitting rays). The pottery repeats the characteristics already recorded at Carthage. In the earliest period we have glazed mushroom-lipped and trefoil-lipped jugs. There are some examples of *chardon* vases and jugs with cylindrical neck and ring and linear designs, while umbilicated plates are quite frequent. There are also interesting animal-shaped vases, large amphorae with peg bottoms (the excavations of Nora have shown the holes in the floor in which they stood), and the typical two-beaked lamps, as well as single-beaked lamps at Sulcis (an indication of great antiquity).

3 Religion

The discovery of numerous *topheths* seems the most obvious characteristic of Phoenician-Punic religion in Sardinia – a characteristic that fits in with the environment of which we have already examined the Carthaginian and Sicilian data. The *topheths*, however, are not the only places of cult to have come to light in Sardinia: there are also the remains of temples.

The Phoenician-Punic pantheon of Sardinia is indicated by inscriptions. As at Carthage, Baal Hammon and Tanit Pene Baal prevail. Furthermore, we note Melqart, Eshmun with the epithet 'Merreh',[15] Baal Shamem (in the form Bashshamem, recorded in an inscription mentioning his temple on the Island of Hawks, now S. Pietro)[16] Baal Addir, and Astarte. Baal Shemem and Baal Addir may be variants or different aspects of Baal Hammon, and the relations between Tanit and Astarte are well known. An inscription from Cagliari mentions Astarte Erycine,[17] and according to some this deity had a sanctuary of her own in Sardinia, while others consider her purely Sicilian. In a late bilingual inscription from Sulcis[18] the mention of Elat may simply refer to the 'goddess' Tanit. From the onomatology we get Sid, known in Carthage, while Pumay, mentioned in the inscription of Nora, goes back to an important Cypriot prototype. Finally, we are not sure of the identity of the Pygmoid god conventionally called Bes and certainly widespread in Sardinia. He seems to serve as a tutelary spirit in the cadre of the current popular superstitions, to judge from the amulets. In this respect the head (probably demonic) carved on the ceiling of a tomb in Monte Sirai is significant.

Finally we note the long persistence of Punic religion in Sardinia, beyond the Roman occupation. This is attested both by the Punic and Neo-Punic inscriptions, and by the survival of religious production of Punic type and its characteristic symbols in art.

CHAPTER 17

SPAIN

1 History

The Phoenicians colonized Spain in order to obtain control of the sources of the metal trade (gold, tin, and, above all, silver), which they later sold in the East at a large profit. The ancient authors tell us of this, and Diodorus, insisting on the essential value of this traffic, leads us to believe that it was the reason for, rather than the result of, the foundation of the colonies:

And the result was that the Phoenicians, as in the course of many years they prospered greatly, thanks to commerce of this kind, sent forth many colonies, some to Sicily and its neighbouring islands, and others to Libya, Sardinia, and Iberia.[1]

We have a series of accounts concerning the period of the colonization of Cadiz. Strabo, quoting Posidonius, tells that various expeditions were sent by the Tyrians to the Pillars of Hercules, and that the third of these expeditions resulted in the foundation of Cadiz with the sanctuary on the eastern part of the island and the city on the western part.[2] Velleius Paterculus specifies that eighty years after the fall of Troy, c. 1110, the Tyrian fleet, which ruled the sea, founded Cadiz at the tip of Spain on an island surrounded by the Ocean and separated from the mainland by a short strait; soon after, he adds, the same Tyrians founded Utica.[3] Since the sources of Utica provide the date of 1101, nothing seems to contradict the foundation of Cadiz in 1110.

From the archaeological point of view, the discovery in 1963 of the necropolis of the Cerro de San Cristobal near Almuñécar (ancient Sexi) and in 1964 of the necropolis of the Cortijo de los Toscanos near Torre del Mar allows us to go back to the eighth century BC. The first of these two necropolises has actually yielded cartouches of pharaohs of the ninth century, but it is obvious that they may have been imported subsequently. From the eighth or seventh century we have a seal with Phoenician inscriptions of a certain Naamel, from Cadiz. Of the seventh century we have a seal of Psammetichus I, found in Alcacer do Sal (near

Salacia) and we can date the ivories of Carmona at about the same time. For these reasons archaeologists, including Donald Harden, have tended to ascribe Phoenician colonization in Spain to a later date. But the general characteristics of Phoenician colonization in the Mediterranean correspond to the installation of trading-posts on the Spanish coasts from *c.* 1100. Indeed, the Phoenicians succeeded the Mycenaeans in trade with the West, and it is at this time that the phenomenon takes place. Cadiz was in a very important position, from the commercial point of view, since it guarded the area of the silver-mines of Tartessus. It was therefore evidently one of the first Phoenician settlements, and the tradition according to which Lixus, on the Moroccan coast, was founded before Cadiz (as Pliny[4] says) is also significant. From these cities the Phoenicians could control the Mediterranean trade routes and at the same time open the routes on the Atlantic coasts. At first there was no need for colonies to be numerous, since it was only possible to control navigation in certain points. This assumption of the Atlantic strongholds was obvious to the ancient historians: Strabo claims that after the Trojan War the Phoenicians sailed beyond the Pillars of Hercules and founded cities there.[5] Finally justifiable emphasis has been given to the fact that Greek colonization began in the eighth century, and that history suggests Phoenician precedence (García y Bellido).

We now come to one of the main problems of Phoenician colonial expansion: the problem of Tarshish-Tartessus, from which an entire aspect of the movement of Mediterranean expansion depends. Starting with the biblical sources, we read with reference to Solomon that 'the king had at sea a navy of Tarshish with the navy of Hiram: once in three years came the navy of Tarshish, bringing gold, and silver, ivory, and apes, and peacocks'.[6] Jeremiah mentions 'silver spread into plates brought from Tarshish, and gold from Ophir'.[7] Ezekiel tells Tyre: 'Tarshish was thy merchant by reason of the multitude of all kind of riches; with silver, iron, tin, and lead, they traded in thy fairs.'[8] From these quotations and others of less importance it seems clear that, even if 'navy of Tarshish' can generically mean 'ocean-going navy', the expression originates from the fact that Tarshish designates a city or a region in the West, particularly rich in metals. The epoch to which the texts refer can be placed around the tenth century and after it.

Passing on to the classical sources, it is obvious that Tartessus is a locality in southern Spain. The poet Stesichorus, who wrote *c.* 600 BC in Sicily, has left us a line quoted by Strabo which mentions 'the unlimited, silver-rooted springs of the river Tartessus'.[9] If this refers to the river, the city is mentioned by the poet Anacreon (*c.* 530), again quoted by Strabo,[10] with reference to Arganthonius, long-lived king of Tartessus.

In the fifth century, but referring to an earlier period, Herodotus tells of the voyage of Kolaios to Tartessus,[11] and of the friendship between the Phocaeans and the local king Arganthonius.[12] Finally, from various authors of the sixth century, the following description of Tartessus was reconstructed:

Tartessus is an illustrious city of Iberia which takes its name from the river Baetis (Guadalquivir) formerly also called Tartessus. This river comes from the Celtic region and has its source in the 'silver mountain'; in its stream it carries, besides silver and tin, a great abundance of gold and bronze. The river Tartessus divides into two arms when it reaches the mouth. Tartessus, the city, stands between the two arms, as on an island.[13]

Now, is the biblical Tarshish definitely the same as the Greek Tartessus? Recent studies tend to give Tarshish a common rather than a proper value, meaning 'mine' (from the Semitic root *ršš*). If this hypothesis is not very probable, we must also mention the fact that Tarshish appears in the genealogy of Genesis,[14] together with Elisha and Kittim, both names indicating the island of Cyprus, which would validate the ancient theory, sustained by Josephus[15] and Eusebius,[16] that Tarshish is to be identified with Tarsus in Cilicia. Whatever the value of these observations, however, it seems certain that at a given moment Tarshish really was taken to denote Tartessus, evidently because of the phonetic affinity.

Tartessus, therefore, was a city and state which extended far and was rich from the trade in metals. What was its relationship with Cadiz? It seems likely that the Phoenicians of Cadiz succeeded to the Tartessian routes and trade, or in any case used and supported them. And this is why the Phoenicians founded Cadiz in the neighbourhood of Tartessus. But where exactly was Tartessus? The traditional Spanish theory places the town on the site of Mesas de Asta, ancient Asta Regia, near Jerez. Others have sought it at Doñana, at the mouth of the Guadalquivir, but excavations have not confirmed this theory. A further possible hypothesis places it in Huelva or in the neighbourhood, on the island of Saltés. In any case, the ancient city, the remains of which have not definitely been identified by archaeology, was in the region of the lower Guadalquivir.

Little is known about the expansion of Phoenician colonization from Cadiz. According to Strabo[17] the Tyrians 'occupied before the age of Homer the best of Iberia and Libya'. We are in no position to extract more than an indication of what appears obvious to us from this account, and that is an expansion on the coast and maybe also into the interior, not so much with an intent to conquer as to reinforce the landing-stages in more points than one.

The gradual establishment of the power of Carthage determined her substitution to Tyre in the control of the ports in the West. With regard to the Spanish area, an account by Timaeus, recorded by Diodorus,[18] informs us that one hundred and sixty years after the foundation of Carthage, in 654–653 BC, the Carthaginians founded a colony at Ibiza in the Baleares. The form of the name Eresos must stand for Ebysos, hence the Latin Ebusos, and present Ibiza. In this case the archaeological finds fully confirm the historical data: from Ibiza, and more exactly from the Isla Plana, now joined to the rest of the island, but then separated, we have terracotta figurines of the type of the Sardinian ones found in Bythia, of which some, at least, go back to the seventh century. The finds of Isla Plana also suggest the first Carthaginian landing-stage, whence the settlers subsequently spread to the larger island.

The occupation of Ibiza is highly significant. The position of the island is decisive for the control of the sea and trade routes on the way to the Spanish ports; the possession of Cadiz, Ibiza, south-western Sardinia and the western tip of Sicily constituted an insurmountable barrier protecting the seas off the African coast. The Greeks, who had tried to reach the Pillars of Hercules and had even founded a colony at Mainake, in the vicinity of Malaga, gradually abandoned trade with southern Spain and turned towards the northern coasts of the Mediterranean. The foundation of Massalia, c. 600, Alalia, c. 560, and Emporion, c. 550, mark the stages of the political and commercial development. And yet Greek prestige in Spain did not die out altogether: according to Herodotus,[19] Arganthonius, king of Tartessus, between the end of the seventh and the middle of the sixth century, distinguished himself by his philhellenism.

The decisive encounter with the Greeks took place at Alalia in 535. In alliance with the Etruscans the Carthaginians defeated the Phocaeans and gained control of the Mediterranean area. Spain was now closed to the Greeks: Mainake must have been destroyed at about that time; if, as its name suggests, Abdera really did start as a Greek colony, it then became Punic; and Tartessus began to decline. In 510 BC the first treaty of Carthage with Rome decreed Punic dominion in the western Mediterranean: the Romans and their allies, stated the treaty, were not to sail beyond the Fair Promontory; that is, according to the most likely explanation, they were not to sail west of the promontory of Carthage.

In 348 BC the second treaty of Carthage with Rome stated that the Romans were not to trade or found cities beyond the Fair Promontory and 'Mastia of Tarseum'. This last city, to be situated near Cartagena, must therefore have formed the eastern border of the Spanish territory controlled by Carthage; and the order not to found cities now implies the extension of Carthaginian colonial dominion to the south of the peninsula. But although the sources give a good indication of the extent and principal cities of this dominion, they give no dates concerning its foundation. We cannot be far from the truth if we assume that the dominion established and consolidated itself between the battle of Alalia (535) and the second treaty with Rome (348).

The main Punic colonies were Sexi, Malaga, and Abdera on the southern coast, which proved their importance by striking their own coins in the Roman era. There must also have been smaller cities dedicated mainly to the industry of curing fish. The eastern limit, which has been confirmed archaeologically, is Baria, now Villaricos, while, as we said, the boundary indicated in the second treaty with Rome is Mastia near Cartagena.

Beyond the Pillars of Hercules, on the Atlantic coast, new centres undoubtedly radiated from ancient Cadiz. The *Ora maritima* of Avienus, in a translation from a Greek text datable soon after 500, says that the Carthaginians 'had peoples and cities' beyond the Pillars of Hercules,[20] and the Periplus of Pseudo-Skylax in the fourth century mentions many Carthaginian trading-posts in the region.[21] García y Bellido drew up a list of Hispano-Portuguese settlements where factories of the Roman era for curing fish were found and which were probably the continuation of Punic centres: Mellaría, Bailon, Baisipo, and beyond Cadiz, Cacella, Antas, Torre de Ares, Praia de Quarteira, Pera de Baixo, Portimão, Vao, N. Senhora de Luz, Bocca do Rio; still farther north, near Troia at the mouth of the Sado, there were more industries of curing fish. In the south-western corner of Spain there were other centres, characterized by the discovery of Punic coins: Asido (Medina Sidonia), Oba, Vesci, Lascuta, Arsa, Iptuci, Ituci, Olont, Turris Regina, etc. Bailon has also yielded coins. Finally, toponymy suggests the Punic origin of Suel and Selambina, in the vicinity of Malaga and Sexi respectively.

That Carthaginian penetration was not restricted to the coastal settlements, but spread a certain distance inland in the southern region, and that it was accompanied by ethnic infiltrations is proved by the repeated reference to 'Libyphoenicians' in the classical sources as the population of the area in question. They were evidently Carthaginian settlers in whom the North African element played a strong part; but the term only applies to this particular zone and does not extend to Cadiz and the Atlantic coast on one side nor to Ibiza on the other.

The second treaty with Rome is followed by a long dearth of information. In 241 BC the First Punic War ended with the loss of Sicily, which was rapidly followed by the loss of Sardinia and Corsica abroad and the war with the mercenaries at home. In Spain we learn that the local population took advantage of the crisis to gain possession of Carthaginian territories in that region. Whether this happened during the First Punic War or in the period between the end of this war (241) and Hamilcar Barca's expedition (237) we cannot say for sure. This last solution seems the most likely, since the crisis of the mercenaries in Carthage and of the possessions in Spain might well have taken place at the same time.

The offensive of the local population against Carthage met with resistance in Cadiz, and it was here that Hamilcar Barca landed in 237, after bringing the war with the mercenaries to a victorious close. Passing beyond the primitive limits of Carthaginian penetration, his reconquest seems more like a genuine policy of territorial annexation – the natural result of the new political and military situation in which the Carthaginians were driven out of the Mediterranean islands. Spain remained the only foothold for revenge against Rome, and plans were favoured by the mineral and agricultural wealth of the region as well as the possibility of recruiting mercenaries.

That the expedition of Hamilcar and his intent to conquer in Spain were the result of an individual policy rather than of a general policy of the Carthaginian senate seems hardly likely. It is more likely that the powerful personality of Hamilcar and his family had made the Barcids an almost independent power in the state, which guided rather than obeyed the common decisions. Hamilcar was wholly successful in his venture, and, within nine years, with military victories and diplomatic skill, he had gained control over the entire southern part of the peninsula. The foundation of Akra Leuke (Castrum Album) marks the zenith of his power in Spain.

After his defeat and death in the battle of Elike (228), Hamilcar was succeeded by his son-in-law, Hasdrubal, who continued his political and military aims. Having reinforced his control of the occupied territory, he founded the new Punic city of Cartagena on the site of ancient Mastia, and, in 226, reached an agreement with Rome in which the Ebro was to mark the limit of Punic expansion. This was a great diplomatic success, at a difficult moment for Rome, which allowed Carthage to expand considerably in the Iberian dominion.

The assassination of Hasdrubal in 221 brought Hannibal to power. He immediately decided to extend his dominion into the interior. Helmantiké (Salamanca) and Arbukala (probably Toro) fell and the enemy was routed at the Tagus. The whole area south of the Ebro fell to Carthage, and the Second Punic War broke out in Saguntum in 218. After the swift advance beyond the Alps, which seems to have ensured Carthaginian dominion over the whole of Spain, the fortunes of the war changed. Scipio conquered Cartagena in 209, Cadiz in 206, and put an end to Phoenician-Punic history in Spain.

2 *Archaeology*

The Phoenician-Punic finds in Spain originate mainly from the necropolises of Cadiz and Ibiza, which are better documented than any other locality. But our knowledge is conditioned by the fact that these finds are scarce in the sphere of civil and non-sepulchral architecture and are principally funerary objects.

Chronologically, in order to distinguish the Phoenician from the Punic phase, we can possibly attribute the ivories of Carmona to the Phoenicians, while the rest of the material discovered must probably be ascribed to the Punic phase, although we cannot give exact dates.

With regard to the general characteristics, we can say that Spanish material seems far more evolved than either the Sardinian or the Sicilian material from Motya, or rather that the archaic elements existing in Sardinia and Sicily are lacking in Spain. The reason for this must be the Punic origin of nearly all this production and the constant contacts with the Greek world which left in Spain a deep mark.

Phoenician-Punic town planning is again confirmed in Spain. Cadiz is a long island lying opposite the coast, from which it is divided by a stretch of sea containing a smaller island. The situation of Motya is repeated, with the addition of a stable settlement on the larger island. Nothing is left of the civil buildings, but there are several remains of factories for curing fish and the production of the *garum* greatly appreciated in Rome, as in Bailon and Baria.

Literary sources inform us of the temples in Cadiz: that of Kronos (Baal Hammon) was in the inhabited area on the northern tip of the island, while the better known one of Heracles (Melqart) was on the southern point.[22] The temple of Heracles was in all probability of Phoenician origin and, according to Strabo,[23] contained two bronze columns bearing a dedication, together with the list of expenses entailed by the building of the temple itself: this is reminiscent both of Solomon's building in Jerusalem and of the Cypriot models of sacred buildings. Strabo adds that the precinct of the temple contained two sweet-water springs which evidently served as holy water for the shrine.[24] According to tradition, the fame of the temple of Heracles was such that the greatest generals always visited it. To this literary information archaeology has only added the identification of an open-air rock shrine, in the locality of Cueva d'es Cuyram in Ibiza, which has yielded about six thousand terracotta figurines. A votive inscription assigns the shrine to Tanit.

So far no *topheths* have come to light in Spain, unless the shrine of Cueva d'es Cuyram was one; but there are numerous necropolises, usually dug into the rock and accessible directly or along a short passage. We have the example of a short *dromos* or gallery in Villaricos. The most important necropolises are those of Punta de la Vaca in Cadiz, with tombs four to five metres deep, datable between the fifth and third century B C, abounding in precious objects; the necropolis of Puig d'es Molins in Ibiza, with tombs two–five metres deep, connected by a short passage, which must have numbered about three or four thousand, abounding in terracotta figurines; and the necropolis of Villaricos, with some tombs almost on ground-level and others accessible through a corridor or *dromos*, which have yielded many jewels and amulets.

The dearth of large statuary is not surprising in the Punic world; but there is a curious absence of the stelae so characteristic of other regions. Nor can we consider a stele from Cartagena with a large figure in the field bearing no resemblance to traditional types, a pointed stele from Villaricos with a plain Punic inscription, and another barely hewn, with a triangle in relief at the summit, from the same locality, as substantial exceptions to the rule. One fact is noteworthy: the absence of stelae coincides with the absence of *topheths*. This may suggest that the absence is not so much the result of insufficient archaeological research as a significant peculiarity of the Punic world in Spain.

On the other hand, a Punic element reappears which did not exist in Sardinia – the anthropoid coffin. Admittedly there is only one, from the necropolis of Punta de la Vaca in Cadiz, found in 1887. The typology is clearly Graecizing, as is proved by the male head with thick hair and flowing beard. The arms are in an interesting position, the right one held close to the body and the left folded on the chest. The problem is whether this copy, with no other parallels in Spain, was not merely imported. In this case the Spanish attestation would be purely apparent.

Of completely round statuettes we can cite an Egypticizing bronze with a gold mask from Cadiz (plate 47), and a seated deity in alabaster from the necropolis of Galera (ancient Tutugi) (plate 36). But most of the material is in terracotta and comes from the necropolis of Puig d'es Molins (Ibiza). Omitting the protomai, which we shall mention with the masks, we come to the numerous completely round figurines, sometimes seated, but usually standing, sometimes naked, but more frequently clad in a long tunic. García y Bellido has distinguished examples of Greek or Graecizing, Egypticizing, and Carthaginian art. To this last group we attribute some extremely crude figurines (plate 57) which suggest directly Phoenician models. We also find certain heads in which Greek influence clearly prevails.

An extremely significant discovery, made on the Isla Plana at Ibiza, was of a group of clay statuettes of the type familiar to us from Bythia (plate 68). Here again the body consists of a vase to which the head, arms, and sexual organs have been attached. We sometimes note necklaces and ornaments round the neck. Like those of Bythia, the figurines were probably intended to commend the sick to the deities (the hands indicating the part of the body concerned). Most of the statuettes of the Isla Plana have eyes superimposed, a characteristic which recurs in certain copies from other localities in Spain (Alcoy, Carmona, Cadiz).

Of the female protomai from the necropolis of Puig d'es Molins at Ibiza we have various examples of the type classified elsewhere as Greek, with a veil, smiling expression, slanting eyes, eyebrows continuing the lines of the nose, pointed nose, and jutting-out chin (plate 58). There do not seem to be any examples of the type classified as Egyptian, but we must admit that the typology is very varied and evidently goes back to numerous models. Furthermore, there are some grotesque male masks in which we can clearly identify the second and fifth group of Cintas's classification (plate 77). Spanish production shows therefore the same tendencies of Sardinian production. The curious negro mask from Cadiz, with accentuated and realistic features, forms a category to itself.

A vast quantity of small amulets of glass paste or hardstone, frequently necklace beads, which characterize the whole Punic world, have appeared in the Punic necropolises of Spain (plate 96). They are particularly abundant in Ibiza, but some also come from Cadiz, Ampurias, Malaga, Sexi, and Villaricos, as well as from various places on the Atlantic coast and the interior, where they were evidently imported. In Spain, too, the divine figurines of Egyptian type, the animal figurines, and the miniature masks are characteristic. And finally, there is no dearth of gold amulet cases.

The necropolis of Puig d'es Molins at Ibiza has yielded certain typical razors which we have already encountered at Carthage. Here again we note the narrow stem in the shape of a bird's head. Certain blades have no depictions, while others have, at the base of the stem, geometrical designs or the familiar bird's wing and a figure of Egypticizing or Graecizing type (plate 113).

A large quantity of ivories has been found in the tombs of the area of Carmona (Cruz del Negro, El Acebuchal, Alcantavilla, and El Bencarrón) as well as at Osuna. Usually they belong to toilet objects, boxes, combs, and bowls. They bear intricately incised geometric motifs, palmettes, lotus flowers, scenes with men, and above all animals, in which the lion, the gryphon, and the gazelle prevail. On a box (fig. 48), for example, we see a kneeling warrior with a helmet, shield, and garb of Greek type fighting with a lion, while a winged gryphon appears at his shoulders. On another we have a huntsman on a horse approaching gazelles protected by a gryphon. On others there are only animals fighting and defending themselves – lions, gryphons, and gazelles. The same applies to the combs, where the animals often form confronting

48   Ivory with warrior from Carmona

couples before a palmette, for symmetrical reasons (fig 49), and the human figure exists, but is rare. Spatulae are more scarce and the depiction is sometimes constituted by the actual shape of the object. It seems possible to date these ivory reliefs around the seventh–sixth century B C. They are connected with a characteristic Phoenician production, but are not so widespread in the West, and have therefore been thought to be direct importations from Phoenicia.

49   Comb from Carmona

Passing on to the jewellery, the masterpieces of Punic goldwork in Spain are those of the treasure of La Aliseda (Cáceres), found by chance in 1920 and today in the archaeological museum of Madrid. They consist of a vast quantity of gold objects which include a belt (plate 95) consisting of sixty-one finely granulated pieces bearing repeated motifs of a man fighting a lion, a winged sphinx, and palmettes. Other elements of the 'treasure' are bracelets with spiral designs, diadems, and pendants with lotus flowers and palmettes, necklaces with amulet-cases, and

239

chains with a fine geometrical design (plate 94). On the whole, it seems that the earliest piece is the belt ascribable to about the sixth century, while the other objects range from the sixth to the third century.

Scarabs and seals of various sorts come from the necropolises. The incisions repeat the Egyptian motifs of the Phoenician homeland and of the colonies, and the seals are usually fitted in rings. The greatest quantity come from the area of Cadiz, mainly Puerta de Tierra and Punta de la Vaca.

The necropolis of Sexi and above all of Villaricos (fig 50) have yielded ostrich eggs (Sexi three examples): they are painted red on a

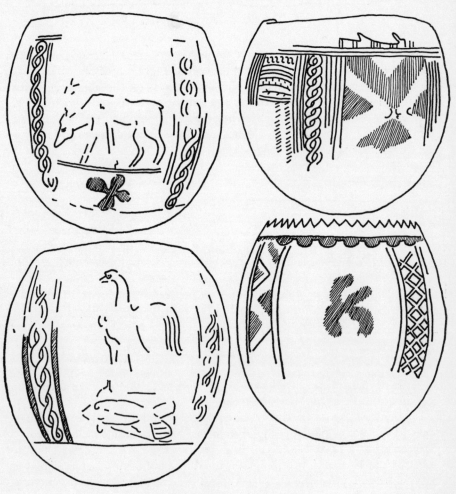

50   Paintings on ostrich eggs

white background with geometric, floral, and, more rarely, animal motifs, distributed in vertical bands, sometimes with internal borders. Polychrome perfume flasks have been found at Ibiza. Coins were struck in Cadiz, Malaga, Sexi, Abdera, Baria (Villaricos), Cartagena, and Ibiza, as well as being imported from North Africa. They have been found in many localities of the southern region (Cadiz, Ituci, Olont, Malaga, Sexi, Abdera). Finally, pottery repeats various forms familiar to us from the rest of the Punic world: the mushroom-lipped jugs of glazed terracotta and the umbilicated plates of the same material (Torre del Mar, Almuñécar), the vases in animal and human form (plate 65), the typical two-beaked lamps, the peg-bottomed amphorae, and other varieties which we already know.

3 Religion

Apart from the coins, there is little consistent epigraphical material in Spain. This fact is significant and limits effective Phoenician, if not Punic, presence in the peninsula, and constitutes a negative element in our means of reconstructing local religious cults. The cult of Melqart, to whom the largest temple in Cadiz was dedicated, points to Phoenician, and particularly Tyrian, origins. The identification of Melqart with Heracles, which was made in the East, is repeated in Spain, where Heracles Gaditanus assumes great importance in the Roman era. We have numerous accounts of his temple at this period and of the cult observed there, but it is obviously difficult to estimate how far this cult reflects the Phoenician and Punic phase. Astarte and Eshmun, who appear as components of proper names in the inscriptions, may go back to the Phoenician phase, while Eshmun's equivalent, Asklepios, had a temple in Carthage and is mentioned by Polybius.[25]

The actual Punic phase is primarily represented by Baal Hammon, who is mentioned in his Greek form of Kronos by Strabo, because of his temple in Cadiz,[26] and by Polybius, because of the cult devoted to him in Cartagena.[27] Tanit also exists and is mentioned as such and had a rock shrine at Ibiza according to a Neo-Punic inscription of the second century BC on bronze leaf:[28] 'This square wall was built, dedicated and restored by Abdeshmun, son of Azarbaal, priest, for our lady the mighty Tanit and for Gad. The builder was he himself, at his expense.'

In Spain, as elsewhere, Tanit was assimilated to Juno Caelestis, and, as such, had a widespread cult. In the shrine of Baal Hammon in Cadiz, according to a late account by Philostratus,[29] Pygmalion (Pumay) was worshipped. This would be of great interest for connexions with Cyprus and Sardinia. Finally we learn from inscriptions about the cult of Reshef-Melqart and Milkashtart, while Chusor may be the Phoenician-

Punic antecedent of the Hephaestus cited by Polybius as a deity worshipped at Cartagena.[30] As for Gad, 'fortune', his name appears on a trophy, and, with the article, in the inscription from Ibiza of the second century B C. It is not certain whether he should be considered an autonomous deity or an attribute of another deity (Tanit). Finally, there is a suggestion by Solá Solé according to which Bes was the main god of Ibiza and gave the Phoenician-Punic name to the city.

The attestations of the Punic cult are few and late. In the temple of Cadiz, according to Silius,[31] the priests had to be celibate and officiated in robes of white linen and bare feet. An interesting oracular activity took place in the shrine. Hannibal and Caesar consulted it, while Caracalla had a proconsul put to death for daring to ask the oracle about the future of the emperor. Another aspect or, rather, problem of the Phoenician-Punic cult in Spain is the human sacrifice. Although no *topheth* has yet been found, the bones of men who met a violent death have been discovered in the necropolis of El Acebuchal, and graves of children in Bolonia, in the far south of the peninsula. Of the two groups of remains, the first can be dated in the seventh or sixth century B C, while the second is late, of the Christian era.

CONCLUSION

The singular nature of the Phoenician civilization should now emerge clearly. It is a civilization for which the sources are either indirect or to be found outside the geographical area of Phoenicia. The homeland is exceptionally lacking in material, in contrast to the Syro-Palestinian and Mesopotamian interior and the colonies overseas, but this seems more the result of chance and archaeological conditions than actual dearth, and we can devise a means of supplying it from the many indications surrounding it and pointing to it. So although we often lack the certainty of the attribution of one single religious, cultural, or artistic element, we are certain that these elements are nearly all Phoenician.

The points of reference and comparison for this civilization are provided by its earlier and later phases (Bronze Age and Hellenistic-Roman Age) on the chronological level and its expansion into the interior and the colonies on the geographical level. So the question is, can we define an autonomous Phoenician civilization, and if so, how?

First of all, we must recall the geographical conditions of the Syro-Palestinian coastal strip and the relative isolation it attained as a result of the penetration into the interior of the new peoples of the Iron Age, like the Israelites and Aramaeans. This resulted in the development of the maritime cities, maritime trade, and finally the unique and distinctive phenomenon of colonization, which was a new dimension peculiar to the Phoenicians. These conditions and facts, which are only verified with the Iron Age and dissolve with the Hellenistic-Roman epoch, can be taken to mark the Phoenician civilization.

On the cultural level Phoenician independence can initially be regarded as a persistence and prolongation of Canaanite civilization in the face of new cultures in the interior. Considering the fact that these cultures brought no appreciable innovations or independent traditions in certain spheres (art, in particular), the cultural manifestations of the Syro-Palestinian interior in the Iron Age are frequently subordinate to those of the Phoenician coast (cf. the temple of Solomon).

Moreover, the autonomy of a culture is determined by its individuality with respect to other cultures, an individuality manifested in this

243

case by the establishment in the Phoenician area of a skilful craftsman-ship which served the interests of trade and was characterized by a production like jewellery, ivories, and metal bowls. Admittedly, these types were not unknown in the preceding era, but it was only in the Iron Age that they asserted themselves to an hitherto unknown extent, while iconography was characterized by the unlimited confluence of Egyptian (prevalent because of the facility of communication with Egypt by sea), Mesopotamian, Aegean, and other motifs, and their dissolution into pure ornamentalization in the so-called minor arts.

If all these elements allow us to define the autonomy of Phoenician civilization, they also define its intrinsic coherence, since they are not found to such a wide extent elsewhere. This coherence does not assume obvious political forms, but nevertheless fits in with the general condi-tions of geography and history.

The present study is thus confirmed by its conclusion, and the civili-zation of the Phoenicians emerges as a primary component in the cultural complex of the ancient Near East and a decisive element in the establishment of fruitful relations between the East and the West throughout the Mediterranean.

The examination of Punic history and culture over an exceptionally wide area shows the permanence of the characteristics of the Phoenician world, and the development and determination, in the focal centre of Carthage, of new elements which subsequently distinguish Punic culture from Phoenician.

And yet we are more struck by the similarities than the differences between these cultures, so where a difference seems to exist we have tried to discover whether it does not depend on the dearth of original sources and whether new finds would not alter the present state of affairs. There are the political institutions characterized by the system of the suffetes, the senate and the prevalence of commercial aristocracy; the pantheon where the Punic deities are usually Phoenician or a development of Phoenician deities, or have assimilated them under a different name; and the cult, with the characteristic open-air shrines and *topheths*, which are a permanent feature of Phoenician-Punic culture. But above all the artistic production is typologically and icono-graphically so recurrent that it often seems to consist of imported material. In the stelae, sarcophagi, figurines, masks, amulets, jewels, ivories, seals, glass, and pottery there is an extraordinary recurrence of objects and motifs, in the framework of a typically commercial pro-duction which encompasses the Mediterranean coasts.

Local production or importation, Punic or Phoenician origin – these problems recur and prove the fundamental unity of the world of the Phoenicians. To find a further solution to them is a task for the future.

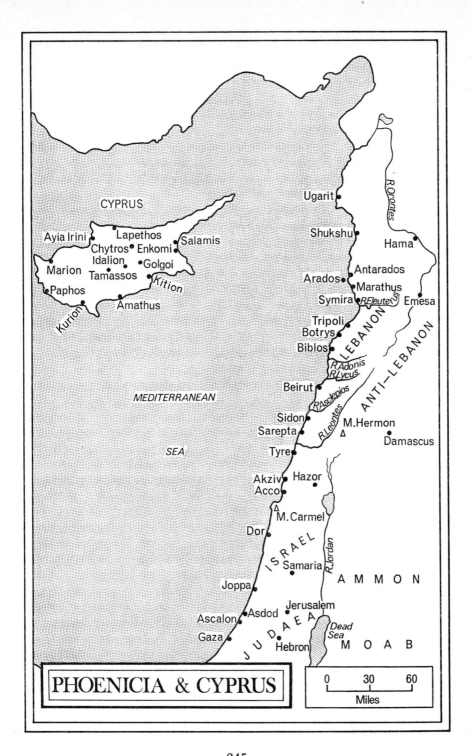

PHOENICIA & CYPRUS

CYPRUS

Ayia Irini
Lapethos
Chytros Enkomi Salamis
Idalion Golgoi
Marion Tamassos
Paphos Kition
Amathus
Kurion

Ugarit
Shukshu
Hama
Antarados
Arados Marathus
Symira R.Eleuteros Emesa
Tripoli
Botrys
Biblos
R.Adonis
R.Lycus
Beirut
R.Asclepios
Sidon R.Leontes M.Hermon
Sarepta Damascus
Tyre

MEDITERRANEAN

SEA

Akziv Hazor
Acco
M. Carmel
Dor
ISRAEL
Samaria
R.Jordan
AMMON
Joppa
Jerusalem
Ascalon Asdod
Gaza Dead
Sea MOAB
Hebron
JUDAEA

LEBANON
ANTI-LEBANON
R.Orontes

0   30   60
Miles

245

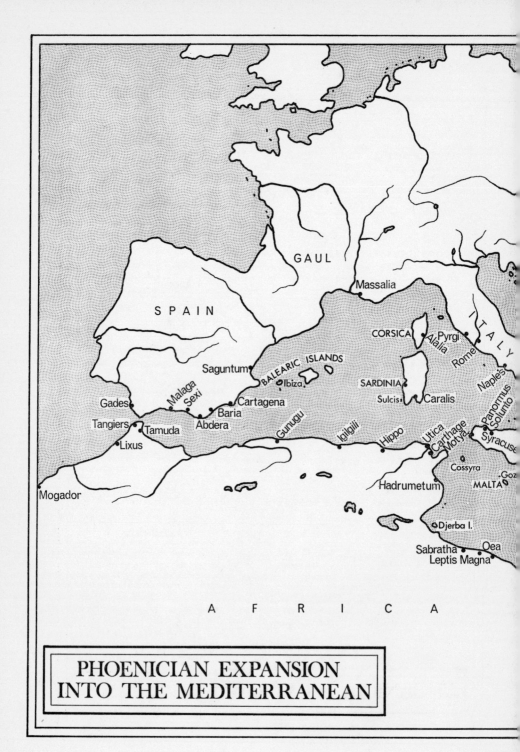

GAUL

Massalia

SPAIN

CORSICA

Pyrgi

Alalia

ITALY

Rome

Saguntum

BALEARIC ISLANDS

Ibiza

SARDINIA

Naples

Malaga

Sexi

Cartagena

Sulcis

Caralis

Panormus

Solunto

Gades

Baria

Gunugu

Igilgili

Utica

Carthage

Syracuse

Tangiers

Tamuda

Abdera

Hippo

Motya

Lixus

Cossyra

Goz

Mogador

Hadrumetum

MALTA

Djerba I.

Sabratha

Oea

Leptis Magna

A F R I C A

PHOENICIAN EXPANSION INTO THE MEDITERRANEAN

THRACE

MACEDONIA

GREECE

PHRYGIA

LYCIA

Sardis

Ephesus

Athens

CILICIA

Karatepe

Tarsus

Alalakh

Ugarit
Arados

CYPRUS

Biblos
Beirut
Sidon
Tyre

CRETE

Joppa
Gaza

Jerusalem

Cyrene

Alexandria

Naucratis
Memphis

Retabe

Philenorum

LIBYA

| 0 | 100 | 200 | 300 | 400 |

Miles

247

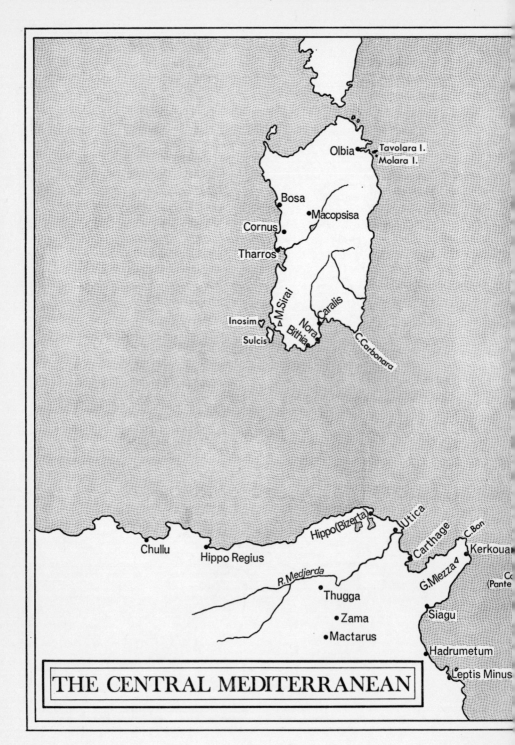

Olbia

Tavolara I.
Molara I.

Bosa

Macopsisa

Cornus

Tharros

M.Sirai

Caralis

Inosim

Nora

Bithia

Sulcis

C.Carbonara

Utica

Chullu

Hippo (Bizerta)

Carthage

C.Bon

Hippo Regius

Kerkoua

R.Medjerda

G.Mezza

Co
(Pante

Thugga

Zama

Siagu

Mactarus

Hadrumetum

Leptis Minus

THE CENTRAL MEDITERRANEAN

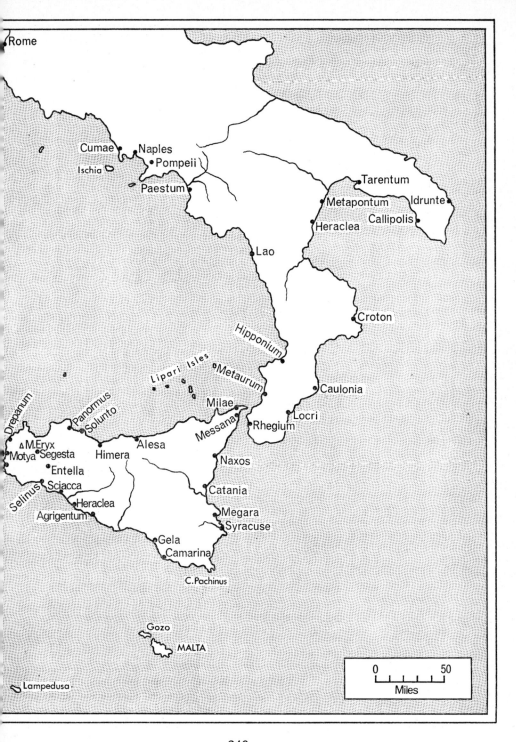

249

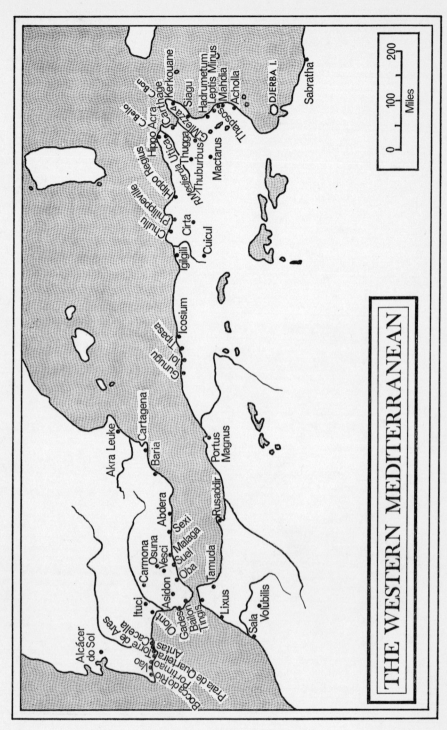

THE WESTERN MEDITERRANEAN

Sabratha
DJERBA I.
Acholla
Mandia
Leptis Minus
Hadrumetum
Siagu
Kerkouane
Carthage
C. bon
Hippo Acra
Utica
Thugga
Tunis
Grazzia
Thapsos
Mactarus
Thuburbus
R. Medjerda
Hippo Regius
C. belio
Philippeville
Chullu
Cirta
Cuicul
Igilgili
Icosium
Tipasa
Iol
Gunugu
Portus Magnus
Cartagena
Akra Leuke
Baria
Abdera
Rusaddir
Sexi
Malaga
Suel
Oba
Carmona
Osuna
Vesci
Tamuda
Asidon
Oba
Lixus
Ituci
Bailon
Tingis
Sala
Olont
Gades
Volubilis
Arias
Torre de Quarteira
Cacella
Alcácer do Sol
Boca do Rio
Vao
Portimao
Praia de Quarteira

200
100
0
Miles

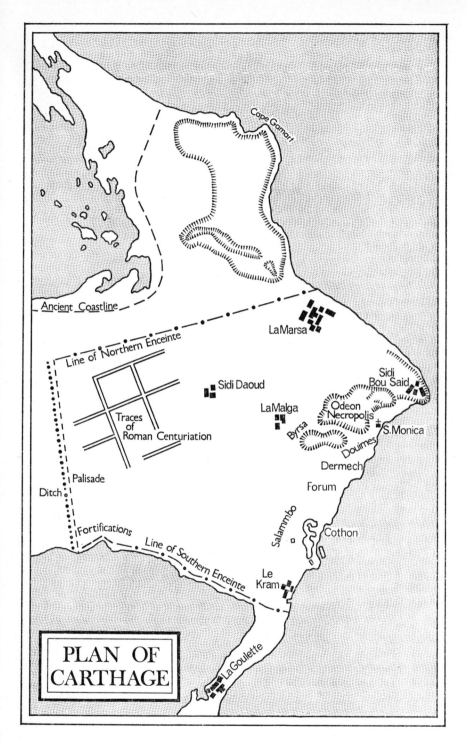

Cape Gamart

Ancient Coastline

Line of Northern Enceinte

La Marsa

Sidi Daoud

Sidi
Bou Said

Traces
of
Roman Centuriation

LaMalga

Odeon
Necropolis

Byrsa

S. Monica

Douïmes

Palisade

Dermech

Ditch

Forum

Fortifications

Line of Southern Enceinte

Salammbo

Cothon

Le
Kram

La Goulette

PLAN OF
CARTHAGE

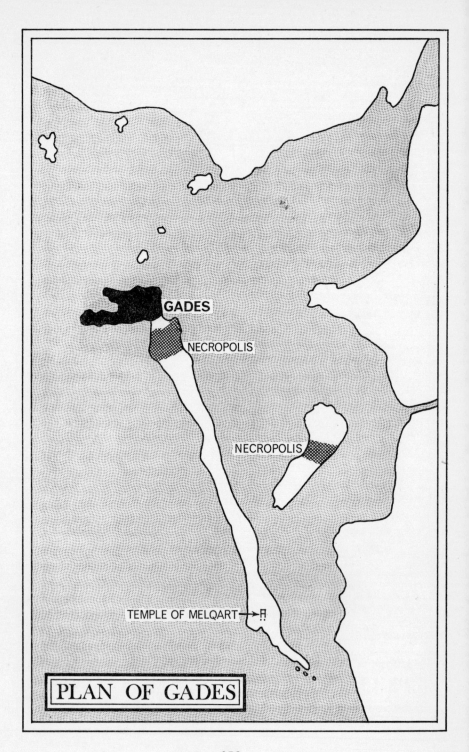

GADES

NECROPOLIS

NECROPOLIS

TEMPLE OF MELQART→

PLAN OF GADES

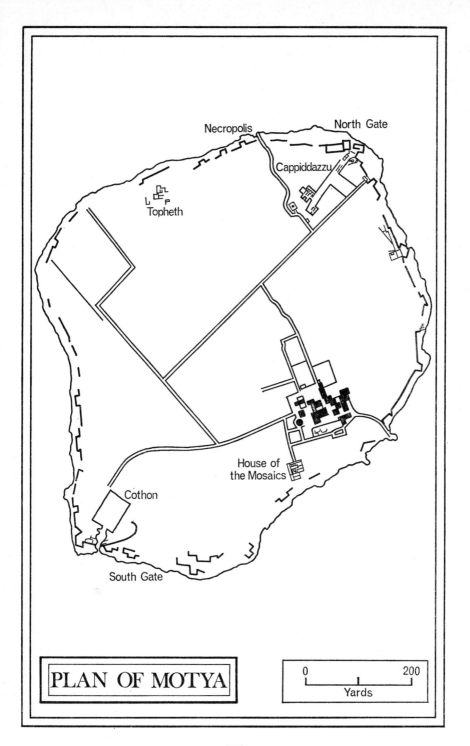

Necropolis

North Gate

Cappiddazzu

Topheth

House of
the Mosaics

Cothon

South Gate

PLAN OF MOTYA

0   200
Yards

NOTES

In these notes the following abbreviations will be used: ARAB = D.D. Luckenbill, *Ancient Records of Assyria and Babylonia*, 2 vols (Chicago, 1926–7); CIS = *Corpus Inscriptionum Semiticarum*; GGM = C. Müller, *Geographi Graeci Minores*, 2 vols (Parisiis, 1855–61); IAKA = R. Borger, *Die Inschriften Asarhaddons Königs von Assyrien*, (Graz, 1956); KAI = H. Donner – W. Röllig, *Kanaanäische und aramäische Inschriften*, 3 vols (Wiesbaden, 1962–5); PG = *Patrologia Graeca*; PL = *Patrologia Latina*; RES = *Répertoire d'épigraphie sémitique*.

Chapter 1

1 Pliny, XXII, 135.
2 Augustine, PL, XXXV, col 2096.
3 Genesis 10, 15.
4 Eusebius, *Praep. Ev.*, 1, 9, 14–19.
5 Herodotus, I, 1; VII, 89.
6 Strabo, XVI, 3, 4.
7 Pliny, IV, 36.
8 Justin, XVIII, 3, 2–4.
9 KAI, 14, 18–19.

Chapter 2

1 Justin, XVIII, 3, 5.
2 Justin, XVIII, 3, 5.
3 ARAB, I, 302.
4 J. H. Breasted, *Ancient Records of Egypt*, IV, 577.
5 KAI, I, 4–7.
6 2 Samuel 24, 6–7.
7 2 Samuel 5, II.
8 Josephus, *Contra Ap.*, I, 118.
9 Josephus, *Contra Ap.*, I, 119.
10 Josephus, *Ant. Iud.*, VIII, 141.
11 1 Kings 5, 1–11.
12 Josephus, *Ant. Iud.*, VIII, 143.

13 1 Kings 9, 10–14.
14 Josephus, *Ant. Iud.*, VIII, 143.
15 Josephus, *Contra Ap.*, I, 114–15.
16 1 Kings 9, 26–28.
17 1 Kings 10, 11.
18 1 Kings 10, 22.
19 Josephus, *Contra Ap.*, I, 121–3.
20 1 Kings 16, 30–32.
21 1 Kings 16, 31.
22 Josephus, *Ant. Iud.*, VIII, 317; IX, 138.
23 Josephus, *Ant. Iud.*, VIII, 324.
24 ARAB, I, 479.
25 ARAB, I, 538.
26 D.J.Wiseman, *Iraq*, XIV, 1952, pp. 24–44.
27 ARAB, I, 611.
28 ARAB, I, 672.
29 F.Safar, *Sumer*, VII, 1951, pp. 3–21.
30 ARAB, I, 578; J.Laesse, *Iraq*, XXI, 1959, pp. 147–57.
31 Josephus, *Contra Ap.*, I, 124–5.
32 ARAB, I, 734, 739.
33 ARAB, I, 770.
34 ARAB, I, 770.
35 ARAB, I, 815, 821.
36 D.J.Wiseman, *Iraq*, XIII, 1954, pp 21–26.
37 ARAB, I, 772, 802.
38 ARAB, I, 801.
39 ARAB, I, 772; D.J.Wiseman, *Iraq*, XVIII, 1956, pp 117–29.
40 KAI, 31.
41 ARAB, I, 803.
42 ARAB, II, 180–9.
43 ARAB, II, 5, 55.
44 ARAB, II, 18.
45 ARAB, II, 118.
46 ARAB, II, 239.
47 ARAB, II, 309.
48 Josephus, *Ant. Iud.*, IX, 284.
49 Josephus, *Ant. Iud.*, IX, 284–7.
50 ARAB, II, 239.
51 ARAB, II, 319.
52 ARAB, II, 511–12; IAKA, 27, 5.
53 IAKA, 109.
54 ARAB, II, 690; IAKA, 27, 21.
55 ARAB, II, 587–91; IAKA, 69.
56 ARAB, II, 556; IAKA, 76.
57 ARAB, II, 710; IAKA, 57.
58 ARAB, II, 547; IAKA, 71.
59 ARAB, II, 779.

60 ARAB, II, 780.
61 ARAB, II, 912.
62 R.F.Harper, *Assyrian and Babylonian Letters*, 992, 14–21.
63 ARAB, II, 783.
64 ARAB, II, 830.
65 Josephus, *Contra. Ap.*, I, 156.
66 Josephus, *Contra Ap.*, I, 157–8.
67 Ezra, 3, 7.
68 GGM, I, pp 78–79.
69 KAI, 14, 18–19.
70 GGM, I, p 78.
71 KAI, 13–16; CIS, 1, 4.
72 KAI, 14, 18–20.
73 KAI, 15, 16.
74 KAI, 14, 3, 13.
75 KAI, 14, 2–3, 12–13.
76 KAI, 10.
77 KAI, 9.
78 KAI, 11.
79 E.Babelon, *Traité des monnaies grecques et romains*, II, 2, vol 537–42; G.F. Hill, *Catalogue of the Greek Coins in the British Museum: Phoenicia*, pp 94–96.
80 Herodotus, VII, 98.
81 KAI, 7.
82 KAI, 4.
83 Eusebius, *Praep. Ev.*, I, 10, 13.
84 KAI, 10, 9.
85 KAI, 16.
86 KAI, 11.
87 KAI, 13, 1–2.
88 KAI, 14, 15.
89 KAI, 14, 16–17, 18–19.
90 KAI, 31.
91 IAKA, 69, Rs III 7.
92 Arrian, II, 15.
93 Diodorus, XV, I, 45.
94 Ezekiel, 27, 9.
95 Josephus, *Contra Ap.*, I, 157.
96 IAKA, 69, Rs III 13–14.
97 cf. note 62.

Chapter 3

1 Genesis, 14, 19.
2 KAI, 4–7.
3 KAI, 10.
4 KAI, 4, 3–6.
5 KAI, 10, 15–16.

6 KAI, 9, B 5.
7 IAKA, 69, Rs IV 14.
8 KAI, 14, 17.
9 KAI, 15–16.
10 1 Kings 16, 31–32.
11 IAKA, 69.
12 Josephus, *Contra Ap.* I, 118–19.
13 1 Kings 11, 5.
14 2 Kings 23, 13.
15 IAKA, 69, Rs IV.
16 Nonnus, LXIII.
17 RES, 234.
18 Eusebius, *Praep. Ev.*, I, 10, 11.
19 Eusebius, *Praep. Ev.*, I, 10, 13.
20 Eusebius, *Praep. Ev.*, I, 10, 10.
21 Damascius, *De princ.*, 125 c.
22 Lucian, *De dea Syra*, 9.
23 Lucian, *De dea Syra*, 8.
24 KAI, 14, 15.
25 1 Kings 18, 19–40.
26 KAI, 11.
27 KAI, 13, 1–2.
28 KAI, 14, 15.
29 Eusebius, *Praep. Ev.*, IV, 16, 6.
30 Theocritus, *Idillia*, XV.
31 KAI, 1, 2.
32 KAI, 13, 3–8.
33 KAI, 14, 4–12.

Chapter 4

1 1 Kings 6–7.
2 Herodotus, II, 44.
3 2 Kings 23, 10.
4 Strabo, XVI, 2, 13, 23.
5 Appian, VIII, 128.
6 1 Kings 22, 39.
7 Pliny, V, 76: XXXVI, 193.

Chapter 5

1 Strabo, XVI, 2, 13.
2 S. Langdon, *Die neubabylonischen Königsinschriften*, 19, IX, 26–45.
3 Pliny, XXXVI, 190–3.
4 Ezekiel 27, 3–25.
5 Isaiah 23, 3.
6 1 Kings 9, 28; 10, 11, 22; 2 Chronicles 8, 18; 9, 10, 21.

7 Herodotus, IV, 42.
8 *Odyssey*, XV, 403–84.
9 *Odyssey*, XIV, 290–7.
10 Herodotus, I, 1.
11 Herodotus, II, 54, 56.

Chapter 6

1 Herodotus, V, 58.
2 Diodorus, V, 74.
3 Pliny, V, 67.
4 Pliny, VII, 192.
5 Tacitus, *Annales*, XI, 14.

Chapter 7

1 Velleius Paterculus, I, 2, 3.
2 Pliny, XVI, 216.
3 Pliny, XIX, 63.
4 Diodorus, V, 20.
5 Thucydides, VI, 2, 6.
6 KAI, 30.
7 KAI, 46.
8 1 Kings 10, 22.
9 Josephus, *Contra Ap.*, I, 119.
10 Herodotus, II, 12.
11 Velleius Paterculus, I, 2, 3.
12 Pliny, XVI, 216.
13 Pseudo-Aristotle, *De mir. auscult.*, 134.
14 Josephus, *Ant. Iud.*, VIII, 324.
15 Sallust, *Bell Iug.*, LXXVII, 1.
16 Silius Italicus, *Punica*, III, 256; Pliny, V, 76.
17 Sallust, *Bell. Iug.*, XIX, 1.
18 Solinus, XXVII, 9.
19 KAI, 64, 1.
20 Diodorus, V, 16, 2–3.
21 Pliny, XIX, 63.
22 P. Cintas, *L'expansion carthaginoise au Maroc*, p 10.
23 Herodotus, IV, 196.

Chapter 8

1 Stephan of Byzantium, *Ethnica* (ed. A. Meineke), p 412, 7.
2 Virgil, *Aeneid*, I, 619–22.
3 Josephus, *Contra Ap*, I, 119; *Ant. Iud.*, VIII, 146.
4 KAI, 30.
5 KAI, 31.

6 ARAB, II, 239, 309, 326.
7 ARAB, II, 690.
8 ARAB, II, 876.
9 KAI, 32.
10 *Frag. Hist. Graec.*, II, p 472, no 12.
11 KAI, 31.

Chapter 9

1 Eusebius, PG, XIX, col 405.
2 Scolium to Euripides, *Trojan Women*, 220.
3 Appian, VIII, 1.
4 Justin, XVIII, 4–6.
5 Dionysius of Halicarnassus, I, 74.
6 Velleius Paterculus, I, 12, 5.
7 Josephus, *Contra Ap.*, I, 125.
8 Quintus Curtius, IV, 2, 10.
9 Diodorus, XX, 14.
10 Thucydides, VI, 2, 6.
11 Diodorus, V, 16.
12 Thucydides, I, 13, 6.
13 Justin, XVIII, 7.
14 Justin, XVIII, 7.
15 Polybius, III, 22.
16 *Fragm. Hist. Graec.*, I, p 264, no III.
17 Diodorus, XI, 1.
18 Diodorus, XIV, 95–96.
19 Polybius, III, 24.
20 Arrian, II, 24, 5.
21 Diodorus, XVIII, 4, 4.
22 Justin, XXI, 6.
23 Diodorus, XX, 8, 2–4.
24 Augustine, PL, XXXV, col 2096.
25 *Inscriptiones Graecae*, XIV, 953.
26 Justin, XIX, 2, 5–6.
27 Aristotle, *Politics*, II, 8, 2–9; III, 1, 7.
28 Aristotle, *Politics*, II, 8, 5.
29 Aristotle, *Politics*, II, 8, 4.
30 Aristotle, *Politics*, II, 8, 3.
31 Diodorus, XX, 55, 4.
32 Polybius, VII, 9, 5.

Chapter 10

1 RES, 17, 1.
2 KAI, 86.
3 G. Levi Della Vida, BASOR, LXXXVII, 1942, pp 29–32.

4 Polybius, VII, 9, 2–3.
5 2 Kings 23, 10.
6 Diodorus, XX, 14, 6.
7 Diodorus, XX, 14, 4–5.
8 Diodorus, XX, 65, 1.
9 Pliny, XXXVI, 39.
10 KAI, 69.

Chapter 11

1 S. Gsell, *Histoire ancienne de l'Afrique du Nord*, IV, p 107.
2 S. Gsell, *Histoire ancienne de l'Afrique du Nord*, IV, pp 107-8.
3 Justin, XX, 5, 13.
4 Appian, VIII, 128.
5 Appian, VIII, 96.
6 Appian, VIII, 95.
7 Polybius, XXXVIII, 7, 3.
8 Diodorus, XXXII, 14.
9 Appian, VIII, 95.

Chapter 12

1 Diodorus, XX, 8, 3–4; Polybius, I, 29, 3.
2 Columella, I, 1, 6.
3 Varro, I, 52, 1.
4 Jerome, PL, XXIV, col 337.
5 Columella, I, 1, 18.
6 Varro, I, 17, 4.
7 Columella, III, 12, 5; III, 15, 4–5.
8 Columella, V, 5, 4.
9 Pliny, XXXVI, 166.
10 Diodorus, XIII, 81, 4–5.
11 Pliny, XVII, 93, 128.
12 Pliny, XVII, 93.
13 Diodorus, XIII, 81, 4–5.
14 Columella, XII, 46, 5–6.
15 Pliny, XVII, 63, 131.
16 Dioscorides, IV, 150.
17 Polybius, XII, 3, 3–4.
18 Varro, II, 1, 27.
19 Columella, VI, 1, 3.
20 S. Gsell, *Histoire ancienne de l'Afrique du Nord*, IV, p 113.
21 Diodorus, V, 20.
22 Aristotle, *Politics*, III, 5, 10–11.
23 GGM, I, 1–14.
24 Athenaeus, II, 44 e.
25 Diodorus, V, 20.

Chapter 14

1 Diodorus, V, 12.
2 Ptolemy, IV, 3.
3 Stephen of Byzantium, *Ethnica* (ed. A. Meineke), p 152, 19-20.
4 GGM, I, p 89.
5 Naevius, *Bell. Pun.*, IV, 31-32.
6 Livy, XXI, 51.
7 Cicero, *In Verrem*, II, 4, 103-4.
8 *Inscriptiones Graecae*, XIV, 953.
9 CIS, I, 124.
10 KAI, 62.
11 Diodorus, V, 12.
12 Ptolemy, IV, 3.

Chapter 15

1 Thucydides, VI, 2, 6.
2 Zenobius, I, 54.
3 Justin, XVIII, 7, 1-2.
4 Diodorus, XIV, 95-96.
5 Diodorus, XV, 15-17.
6 Diodorus, XVI, 72-73.
7 Polybius, III, 25, 4-5.
8 KAI, 63.
9 Diodorus, IV, 83.

Chapter 16

1 Pausanias, X, 17.
2 Solinus, IV, 1.
3 KAI, 46.
4 Justin, XVIII, 7, 1-2.
5 Justin, XIX, 1, 3.
6 Strabo, V, 2, 7.
7 Diodorus, IV, 29, 6.
8 Polybius, II, 22, 8-9.
9 Diodorus, V, 15, 4-5.
10 KAI, 66.
11 KAI, 172.
12 Diodorus, XV, 24.
13 Diodorus, XV, 27, 4.
14 Polybius, III, 24, 11.
15 KAI, 66.
16 KAI, 64.
17 CIS, I, 140.
18 KAI, 172.

Chapter 17

1 Diodorus, V, 35, 5.
2 Strabo, II, 5, 5.
3 Velleius Paterculus, I, 2, 3.
4 Pliny, XIX, 63.
5 Strabo, I, 3, 2.
6 1 Kings 10, 22.
7 Jeremiah, 10, 9.
8 Ezekiel, 27, 12.
9 Strabo, III, 2, 11.
10 Strabo, III, 2, 14.
11 Herodotus, IV, 152.
12 Herodotus, I, 163.
13 A. Schulten, *Avieni Ora Maritima*, p 135.
14 Genesis 10, 4.
15 Josephus, *Ant. Iud.* IX, 208.
16 Eusebius, PG, XIX, col 118.
17 Strabo, III, 2, 14.
18 Diodorus, V, 16, 2–3.
19 Herodotus, I, 163.
20 Avienus, *Ora maritima*, 375–77.
21 GGM, I, p 16.
22 Strabo, III, 5, 3.
23 Strabo, III, 5, 6.
24 Strabo, III, 5, 7.
25 Polybius, X, 10, 8.
26 Strabo, III, 5, 3.
27 Polybius, X, 10, 11.
28 KAI, 72 B.
29 Philostratus, *Vita Apollonii*, V, 5.
30 Polybius, X, 10, 4.
31 Silius, III, 28.

BIBLIOGRAPHY

The best and most recent general works are: G. Contenau, *La civilisation phénicienne* (Paris, 1949); D. Harden, *The Phoenicians* (London, 1962). There is also a useful article by O. Eissfeldt, *Phoiniker und Phoinikia*, Pauly-Wissowa, *Realencyklopädie der classischen Altertumswissenschaft*, XX, 1, 1941, col 350–80. These works contain ample bibliographies for earlier publications. It is also worth mentioning the periodical *Bibliographie sémitique* in *Orientalia*. The bibliography that follows is necessarily selective.

The following abbreviations will be used: AEA = *Archivo Español de Arqueologia*; AJA = *American Journal of Archaeology*; CB = *Cahiers de Byrsa*; CRAIB = *Comptes Rendus de l'Académie des Inscriptions et Belles-Lettres*; MAL = *Monumenti Antichi dell'Accademia Nazionale dei Lincei*; MANL = *Memorie dell'Accademia Nazionale dei Lincei*; MUSJ = *Mélanges de l'Université Saint-Joseph*; PBSR = *Papers of the British School at Rome*; RHR = *Revue de l'Histoire des Religions*; Sef = *Sefarad*; SS = *Studi Sardi*.

Part I The Phoenicians in the East

1 Name, people, and religion – The name: E. A. Speiser, 'The Name Phoinikes', *Language*, XII, 1936, pp 124–5; G. Bonfante, 'The Name of the Phoenicians', *Classical Philology*, XXXVI, 1941, pp 1–20; S. Moscati, *Sulla storia del nome Canaan*, Studia Biblica et Orientalia III (Roma, 1959) pp 266–9. The people: H. Field, *Ancient and Modern Man in South-Western Asia* (Coral Gables, 1956); S. Moscati, *La questione fenicia Rendiconti dell'Accademia Nazionale dei Lincei*, ser VIII, XVIII, 1963, pp 483–506. The region: P. Birot–J. Dresch, *La Méditerranée et le Moyen Orient* II (Paris, 1956); M. Dunand, *De l'Amanus au Sinaï. Sites et monuments* (Beyrouth, 1953).

2 History – General: E. Meyer, *Geschichte des Altertums* II, 2², (Stuttgart–Berlin, 1931) pp 61–186. The origins: W. F. Albright, 'The Role of the Canaanites in the History of Civilisation', *The Bible and the*

Ancient Near East (London, 1961) pp 328–62; J. Gray, *The Canaanites* (London, 1964). Tyre: W. B. Fleming, *History of Tyre* (New York, 1915); J. Liver, 'The Chronology of Tyre at the Beginning of the First Millennium BC', *Israel Exploration Journal*, III, 1953, pp 113–20; J. M. Peñuela, 'La inscripcion asiria IM 55644 y la cronologia de los reyes de Tiro', *Sef*, XIII, 1953, pp 217–37; XIV, 1954, pp 3–42; B. Mazar, 'The Philistines and the Rise of Israel and Tyre', Proceedings of the Israel Academy of Sciences and Humanities, I, 7, 1964, pp 1–22. Sidon: F. C. Eiselen, *Sidon. A Study in Oriental History* (New York, 1907); K. Galling, 'Eschmunazar und der Herr der Könige', *Zeitschrift des Deutschen Palästina-Vereins*, LXXIX, 1963, pp 140–51. Byblos: P. Montet, *Byblos et l'Egypte* (Paris, 1928); W. Herrmann, 'Der historische Ertrag der altbyblischen Königsinschriften', *Mitteilungen des Instituts für Orientforschung*, VI, 1958, pp 14–32. Relations with the Philistines: O. Eissfeldt, *Philister und Phönizier* (Leipzig, 1936).

3 Religion – General: R. Dussaud, *La religion des Hittites et des Hourrites, des Phéniciens et des Syriens*[2] (Paris, 1949). Sanchuniathon and Philo of Byblos: O. Eissfeldt, *Ras Schamra und Sanchunjaton* (Halle, 1939); R. Follet, 'Sanchunjaton, personnage mythique ou personne historique?' *Biblica*, XXXIV, 1953, pp 81–90; O. Eissfeldt, 'Art und Aufbau der phönizischen Geschichte des Philo von Byblos', *Syria*, XXXIII, 1956, pp 88–98. The gods: W. W. Baudissin, *Adonis und Esmun* (Leipzig, 1911); G. von Lucken, 'Kult und Abkunft des Adonis', *Forschungen und Fortschritte*, XXXVI, 1962, pp 240–5; R. du Mesnil du Buisson, 'Origine et évolution du panthéon de Tyr', RHR, CLXIV, 1963, pp 133-63; R. Dussaud, 'Melqart', *Syria*, XXV, 1946–8, pp. 205-30; id., 'Melqart d'après de récents travaux', RHR, CLI, 1957, pp 1–21; O. Eissfeldt, 'Ba'alšamem und Jahwe', *Zeitschrift für Alttestamentliche Wissenschaft*, LVII, 1939, pp 1–31; id., *Baal Zaphon, Zeus Kasios und der Durchzug der Israeliten durchs Meer* (Halle, 1932). Mythology: C. Clemen, *Die phönikische Religion nach Philo von Byblos* (Leipzig, 1939); O. Eissfeldt, *Phönikische und griechische Kosmogonie, Eléments orientaux dans la religion grecque ancienne* (Paris, 1960) pp 1–15; M. H. Pope–W. Röllig, *Syrien. Die Mythologie der Ugariter und Phönizier*; H. W. Haussig, *Wörterbuch der Mythologie* (Stuttgart s.a.) pp 217–312.

4 Art – General: G. Perrot–C. Chipiez, *Histoire de l'art dans l'Antiquité*, III. *Phénicie-Chypre* (Paris, 1885); R. Dussaud, *L'art phénicien du IIe millénaire* (Paris, 1949); H. Frankfort, *Art and Architecture of the Ancient Orient* (Harmondsworth, 1954). Excavations: L. Hennequin, 'Fouilles et champs de fouilles en Phénicie', *Dictionnaire de la Bible, Supplément*, III, 1938, col 436–85. More recent information in journals is to be found in: *Annales Archéologiques de Syrie; Berytus; Bulletin du Musée de Beyrouth; Israel*

Exploration Journal. Tyre: A. Poidebard, *Tyr, un grand port disparu* (Paris, 1939). Sidon: G. Contenau, *Mission archéologique à Sidon* (Paris, 1921–4); A. Poidebard–J. Lauffray, *Sidon. Aménagements antiques du port de Saïda* (Beyrouth, 1951). Berytus: R. Mouterde, 'Regards sur Beyrouth phénicienne, hellénistique et romaine', MUSJ, XL, 1964, pp 145–90. Byblos: M. Dunand, *Fouilles de Byblos* (Paris, 1939–54). Architecture: A. Ciasca, *Il capitello detto eolico in Etruria* (Roma, 1962). Sculpture: M. Dunand, 'Les sculptures de la favissa du temple d'Amrit', *Bulletin du Musée de Beyrouth*, VII, 1944–5, pp 99–107; VIII, 1946–8, pp 81–107; N. Aimé-Giron, 'Un naos phénicien de Sidon', *Bulletin de l'Institut Français d'Archéologie Orientale*, XXXIV, 1934, pp. 31–42; M. Haran, 'The Bas-Reliefs on the Sarcophagus of Ahiram in the Light of Archaeological and Literary Parallels from the Ancient Near East', *Israel Exploration Journal*, VIII, 1958, pp 15–25; E. Kukahn, *Anthropoide Sarkophage in Beyrouth* (Berlin, 1955). Ivories: C. Decamps de Mertzenfeld, *Inventaire commenté des ivoires phéniciens et apparentés découverts dans le Proche-Orient* (Paris, 1954); R. D. Barnett, *A Catalogue of the Nimrud Ivories* (London, 1957); id., 'Hamath and Nimrud', *Iraq*, XXV, 1963, pp 81–85. Terracotta: M. Chéhab, *Les terres cuites de Kharayeb* (Paris, 1951–4).

5 Economy and trade – Economy: L. B. Jensen, 'Royal Purple of Tyre', *Journal of Near Eastern Studies*, XXII, 1963, pp 104–18. Trade: J–G. Février, 'L'ancienne marine phénicienne et les découvertes récentes', *La Nouvelle Clio*, I–II, 1949–50, pp 128–43; J. Pirenne, 'A propos de droit commercial phénicien antique', *Bulletin de l'Académie Royale de Belgique*, Ve série, XLI, 1955, pp 586–614; R. D. Barnett, 'Early Shipping in the Near East', *Antiquity*, XXXII, 1958, pp 220–30.

6 Script and language – Script: G. R. Driver, *Semitic Writing from Pictograph to Alphabet*[2] (London, 1954); M. Cohen, *La grande invention de l'écriture et son évolution* (Paris, 1958); D. Diringer, *Writing* (London, 1962). Language: Z. S. Harris, *A Grammar of the Phoenician Language* (New Haven, 1963); J. Friedrich, *Phönizisch-punische Grammatik* (Roma, 1951); G. Garbini, *Il semitico di nord-ovest* (Napoli, 1960). Inscriptions: *Corpus Inscriptionum Semiticarum. Pars prima inscriptiones Phoenicias continens* (Paris, 1881 ss.); *Répertoire d'epigraphie sémitique* (Paris, 1900 ss.); H. Donner–W. Röllig, *Kanaanäische und aramäische Inschriften* (Wiesbaden, 1962–4).

7 Phoenician expansion – K. J. Beloch, *Griechische Geschichte*[2] I, 2 (Strassburg, 1913); A. Garcia y Bellido, *Fenicios y Carthaginenses en Occidente* (Madrid, 1942); D. B. Harden, 'The Phoenicians on the West Coast of Africa', *Antiquity*, XXII, 1948, pp 141–50; P. Bosch-Gimpera, 'Phéniciens et Grecs dans l'Extrême-Occident', *La Nouvelle Clio*, III, 1951, pp. 269–96; T. J. Dunbabin, *The Greeks and their Eastern Neigh-*

bours (London, 1957); R. Carpenter, 'Phoenicians in the West', AJA, LXII, 1958, pp 35–53; W. Culican, 'Aspects of Phoenician Settlement in the West Mediterranean', *Abr-Nahrain*, I, 1961, pp 36–55; G. Garbini, 'L'espansione fenicia nel Mediterraneo', *Cultura e Scuola*, VII, 1963, pp 92–97.

8 The Phoenicians in Cyprus – History: G. Hill, *A History of Cyprus* I (Cambridge, 1940); E. Gjerstad, 'Four Kings', *Opuscula Archeologica*, IV, 1946, pp 21–24; E. S. G. Robinson, 'Kings of Lapethos', *Numismatic Chronicle*, VIII, 1948, pp 60–65. Archaeology: S. Casson, *Ancient Cyprus. Its Art and Archaeology* (London, 1937); E. Gjerstad, *The Swedish Cyprus Expedition* IV, 2 (Stockholm, 1948). Religion: O. Masson, *Cultes indigènes, cultes grecs et cultes orientaux dans la religion grecque ancienne. Eléments orientaux dans la religion grecque ancienne* (Paris, 1960), pp 129–42.

Part II The Phoenicians and Carthaginians in Africa

General works on North Africa: S. Gsell, *Histoire ancienne de l'Afrique du Nord*[2] I–IV (Paris, 1921–4) (essential); C. A. Julien–C. Courtois, *Histoire de l'Afrique du Nord*[2] (Paris, 1951). General works on Carthage: G.-G. Lapeyre–A. Pellegrin, *Carthage punique* (Paris, 1942); C. Picard, *Carthage* (Paris, 1951); G. Picard, *Le monde de Carthage* (Paris, 1956); M. Hours-Miédan, *Carthage*[2] (Paris, 1959); B. H. Warmington, *Carthage* (London, 1960); F. Barreca, *La civiltà di Cartagine* (Cagliari, 1964).

9 History – Foundation: E. Frézouls, 'Une nouvelle hypothèse sur la fondation de Carthage', *Bulletin de Correspondance Hellénique*, LXXIX, 1955, pp 153–76. Relations with the Etruscans: M. Pallottino, 'Les relations entre les Etrusques et Carthage du VIIe au IIe siècle avant J.-C. Nouvelles données et essai de périodisation', *Cahiers de Tunisie*, XI, 1963, pp 23–29. Internal development: L. Maurin, 'Himilcon le Magonide. Crises et mutations à Carthage au début du IVe siècle avant J.-C., *Semitica*, XII, 1962, pp 5–43. The colonies in general: R. Bartoccini, 'Le antichità della Tripolitania', *Aegyptus*, VII, 1926, pp 49–96; J. L. Ferron, 'La Byzacène à l'époque punique', CB, XI, 1963, pp 31–46; J. Carcopino, *Le Maroc antique*[2] (Paris, 1948); P. Cintas, *Contribution à l'étude de l'expansion carthaginoise au Maroc* (Paris, 1954); M. Tarradell, *Marruecos punico* (Tetuan, 1960). Leptis Magna: R. Bianchi Bandinelli *et al.*, *Leptis Magna* (Roma, 1963). Sabratha: R. Bartoccini, 'La necropoli punica di Sabratha e il culto delle divinità egiziane in Tripolitania', *Annali dell'Instituto Universitario Orientale di Napoli*, III, 1949, pp 35–53. Susa: P. Cintas, 'Le sanctuaire punique de Sousse', *Revue Africaine*, XC, 1947, pp 1–80; L. Foucher, *Hadrumetum* (Paris, 1964). Djebel Mlezza: P. Cintas–E. G. Gobert, 'Les

tombes du Jbel Mlezza', *Revue Tunisienne*, XXXVIII–XL, 1939, pp 135–98. Utica: P. Cintas, 'Deux campagnes de fouilles à Utique', *Karthago*, II, 1951, pp 1–88; id., *Nouvelles recherches à Utique*, ibid., V, 1954, pp 89–155. Hippo Regius: E. Marec, *Hippone la Royale, antique Hippo Regius*[2] (Alger, 1954). Cirta: A. Berthier–R. Charlier, *Le sanctuaire punique d'El-Hofra à Constantine* (Paris, 1955(. Djidjelli: J. and P. Alquier, 'Tombeaux phéniciens à Djidjelli', *Revue Archéologique*, XXXI, 1930, pp 1–17; M. Astruc, 'Nouvelles fouilles à Djidjelli', *Revue Africaine*, XXX, 1937, pp 199–253. Algiers: J. Cantineau–L. Leschi, 'Monnaies puniques d'Alger', CRAIB, 1941, pp 263–78. Tipasa: P. Cintas, 'Fouilles puniques à Tipasa', *Revue Africaine*, XCII, 1949, pp 1–68; L. Leschi, *Tipasa de Maurétanie* (Alger, 1950); J. Baradez, *Tipasa* (Alger, 1952). Cherchel: S. Gsell, *Cherchel, antique Jol-Caesarea* (Alger, 1952). Gouraya: F. Missonnier, 'Fouilles dans la nécropole punique de Gouraya (Algérie)', *Mélanges de l'Ecole Française de Rome*, L, 1933, pp 87–119; M. Astruc, 'Supplément aux fouilles de Gouraya', *Lybica*, II, 1954, pp 9–48. Les Andalouses: G. Vouillemot, 'Vestiges puniques des Andalouses', *Bulletin de la Société de Géographie et d'Archéologie de la Province d'Oran*, LXXIV, 1951, pp 55–72. Rachgoun: G. Vuillemot, 'La nécropole punique du phare dans l'île de Rachgoun (Oran)', *Lybica*, III, 1955, pp 7–76. Mersa Madakh: G. Vuillemot, 'Fouilles puniques à Mersa Madakh', *Lybica*, II, 1954, pp 299–342. Melilla: F. de Castro, *Melilla prehispanica* (Madrid, 1945); M. Tarradell, *La necropolis punico-mauritana del Cerro de San Lorenzo en Melilla*, I Congreso Arqueologico del Marruecos Español (Tetuan, 1956), pp 253–66. Tamuda: P. Quintero–C. Gimenes, *Excavaciones en Tamuda* (Madrid-Tetuan, 1941–5). Tangier: A. Beltran, 'Las monedas de Tingi y los problemas arqueologicos que su estudio plantea', *Numario Hispanico*, I, 1952, pp 89 et seq. Lixus: M. Tarradell, *Lixus* (Tetuan, 1959). Mogador: M. Jodin, 'Les fouilles exécutées à Mogador en mai et juin, 1956', *Bulletin Archéologique*, 1957, pp 118–25.

10 Religion – General: G. C. Picard, *Les religions de l'Afrique antique* (Paris, 1954). The gods: P. Ronzevalle, 'Traces du culte de Tanit en Phénicie', MUSJ, V, 1912, pp 75–83; J. G. Février, 'A propos de Ba'al Addir', *Semitica*, II, 1949, pp. 21–28; A. Caquot, 'Chadrapha. A propos de quelques articles récents', *Syria*, XXIX, 1952, pp 74-88; J. G. Février, 'A propos du serment d'Hannibal', CB, VI, 1956, pp 13–22. The cult: R. Charlier, 'La nouvelle série de stèles puniques de Constantine et la question des sacrifices dits "molchomor", en relation avec l'expression "BSRM BTM"', *Karthago*, IV, 1953, pp 1–48; J. G. Février, 'Molchomor', RHR, CXLIII, 1953, pp 8–18; id., 'Le vocabulaire sacrificial punique', *Journal Asiatique*, CCXLIII, 1955, pp 49–63; id., 'Remarques sur le Grand Tarif dit de Marseille',

CB, VIII, 1958–9, pp 35–43; id., 'Essai de reconstitution du sacrifice molek', *Journal Asiatique*, CCXLVIII, 1960, pp 167–87.

11 Art – General: M. P. Fouchet, *L'art à Carthage* (Paris, 1962). Architecture: A. Lézine, *Architecture punique. Recueil de documents* (Paris, 1962); R. Duval, 'Mise au jour de l'enceinte extérieure de la Carthage punique', CRAIB, 1950, pp 53–59; J. Baradez, 'Nouvelles recherches sur les ports antiques de Carthage', *Karthago*, IX, 1958, pp 45–78; L. Poinssot–R. Lantier, 'Un sanctuaire de Tanit à Carthage', RHR, LXXVII, 1923, pp. 32–68; P. Gauckler, *Nécropoles puniques de Carthage* (Paris, 1915). Sculpture, cippi, stelae: P. Cintas, 'Tête archaïque d'époque punique', *Karthago*, VI, 1955, p 128; id., 'La "Grande Dame" de Carthage', CRAIB, 1952, pp 17–20; M. Hours-Miédan, 'Les représentations figurées sur les stèles de Carthage', CB, I, 1951, pp 15–160. Masks, amulets, razors, jewels, scarabs, other minor products: J. Vercoutter, *Les objects égyptiens et égyptisants du mobilier funéraire carthaginois* (Paris, 1945); P. Cintas, *Amulettes puniques* (Tunis, 1946); M. Astruc, 'Traditions funéraires de Carthage', CB, VI, 1956, pp 29–58. Pottery: P. Cintas, *Céramique punique* (Paris, 1950); id., 'Céramique rouge brillante de l'Ouest méditerranéen et de l'Atlantique', CRAIB, 1953, pp 72–77.

12 Economy and Trade – Economy: G. Picard–C. C. Picard, *La vie quotidienne à Carthage au temps d'Hannibal* (Paris, 1958). Trade: J.-E. Casariego, *El Periplo de Hannon de Cartago* (Madrid, 1947); G. Germain, 'Qu'est-ce que le Périple d'Hannon? Document, amplification littéraire ou faux intégral?' *Hespéris*, XLIV, 1957, pp 205–48.

13 Script and Language: cf. notes on chapter 6.

Part IIIB The Colonies in the West

14 Malta, Gozo, Pantelleria – General: A. Mayr, *Die Insel Malta im Altertum* (München, 1909); id., 'Pantelleria', *Mitteilungen des K. Deutschen Archäologischen Instituts*, XIII, 1898, pp 367–98; P. Orsi, 'Pantelleria', MAL, IX, 1899, col 449–540. Archaeology: M. Cagiano de Azevedo et al., *Missione archeologica italiana a Malta. Rapporto preliminare della campagna 1963* (Roma, 1964); id., *Missione archeologica italiana a Malta. Rapporto preliminare della campagna 1964* (Roma, 1965); A. Mayr, 'Aus den phönikischen Nekropolen von Malta', *Sitzungsberichte der K.B. Akademie der Wissenschaften zu München*, 1905, pp 467–509; J. G. Baldacchino, 'Punic Rock-Tombs near Pawla, Malta', PBSR, XIX, 1951, pp 1–22; id., T. J. Dunbabin, 'Rock Tomb at Ghajn Qajjet, near Rabat, Malta', PBSR, XXI, 1953, pp 32–41; id., *Die antiken Münzen der Inseln Malta, Gozo und Pantelleria* (München, 1895); C.

Seltman, 'The Ancient Coinage of Malta', *Numismatic Chronicle*, VI, 1946, pp 81–90.

15 Sicily – General: B. Pace, *Arte e civiltà della Sicilia antica*[2] I (Milano–Roma–Napoli, 1958); L. Pareti, *Sicilia antica* (Palermo, 1959). History: L. Pareti, 'Sui primi commerci e stanziamenti fenici nei paesi mediterranei e specialmente in Sicilia', *Archivio Storico per la Sicilia Orientale*, XII, 1934, pp 3–28. Archaeology: V. Tusa, 'Testimonianze fenicio-puniche in Sicilia', *Kokalos*, 1965. Motya: J. I. S. Whitaker, *Motya, a Phoenician Colony in Sicily* (London, 1921); B. S. J. Isserlin *et al.* 'Motya 1955', PBSR, XXVI, 1958, pp 1–29; id., 'Motya, a Phoenician-Punic Site near Marsala, Sicily. Preliminary Report of the Leeds-London-Fairleigh Dickinson Excavations, 1961–1963', *Annual of Leeds University Oriental Society*, IV, 1962–3, pp 84–131; V. Tusa *et al.*, *Mozia – I* (Roma, 1964). Panormus: M. O. Acanfora, 'Panormos preromana', *Archivio Storico Italiano*, IV, 1950–1, pp 7–182. Solunto: C. Citro, 'Topografia, storia, archeologia di Pizzo Cannita', *Atti della Accademia di Scienze, Lettere e Arti di Palermo*, XII, 1952–3, pp 265–99; V. Tusa, 'Scavi a Solunto', *Oriens Antiquus*, III, 1964, pp 138–9. Selinunte: A. Di Vita, 'L'elemento punico a Selinunte nel IV e nel III sec. a.C.', *Archeologia Classica*, V, 1953, pp 39–47. Sculpture; S. Chiappisi, *Il Melqart di Sciacca e la questione fenicia in Sicilia* (Roma, 1961); P. Mingazzini, 'La statua fenicia di Marsala', *Bollettino d'Arte*, XXXI, 1938, pp 505–9; E. Gabrici, 'Stele sepolcrali di Lilibeo a forma di Heroon', MAL, XXXIII, 1929, col 41–60.

16 Sardinia – General: E. Pais, 'La Sardegna prima del dominio romano', MNAL, serie III, III, 1881, pp 259–378; G. Pesce, *Sardegna punica* (Cagliari, 1961). Relations with Proto-Sardinian civilization: G. Lilliu, 'Rapporti tra la civiltà nuragica e la civiltà fenicio-punica in Sardegna', *Studi Etruschi*, XVIII, 1944, pp 323–70. Nora: G. Pesce, *Nora* (Bologna, 1957). Monte Sirai: F. Barreca *et al.*, *Monte Sirai – I* (Roma, 1964); id., *Monte Sirai – II* (Roma, 1965). Tharros: G. Pesce, 'Il primo scavo di Tharros', SS, XIV–XV, 1955–7, pp 507–72; id., 'Il tempio monumentale di Tharros', MAL, XLV, 1961, col 333–440. Bythia: G. Pesce, *Le statuette puniche di Bithia* (Roma, 1965). Olbia: D. Panedda, *Olbia nel periodo punico e romano* (Roma, 1952); D. Levi, 'Le necropoli puniche di Olbia', SS, IX, 1950, pp 5–120. Architecture: F. Barreca, 'La città punica in Sardegna', *Bollettino del Centro Studi per la Storia dell'Architettura*, XVII, 1961, pp 27–47. Stelae: G. Patroni, 'Nora colonai fenicia in Sardegna', MAL, XIV, 1904, col 109–268; G. Lilliu, 'Le stele puniche di Sulcis (Cagliari)', MAL, XL, 1945, col 293–418. Razors: G. Pesce, 'I rasoi punici di Sardegna', *Bollettino d'Arte*, IV, 1961, pp 293–9. Coins: E. Birocchi, 'La monetazione punico-sarda', SS, II, 1935, pp 64–164; L. Forteleoni, *Le emissioni monetali della*

Sardegna punica (Sassari, 1961). Religion: U. Bianchi, 'Sardus Pater', *Rendiconti dell'Accademia Nazionale dei Lincei*, XVIII, 1963, pp 97–112.

17 Spain – General: A. Garcia y Bellido, *Protostoria: Tartessos. Colonizacion punica*; R. Menendez Pidal, *Historia de España*[2] I, 2 (Madrid, 1960), pp 281–492 (essential). Tartessus: S. de Ausejo, 'El problema de Tartesos', *Sef*, II, 1942, pp 171–91; A. Schulten, *Tartessos*[2] (Madrid, 1945); J. M. Solá Solé, 'Tarshish y los comienzos de la colonizacion fenicia en Occidente', *Sef*, XVII, 1957, pp 23–35; G. Garbini, 'Tarsis e Gen. 10, 4', *Bibbia e Oriente*, VII, 1965, pp 13–19. Place-names: A. Dietrich, *Phönizische Ortsnamen in Spanien* (Leipzig, 1936); J. M. Millas Vallicrosa, 'De toponimia punico-española', *Sef*, I, 1941, pp 313–26. Cadiz: P. Quintero, *La necropolis anterromana de Cadiz* (Madrid, 1915); C. Peman, *Memoria sobre la situacion arqueologica de la provincia de Cadiz en 1940* (Madrid, 1954). Cerro del Peñon: H. G. Niemeyer–M. Pellicer–H. Schubart, 'Eine altpunische kolonie am Rio Velez', *Archäologischer Anzeiger*, III, 1964, col 476–93. Almuñecar: M. Pellicer Catalan, *Excavaciones en la necropolis punica 'Laurita' del Cerro de San Cristobal (Almuñecar, Granada)* (Madrid, 1963) Villaricos: M. Astruc, *La necropolis de Villaricos* (Madrid, 1951). Ibiza: C. Roman, *Antiguedades Ebusitanas* (Barcelona, 1913); A. Vives, *La necropolis de Ibiza* (Madrid, 1917); J. L. Macabich, *Pithyusas, ciclo fenicio* (Palma, 1931); J. M. Maña de Angulo, *La Isla Plana* (Ibiza, 1954). Architecture: J. M. Blasquez Martinez, 'El Herakleion Gaditano, un templo semita en Occidente', *Congreso arqueologico del Marruecos español*, 1963, pp 309–18. Terracotta: J. Colomines Roca, *Les terracuites cartagineses d'Eivissa* (Barcelona, 1938); M. Astruc, 'Empreints et reliefs de terre cuite d'Ibiza', AEA, XXX, 1952, pp 139–91. Ivories: J. Bonsor, *Early Engraved Ivories* (New York, 1928); A. Blanco Freijeiro, 'Los marfiles de Carmona', AEA, XX, 1947, pp 3–25. Jewellery: J. R. Melida, *Tesoro de Aliseda* (Madrid, 1921); A. Blanco Freijeiro, 'Orientalia. Estudio de objetos fenicios y orientalizantes en la Peninsula', AEA, XXIX, 1956, pp 3–51. Ostrich eggs: M. Astruc, 'Exotisme et localisme, Etudes sur les coquilles d'oeufs d'autruche décorées d'Ibiza', *Archivo de Prehistoria Levantina*, VI, 1957, pp 47–112. Coins: A. Vives y Escudero, *La moneda hispanica* (Madrid, 1924–6); J. M. Millas–F. Mateu, 'Sobre las inscripciones monetarias punicohispanas', *Sef*, IX, 1949, pp 432–41; E. S. G. Robinson, *Punic Coins of Spain, Essays in Roman Coinage Presented to H. Mattingly* (Oxford, 1956), pp 34–53; A. M. Guadan, *Las monedas de Gades* (Barcelona, 1963). Pottery: A. Garcia y Bellido, 'Inventario de jarros punico-tartessicos', AEA, XXXIII, 1960, pp 44–63. Religion: A. Garcia y Bellido, 'Deidades semitas en la España antigua', *Sef*, XXIV, 1964, pp 12–40, 237–75; id., 'Hercules Gaditanus', AEA, XXXVI, 1964, pp 68–153.

INDEX